D1047314

An American Quality Legend

An American Quality Legend

How Maytag Saved Our Moms, Vexed the Competition, and Presaged America's Quality Revolution

Robert Hoover

John Hoover

McGraw-Hill, Inc.

New York San Francisco Washington, D.C. Auckland Bogotá
Caracas Lisbon London Madrid Mexico City Milan
Montreal New Delhi San Juan Singapore
Sydney Tokyo Toronto

Library of Congress Cataloging-in-Publication Data

Hoover, Robert.
    An American quality legend : how Maytag saved our moms, vexed the
competition, and presaged America's quality revolution / Robert
Hoover, John Hoover.
        p.   cm.
    Includes index.
    ISBN 0-07-030309-6
    1. Maytag Company—History.   2. Electric household appliances
industry—United States—History.   3. Quality of products—United
States—History.   I. Hoover, John.   II. Title.
HD9971.5.E544M394   1993
338.7'68388'0973—dc20   93-19142
                                                                        CIP

1 2 3 4 5 6 7 8 9 0   DOC/DOC   9 9 8 7 6 5 4 3

ISBN 0-07-030309-6
134189

*The sponsoring editor for this book was James H. Bessent, Jr., and the
production supervisor was Suzanne W. Babeuf. It was set in Baskerville
by North Market Street Graphics.*

Printed and bound by R. R. Donnelley & Sons Company.

Contents

2. Maytag's Unwritten Credo
Complete Customer Satisfaction (An Intricate Endeavor)   31

3. Quality Is Flesh and Blood
Flashback: The Origins of Maytag's Customer Orientation   57

6. The Dawn of Social Responsibility in Manufacturing
Evolving Attitudes on Company Stakeholders—
The Turbulent Thirties   **123**

7. Enlightened Self-Interest
From Philanthropy to a Formal Policy
of Community Service   **149**

Preface

The idea for a book about Maytag has been bugging John Hoover for years, both because he grew up in Newton and because his father, Robert, knew his way through company closets after a lifetime Maytag career. But his attempts to interest Maytag executives fell on deaf ears.

Finally, after a retired Robert had freed up some time, the two produced a treatment upon the invitation of a publisher. One publisher later, the book got written.

Maytag was not consulted in the matter, but cooperated once the project got underway. Meanwhile, the company was busy planning for their 1993 centennial activities, including their own history.

Robert's Maytag career reached from the days when everyone's mother had a Maytag to being beset with Old Lonely lines from amateur and professional comedians alike. He was party to the quality culture from the leadership of Fred Maytag II to recently retired Dan Krumm. Researching this book verified that the roots of that culture did indeed extend back to the founder. Maytaggers used to joke that a Cadillac was the Maytag of automobiles. Today they probably say the same about a BMW or Mercedes.

The authors are extremely grateful to Maytag archivist Orville Butler for his monumental assistance in gathering information and illustrations for this book. Thanks go also to Barb Richards and Karen O'Roake of Maytag for their patience and help in gathering material. In addition to Maytag Company and Maytag Corporation, assistance also came from Leo Burnett, current Maytag advertising agency, and the Jasper County Historical Museum.

Robert Hoover
Newton, Iowa

1
Old Lonely

Marketing the Quality Legend

Product quality is defined in a variety of ways depending on who's doing the defining. Some will argue that giving a consumer superior performance—meaning that the product actually does what it's designed to do, if only for a short time—is a mark of quality. Others counter that slightly compromised performance, maintained over the long haul is a more appropriate definition. The fact is that no universal definition of quality exists, not even among the experts.

Dictionaries define *quality* as the basic or essential character or nature of something. Threshing crews in the American heartland handed Maytag Company founder F.L. Maytag their own definition for acceptable and unacceptable quality back in 1893. At that time, Maytag was a partner in the manufacturing and sales of an automatic feeder for threshing machines. When one of his feeders failed on the job, the hot, sweaty, cantankerous crew members would discard it in the field and move on. Because the automatic feeders were sold on credit, payments stopped when the product failed. How many manufacturers could survive such unforgiving customer behavior in the 1990s?

To stay in business, Maytag's home office people followed threshing crews from farm to farm, repairing the feeders by night so the crews could use them by day. The repair crews brought the company face to face with the essential nature of the customer, and the concept of continuous improvement was born. The Maytag definition of quality and dependability that evolved turns on two primary concepts: *superior performance* and *reliability*.

In 1959, F.L. Maytag's grandson, Fred Maytag II, told an audience:

> It has long been our objective to deliver to the dealer a product that [can be installed] in a customer's home with confidence that it will require no major repair for ten years.

1

He was talking about automatic washing machines, but Maytag had long since surpassed that goal with its wringer washers. During most of the 76 years that Maytag manufactured wringer washers, beginning in 1907, they utterly dominated the market. The wringer washer was Maytag's *only* product for an entire generation (1922–1949).

Maytag's success with the wringer washer was a direct result of overwhelming customer satisfaction. Industry-leading sales over such a long period of time established a quality benchmark for the appliance industry that remained unchallenged even after Maytag stopped making wringer washers in 1983. At Maytag, customer satisfaction defines product quality.

Consumers respond to a company that learns to meet and even anticipate their needs. Maytag has historically been the most profitable company in the home appliance industry, indicating that long-term profitability is tied to long-term quality.

Maytag is often asked about the secret of its success. Fred Maytag II's comment about that question in 1959, up to that time Maytag's second best year for sales and earnings, was:

> They are always disappointed when I tell them that *there is no secret*—that our success did not result from any particular or peculiar thing that we alone are doing; rather it resulted from a combination of a great many policies and practices over a long period of time.

Perhaps he didn't realize in 1959 that Maytag's secret weapon was a management philosophy that was from the beginning and still is customer-driven. In his own words:

> Any business enterprise can succeed only as it serves the needs of the economy and the society. The degree of success should be and generally is in direct proportion to how well the individual enterprise serves the public good.

In 1961, the year before his death, Fred Maytag II helped dedicate the current Maytag headquarters building in Newton, Iowa. At that time a plaque bearing his signature was mounted on the lobby wall (see Figure 1-1).

For Fred Maytag, balance meant not letting the interests of shareowners or employees get ahead of customer focus. He observed:

> The public, of course, does not make organized demands on a corporation, but the collective result of the individual choices of customers, in a free market, is swift and certain. It is obvious that there will be no dividends for shareowners, no wages for employees—indeed, no corporation—unless there are buyers for its products.

Maytag's words are still true. Keeping the customer satisfied is no secret. But if it's no secret, then why have so few companies over the years made it

> OUR MANAGEMENT MUST MAINTAIN A JUST BALANCE AMONG THE INTERESTS OF CUSTOMERS, EMPLOYEES, SHAREOWNERS AND THE PUBLIC. ALTHOUGH THE GROUPS MAY APPARENTLY COMPETE IN SHORT-TERM GOALS, THEIR LONG-RANGE INTERESTS COINCIDE, FOR NONE CAN LONG BENEFIT UNLESS THE NEEDS OF ALL ARE SERVED.

Figure 1-1. Fred Maytag II's philosophy of doing business stressed fairness, long-term thinking, and customer focus.

their consummate objective? The fact that customer-driven policy pays big dividends is best illustrated by the unexpected and unbridled success of Maytag's most famous ambassador of quality.

Still Lonely After All These Years

The most visible player in the Maytag quality story is "Old Lonely." He is portrayed as perennially isolated and relegated to inactivity by the proverbial reliability of Maytag products (see Figure 1-2). Is it image or reality? In 1992, celebrating 25 years of unceasing vigil waiting for a Maytag product to fail, Old Lonely was honored as the longest-running advertising campaign in the history of network television featuring a real-life character.

In the fickle world of advertising, 25 months is considered an eternity for a single advertising campaign. But the quarter century that Old Lonely has been on the air offers a clue to much more than advertising creativity. More than anything else, the longevity of the Old Lonely advertising campaign indicates that consumers believe the credibility claims associated with Maytag products.

According to the Maytag people, consumers' positive experiences with Maytag products drive the success of their advertising campaign. This assertion is contrary to the advertising industry rule that claims made by companies on behalf of products or services are supposed to present an image that consumers *hope* to experience in real life. Some puffery is expected.

By contrast, Maytag claims that consumers' real-life experiences with its products validate the reliability espoused by Old Lonely's repose. To better understand why Maytag feels that consumers' experience accounts for Maytag customer loyalty, it helps to trace the history of advertising at Maytag. For the rest of this chapter, we'll take you through Maytag's marketing and advertising story, starting with Old Lonely, then flashing back to the beginning, and finally coming full circle to the present.

If Maytag's assertion is correct, Old Lonely's toolbox will continue gathering cobwebs as long as Maytag products deliver the superior performance and reliability they've come to be known for. If Maytag manages to keep its name synonymous with quality and value over time, some actor, now in his or her adolescence, will be playing the part of Old Lonely when the fiftieth anniversary rolls around.

The Gamble

Credibility—public acceptance of something as believable—can't be assumed when launching an advertising campaign despite pretesting and research. Public response to claims made on behalf of a product manufacturer or service provider can cut both ways. There's no way to be absolutely sure which will be the case until a company steps off the cliff with its ad campaign strapped to its back like a parachute. When the rip cord is pulled, the truth will be known.

By hindsight, some might insist that Old Lonely couldn't have missed. But when the campaign was first launched in 1967, Maytag had no way of being certain consumers would accept the claim that Maytag products are so dependable that service people find it difficult to keep busy. However, when Maytag, free-falling off that 1967 cliff, pulled the rip cord, out came Old Lonely and the company's image has been floating gracefully ever since.

The advertising campaign tapped a reservoir of public sentiment much larger than anyone at Maytag or Leo Burnett, Maytag's Chicago-based advertising agency, had expected. Although Maytag's corporate culture seems to have been driven from the earliest days by a commitment to long-term customer satisfaction through product reliability and performance, the degree of acceptance among Maytag customers had never before been fully measured.

A Lesson From Mother

In the language of total quality management, Maytag had more than a few "lessons learned" under its belt prior to launching Old Lonely in 1967. Specifically, the company had a vast depository of service records, industry statistics, and independent surveys that chronicled a long history of product superiority. What Maytaggers didn't fully appreciate in those pre–Old Lonely days was that consumers already knew how good they were.

For most of the twentieth century, it was not uncommon for people meeting a Maytag employee to say, "You know, my mother had a Maytag." Few people associated with the company for any portion of the past 75 years

Figure 1-2. Old Lonely, a.k.a. the Maytag repairman.

haven't heard that unsolicited comment at least once during the course of their Maytag career. For many, to hear it once a month was not unusual. Without realizing it, these consumers were collectively acknowledging that Maytag had quietly generated the most fundamental form of product credibility by maintaining consistently high quality and dependability standards through succeeding generations. People who remembered that their mothers owned Maytag washers were also clearly implying that their mothers' experiences with Maytag products had been positive.

Good News Travels Fast

Although Old Lonely entered the advertising arena on a meager budget, he became an immediate success, riding on the Maytag reputation that had preceded him. It wasn't long before everyone from comedians to editorial writers began to use the Maytag repairman as a metaphor for loneliness. Being as "lonely as a Maytag repairman" needed no explanation. The speed with which Old Lonely raced toward celebrity status amazed everyone associated with the company.

The Old Lonely campaign wasn't a campaign at all in the beginning. It started as a single commercial, and with relatively limited exposure compared with other national advertisers, it didn't warrant such a rapidly accelerating recognition factor. It was as if everyone who ever spontaneously exclaimed "My mother had a Maytag" suddenly joined voices in saying to the company, "That's what we've been telling you. Maytag has made believers out of us." Old Lonely's virtual overnight success was both a pleasant surprise and another "lesson learned" for Maytag.

Nearly a Miss

Like many successful ideas, Old Lonely very nearly never was. The idea of a lonely Maytag repairman was offered almost as an afterthought at an advertising agency client presentation. Veteran actor Jesse White was cast in the role of a drill instructor training new Maytag service people. Old Lonely marched in five recruits and called the roll (see Figure 1-3).

At ease men. Now you have all volunteered to be Maytag repairmen, so I'm gonna give it to ya straight. Maytag washers and dryers are built to last. That makes a Maytag repairman the loneliest guy in town. See this rugged motor, this almost indestructible pump? Take a good look because most of you may never see the inside of one again. This is your survival kit. Playing cards for solitaire. Crossword puzzles. Beadwork.

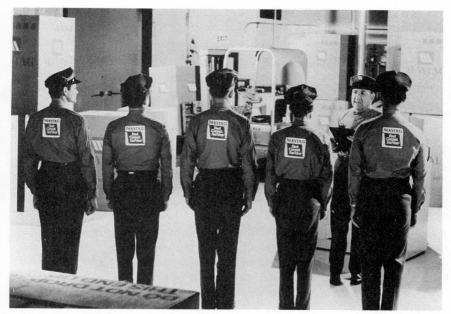

Figure 1-3. The "Drill Instructor" ad, Maytag's first Old Lonely segment, started as an experiment. © Leo Burnett.

Keep this with you at all times. Okay men, wear your Maytag emblem proudly; the sign of dependable washers and dryers. So what if nobody needs you? It takes a real man to fight off loneliness, a *Maytag* repairman, the *loneliest guy in town.*

At first, it was the enthusiastic response from Maytag employees and dealers the day after the television ad first aired that prompted the company to authorize additional commercials. Soon thereafter, affirmation from the consuming public set the wheels in motion for what, to date of this publication, have been 87 different Old Lonely scenarios. Over the years, Old Lonely has occupied his time with a variety of activities, including teaching a parrot to talk. One spot features Old Lonely, with his feet up on the desk, snoring peacefully through the entire 30-second commercial. One of the most memorable episodes involved Old Lonely being picked up at a boat dock by a lighthouse keeper.

OLD LONELY: Maytag won't run, eh?

LIGHTHOUSE KEEPER: Yup. comes the down-east reply.

Arriving at the lighthouse, Old Lonely finds only a broken electrical plug.

OLD LONELY: (disappointed that the repair wasn't more of a challenge) Just a broken plug.

LIGHTHOUSE KEEPER: Yup, coulda fixed it myself.

OLD LONELY: Why did you call me?

LIGHTHOUSE KEEPER: Kinda lonely out here.

OLD LONELY: ...lonely, I know what you mean.

More Products Not to Repair

Maytag manufactured nothing but washers from 1922 until 1954. With the company now manufacturing other appliances that lack the historic track record of Maytag washers, Old Lonely's role has gradually shifted from star to cameo player. Following a product-centered message, Old Lonely pops into the picture looking basset-hound depressed as a subtle reminder of Maytag quality. Eventually, Old Lonely was joined in these cameo appearances by a real basset hound that needed no prompting to look depressed. Old Lonely's canine companion was named Newton, after the small Iowa town where the Maytag Company was born and continues to be headquartered (see Figure 1-4).

Figure   1-4. Newton,   repairman's best friend.

A recent commercial featuring the new Old Lonely, Gordon Jump, shows Newton alert and keeping an eye on Old Lonely, who is sound asleep. There is no dialogue until a voice-over announcer says, "This message is brought to you by Maytag." Another commercial closes with a vignette of Old Lonely making a sandwich, with the voice-over, "All he gets to fix is lunch."

Old Lonely's role changed with the introduction of nonlaundry appliances because the role of quality itself changed. Research indicated that, with dishwashers, introduced by Maytag in 1967, durability of the machine was less important to consumers than clean dishes—that is, performance. Consumers also consider product reliability to be fairly universal in refrigerators. With consumers looking first for flexibility and storage arrangements in refrigerators, Maytag advertising messages are tailored to the product's versatility while Old Lonely's presence supplies the generic message of Maytag dependability.

Measuring the effectiveness of a long-running campaign is difficult. It must be determined whether or not the campaign has reached a point of diminishing returns or has ceased to be effective altogether. According to Maytag advertising director Norman Boyle, the company uses two yardsticks—*product awareness* and *product preference*. In the modern era of automatic washers, Maytag has traditionally been second only to Sears in the laundry product awareness category, and the gap between Maytag and number three is growing. In brand preference, twice as many consumers chose Maytag first over second-place Sears.

Both product awareness and product preference are determined by independent market researchers, primarily Marketfax. The researcher asks a sample audience to list all brands that can be recalled for a specified product. The same audience is then asked which brand is preferred if the product were to be purchased that day. In addition to dominating the laundry category, Maytag ranks first, second, or third in every product category it represents. In Canada, for example, the Maytag dishwasher ranks first in both the awareness and preference categories.

At least once every three years Maytag uses Marketfax to verify the validity of its claim that Maytag washers last longer and need fewer repairs than other brands. Marketfax researchers ask consumers how old their washers are and how many repairs they require.[1] Newer Maytag products, including

---

[1] Consumer preference surveys are not new to Maytag. In 1932, Cramer-Krasselt Company, Maytag's advertising agency at the time, surveyed 7000 homemakers nationwide and learned that 45.4 percent preferred Maytag. The nearest competitor, Easy, was preferred by 17.5 percent. ABC (Aldorfer Brothers Co.) was preferred by 3.6 percent, the 1900 Corporation (later Whirlpool) by 2.4 percent, and General Electric by 1.9 percent. Automatic Washer Co., also in Newton, and Universal had 1.7 percent each, Apex 1.6 percent, Voss 1.5 percent, and One Minute, another Newton company, 1.4 percent.

dishwashers, ranges and refrigerators, continue to gain in both the awareness and preference categories, prompting company officials to conclude that Old Lonely's subtle assurance extends beyond laundry products.[2]

Maytag appears to carefully weigh objective outside feedback. In both 1991 and 1992, Maytag received a gold Effie award from the New York chapter of the American Marketing Association. Considered more prestigious than other advertising awards based solely on creativity, the Effie recognizes efficiency in advertising by requiring proof of a campaign's results. Norm Boyle points out that Old Lonely's success depends entirely upon Maytag's ability to continue providing products that last longer and need fewer repairs than competing products.

The Gradual Evolution of a Quality Icon

Even though Old Lonely is, by advertising standards, ancient, Maytag's relationship with the advertising agency that created the Old Lonely campaign is even older. Staying with one agency for a long period of time is common course and performance for Maytag. The company has worked with only three advertising agencies in its entire 100-year history.

Beginning about 1911, the first agency, Cramer-Krasselt Company of Milwaukee, produced ads for *The Saturday Evening Post, Country Gentleman,* and other magazines (see Figure 1-5). In 1915, the first year that sales of Maytag washing machines surpassed sales of Maytag farm implements, L.B. (Bud) Maytag, the younger of founder F.L.'s two sons, asked his father for $50,000 to finance a national advertising campaign to promote washers. At the time, a full page in *The Saturday Evening Post* cost about $5000. The reluctant company founder gave his son $22,000.

L.B.'s initial campaign was so successful that within three years, the Maytag annual advertising budget had climbed to six figures. In 1925, Maytag began monthly advertisements in *House and Garden* magazine, and F.L. instituted a policy of loaning a Maytag washer to the domestic sciences department of any college with a student enrollment of 300 or more. Even though the dependability theme was mentioned in early advertising, the public had to first be sold on the idea of a washing machine.

In 1926, Maytag erected a $70,000 electric sign at the corner of 49th Street and Broadway in New York City. By the end of 1927, with the Maytag sign helping to light up Times Square, Maytag was the world's seventh

---

[2] Quality remains an important, if not primary, issue for consumers in any appliance category. In 1990, Maytag launched an advertising campaign that featured a unique 10-year guarantee—until the year 2000—that was instrumental in quadrupling brand awareness for Maytag refrigerators in a single year.

Figure 1-5. One of the Cramer-Krasselt ads for the Multi-Motor washer, from *Country Gentleman* magazine.

largest newspaper advertiser. By the time the company produced its one-millionth washer in 1927, its overall advertising budget exceeded a million dollars. At that time, Maytag owned 43 percent of the American washing machine market.

On the Air: *The Maytag Happiness Hour*

In 1928, the largest independent radio network of its day was created to broadcast a Maytag program. Company founder F.L. Maytag had left his two sons, Elmer and Bud, to run the company in Newton around 1910 when he shifted his focus to Chicago, 300 miles to the east. Along the way he discovered an inventor who had developed a method of producing phonograph records that sounded live. The high fidelity and transcribability of these recordings made it possible to air the same program simultaneously on several radio stations and still sound live. F.L. was hooked. His discovery gave birth to *The Maytag Happiness Hour,* which premiered in 1928.

F.L. had dabbled in radio from the earliest days of station WHO in Des Moines, 30 miles west of Newton. In 1924, he sponsored a vocal ensemble called the Maytag Troubadours. In 1927, he tested a 30-minute entertainment program on station WHT in Chicago, Tuesday through Saturday at 9 p.m., and sponsored *Household Talks* every afternoon.

The Maytag Happiness Hour was a weekly 30-minute program recorded in Chicago and featuring The Maytag Orchestra.[3] In those early days, while Maytag was still building the tradition of dependability upon which it based its later advertising, F.L. set out to entertain the nation's socks off. At first, the Maytag network included six stations—KDKA in Pittsburgh, WHT in Chicago, WCCO in Minneapolis, WBAP in Fort Worth, WHO in Des Moines, and KEX in Portland, Oregon. Later that first year, KSL in Salt Lake City, KLZ in Denver, CFCA in Toronto, and WBZ in Boston all signed on for *The Maytag Happiness Hour.* The radio budget for 1928 was $425,000. Every program ended with the soon familiar theme song:

Let a smile be your umbrella and a Maytag your washer

By 1930 the Depression was beginning to erode Maytag's profits, and like many other companies, Maytag trimmed its advertising budget. In 1934, national advertising was resumed, using smaller ads in key city newspapers to feature a 45 percent reduction from 1929 prices. The advertising budget in 1934 was $18,000 per month.

---

[3] The Maytag Orchestra sounded remarkably similar to the band at Chicago's Edgewater Beach Hotel. The program also featured a cast of soap opera style players and vocalists. A trio from the Chicago Philharmonic—Theodore Katz, Doris Wittisch, and Louis Colburn-Bicht—became known as the Maytag Ramblers. The vocalists included tenor Wolfgang Wittisch and baritone Charles Livingstone, with Al Carney at the organ. Pat Barnes, station manager from WHT in Chicago, was the announcer.

Continuing his belief in radio, F.L. announced in 1935 that Maytag would sponsor broadcasts of University of Iowa football games with announcer Ronald "Dutch" Reagan. Always loyal to his sponsors, Reagan officiated several years later at the dedication of the Fred Maytag Park swimming pool in Newton. The football sponsorship continued in 1936, the year Reagan left Iowa—bound for Hollywood—but not before he delivered a farewell speech to the Newton Jaycees.

Changing Agency Allegiance: McCann-Erickson and Early Television Advertising

In the late 1930s, Maytag switched to McCann-Erickson, a New York advertising agency that handled the Maytag account out of its Chicago office. In addition to producing color print ads for the "seven sisters" women's service magazines (*Ladies Home Journal, McCalls, Redbook, Family Circle, Woman's Day, Better Homes & Gardens,* and *Good Housekeeping*), McCann introduced Maytag to early television.

Early television adopted its commercial methods and techniques from radio. Not only were programming formats copied from one medium to another, but actual programs that had been created and flourished on radio were transferred to television. Jack Benny, Edgar Bergen and Charlie McCarthy, Lawrence Welk, and Milton Berle are a few examples of radio personalities who successfully made the leap to television.

With these established programs and entertainers came their sponsors. In those days, most programs were identified by a single sponsor and vice versa. Daytime dramas earned the moniker "soap operas" by virtue of their principal sponsor, Procter & Gamble. A few early magazine format programs, like the original *Today Show,* sold commercial time to a variety of sponsors, allowing smaller advertisers like Maytag to participate. The term *magazine,* when applied to a television format, referred to a program with multiple sponsors.

By this time, the public was already convinced of Maytag dependability. However, the company didn't yet fully realize it. Maytag's first television commercials appeared in the spring of 1954 on NBC's original early-morning *Today Show,* starring Dave Garroway and his simian friend, J. Fred Muggs. To honor his new sponsor, Garroway interviewed then company president, Fred Maytag II, on live television, at dawn, in New York City. Maytag brought a replica of the *Pastime,* the company's first hand-operated washer, as a visual aid. Even on live television at an hour of day not fit for man or beast, nonperformer Fred Maytag managed to hold his own with both Garroway and the monkey (see Figure 1-6).

Despite the early hour, television sets were set up in each of the Maytag's 12 branch and distributors' offices, and as part of a sales meeting, all Maytag

Figure 1-6. Fred Maytag II showing the nation a replica of Maytag's Pastime washer on Dave Garroway's *Today Show,* 1954.

sales people were called in to watch Fred, live, on the Garroway show. Soon Maytag dealers were distributing thousands of hand puppets of J. Fred Muggs as a giveaway promotion. Maytag commercials on the *Today Show* were done live by Garroway himself or by the show's announcer, Jack Lescoulie.

A Collaborative Opportunity

In the early fall of 1954, Maytag received a call from executives at Amana, an Iowa manufacturer of freezers and refrigerators, to join them in advertising on NCAA football games aired by the ABC network. The principal sponsor of the ABC contract, General Motors, had dropped out at the last minute. As appliance manufacturers, Amana (which was not yet part of electronics manufacturer Raytheon) and Maytag were known as "white goods" companies, so named after the color of their products. Amana also called upon Zenith, a "brown goods" manufacturer of radio and television sets, to be the third player to pick up the vacated ABC contract.

With less than a week's notice, the decision was made and Maytag's young advertising manager, Ralph Nunn, flew to Chicago on a Monday to sign the ABC contract. Nunn then flew on to New York with McCann's Chicago account executive to hire an announcer, Bob Williams, and prepare seven or eight commercials, which had to be ready before Saturday's first game. During Saturday's game, Maytag's hastily prepared commercials were done live from a New York City studio.

Three sets located in the ABC studio loft were used for commercials by the three sponsors. Zenith, Amana, and Maytag all had eight or ten 60-second commercials ready. The busiest guy in the studio was the McCann writer from Chicago who had to prepare all the spots for Williams to read from the prompter. The commercials focused on product features. In one, Williams washed light bulbs to demonstrate Maytag's gentleness. Company president Fred Maytag II appeared in the opening commercial, having arrived by train from a Washington, D.C., meeting with just moments to spare.

The Move to Leo Burnett

It was considered unethical for an advertising agency to simultaneously represent competing clients. By the nature of their work, agencies are privy to company plans and secrets that shouldn't be shared with the competition. On the other hand, agencies sometimes prefer to jump to a larger account, and if they can get away with it, have their cake and eat it too. Maytag's intolerance for such dealings on the part of suppliers and business associates set the stage for the fracture that separated Maytag from McCann-Erikson.

The year was 1955. The McCann/Maytag account executive, Neal Gilliatt, and Ralph Nunn walked into Fred Maytag II's office for a routine discussion of advertising concepts just as the president was completing a fateful telephone conversation with a competing advertising agency. As soon as he hung up the telephone, Fred asked the McCann executive, "What's this about your agency representing Westinghouse?"

According to Nunn, Maytag went on to say that the telephone call had come from Fuller, Smith & Ross, a Cleveland advertising agency that had lost the Westinghouse account to McCann and wanted to solicit Maytag's business. The Chicago-based McCann executive wasn't aware of the change, although he knew that McCann's New York office handled the Westinghouse *Studio One* television program. While able to overlook *Studio One* because it was new to television, Maytag was offended that the agency would take on the entire account of a major competitor.

The McCann executive felt sufficiently subverted by the timing and implications of the discovery that he borrowed a secretary in Nunn's advertising department and dictated his letter of resignation to McCann-Erickson.[4] Fred canned McCann straightaway.

[4] The agency persuaded the account executive to stay and he later became vice chairman of the parent company, The Interpublic Group.

Maytag's approach to selecting a new advertising agency was an example of how the company learned from experience and applied the lessons to continuous improvement in all aspects of the business. Foregoing the traditional "who you know" approach to seeking a new agency, Maytag engaged in an objective analysis and issued a detailed questionnaire to some 75 advertising agencies.[5] From the responses, the field was narrowed to six agencies, all of which were based in Chicago or had Chicago offices. A Maytag marketing delegation visited each agency and witnessed a half-day presentation. Three agencies were invited to visit Maytag's headquarters in Newton to make final presentations on successive days. Finally, Leo Burnett won the account.

Burnett brought television experience to the Maytag account. Burnett was responsible for the only television program that ever identified Maytag as a cosponsor, along with Sheaffer Pen company, another Iowa manufacturer. The show was *Navy Log,* which aired on CBS Monday nights at seven o'clock. There were three 60-second commercials in the half-hour program, plus an opening and closing announcement. The two sponsors alternated with the odd commercial. Burnett filmed the commercials in Hollywood.

By 1955, varied technologies were being joined to modernize the media. Film, which had no role in radio, was now being used to record television commercials, allowing them to be played again and again, much like the phonograph discs that had captured F.L. Maytag's attention over 30 years earlier.

Showdown With the Bean Counters

Within Maytag, as with most companies, there exists a "dynamic tension" between those anxious to spend advertising and marketing money and those dedicated to preventing such expenditures. Almost invariably, the bean counters from the financial division behave as if the company's money is their own. So it came as no surprise when executive vice president George Umbreit, who had worked his way up through the financial ranks, wanted to pull in the reigns on what he felt were excessive advertising expenditures.

Umbreit visited Nunn's office regularly, demanding some justifiable measurement of benefit from the company's vastly increased advertising expenditures. Nunn's inability to provide hard, statistical data on advertising results eventually led to his losing the battle for advertising funds. As a

---

[5] A similar technique was used to select a public relations firm in 1956.

result, Maytag abandoned the television show sponsorship approach, and from that time to the present, Maytag has bought more economical and versatile spot time on television.

It would probably have cost more to go about scientifically measuring absolute advertising effectiveness than to produce the actual advertising being evaluated. At least Maytag never tried. Readership, viewership, message retention, credibility, and other criteria can be measured for most products and services. Yet no qualitative instrument exists to measure the precise relationship between advertising and sales, independent of other influences.

According to Norm Boyle, Maytag continues to spend somewhat less on advertising than its competitors, but the company tries to stay in the ball park. Through advertising analysis, Boyle maintains that Maytag seems to get more bang for its buck by staying with a single theme rather than shotgunning its messages. Boyle feels that the best test of advertising success is the measurable increase in product awareness.

Following Umbreit's reduction in advertising allocations in 1956, Maytag shifted the majority of its advertising budget back to magazines. The Leo Burnett print ads were dominated by large illustrations of product features shown in arresting color, a common practice in appliance advertising of that time. The first five years featured a couple of major national promotions—firsts for Maytag. Despite the promotions, the advertising seemed uninspired.

At a 1960 field meeting in Los Angeles, Ralph Nunn told Burnett account executive Chuck Jones that Burnett was in danger of losing Maytag as a client. Nunn explained to Jones that Fred Maytag felt that a company as distinctive as Maytag ought to have a more distinctive approach to advertising. Independently, Claire Ely, marketing vice president, had a similar conversation with Jim Love, Burnett's account supervisor for Maytag. Both carried the message back to Leo in Chicago, and Burnett responded immediately. Even though Maytag was one of his smaller accounts, Burnett had a fondness for the company, relishing its small-town integrity and reputation.

Discovering the Power of Customer-Driven Quality: A Prelude to Old Lonely

Burnett gathered together all the top creative people in his agency along with several outside consultants and asked each of them to create new ads for Maytag. Out of the resulting ideas emerged the concept of focusing on the *user* rather than the product itself, and the first dependability ad was born. The black-and-white ad featured a little girl and a big headline that read, "She will buy a Maytag before her mother needs another." With the

Life magazine deadline for the ad rapidly approaching, the Burnett creative director had yet to select the photograph he liked best of the little girl. Creative directors at advertising agencies take their roles very seriously, and an account executive is not considered "creative." Anxious to make the deadline, Jones nevertheless took it upon himself to choose a photo and later got roundly chewed out for overstepping his role (see Figure 1-7).

All together, Burnett presented Maytag with 127 different ads resulting from the brainstorming ordered by the agency. Half the ideas had nothing to do with dependability. The dependability concepts included comparisons of Maytag products with the Rock of Gibraltar and with Old Faithful at Yellowstone Park. The idea of using consumer testimonials was discussed, but there was concern over where to find testimonials in a hurry.

Real People With Real Stories: Delving Into Maytag's Secret Treasure

As luck would have it, files at company headquarters in Newton held volumes of "fan mail" from satisfied customers. Burnett was about to tap a mother lode of consumer loyalty in response to Maytag's commitment to customer satisfaction that hadn't previously been measured. So, several years before the advent of Old Lonely, Leo Burnett started making the case for the credibility of a lonely service person. Maytag magazine ads began to feature real people with real stories discovered in the archives of unsolicited testimonial letters. The first of the series pictured a bride and her Maytag with the caption, "Married in 1932, got Maytag in 1933. Both marriage and Maytag still working." (See Figure 1-8.)

The series also publicized stories of washers subjected to unusual hardships, such as operation in the freezing Arctic, on board ships, or in desolate regions serving missionaries. Stories of Maytag washers serving large families played well. The popular Lennon Sisters of Lawrence Welk fame were featured in three ads. There were 11 Lennon children, plus a son-in-law in the second ad.[6] Figure 1-9 shows the first Lennon family ad.

"Sister Charity Marie says you don't even have to be a housewife to appreciate a Maytag," headlined an ad featuring a nun with a conventful of laun-

---

[6] With so many testimonials featuring large families of eight or more children—beaming, neat, and clean—Maytag began hearing from birth control advocates and eventually knuckled under to their crusade to reduce the size of the families in the ads. The federal government got into the act and challenged Maytag on the basis that showing its washers functioning in so many abnormal situations consitituted misleading advertising. So, although all of Maytag's claims came directly from unsolicited testimonies, the company voluntarily limited the scope of its product representations to appease activists and overly zealous government bureaucrats.

She will buy a new Maytag
before her mother needs another

Married in 1932

Got Maytag in 1933

Both marriage and
Maytag still working

"We had 11 good reasons for buying a Maytag"

Sister Charity Marie says you
don't even have to be a housewife
to appreciate a Maytag.

Figure 1-7. Maytag's first user-oriented "dependability" ad. **Figure 1-8.** Unsolicited customer letters were used as the basis for a series of ads. **Figure 1-9.** The Lennon family combined celebrity status and a large household. **Figure 1-10.** If you can't trust a nun to be telling it like it is, then who? © Leo Burnett.

dry to clean (see Figure 1-10). Another ad claimed, "You don't buy a Maytag, you adopt it."

On and on went the testimonials:

"When our 20-year-old Maytag needed parts, we figured it was finished."

"Mrs. Gonder (den mother) feels her Maytags have earned a merit badge or two these past 12 years."

"Mrs. Trevisan babied every one of her seven children but never her Maytag."

"Mrs. Hands got her Maytag the same week *The Spirit of St. Louis* flew the Atlantic. The airplane is in a museum, the Maytag's still going strong."

"From Montreal to the steaming Amazon jungle, my Maytag never let me down."

"My husband, the chimney sweep, made our Maytag prove its dependability in more ways than one."

"With the nearest repairman 100 miles away from the ranch, Mrs. Royer really appreciates Maytag dependability."

Figure 1-11 is an example of the kind of letter Maytag receives so often. Figure 1-12 shows the ad it inspired.

Banking on Dependability

The dependability series that grew from Fred Maytag's desire for advertising as distinctive as his company scored big. Advertising industry research revealed that it was a Maytag ad that enjoyed the highest readership of any ad in an issue of *Life* magazine. The Maytag human interest stories, told in black and white, outpulled all other advertising in the nation's leading magazine during that period, including many glamorous full-color spreads.[7]

---

[7] Burnett always used the same photographer for the dependability photographs and it was suspected by some that the photographer's not quite accurate focus added a subtle innocence to the look of the ad. Perhaps this was yet more genius on the part of Leo Burnett not to make the ad look too slick and professional in order for it to appear genuine and believable. So it was that Maytag testimonial ads remained black and white at a time when the advertising industry was obsessed with color.

Contests and Promotions

One 1974 dependability ad featured an Iowa family who owned the oldest still-working Maytag automatic washer, which had been discovered in a national contest. It was a 1949 Maytag that turned out to be the twelfth of its model ever manufactured. In the firm belief that anything that works is worth doing again, Maytag followed with a search for the oldest Maytag washer of any kind still in service. A 1914 wooden tub model, only seven years younger than the first Maytag washers built in 1907, was found still in service in Lethbridge, Ontario.* Many Maytag dealers followed suit and ran their own oldest-washer contests.

To commemorate its 1993 Centennial, Maytag sponsored yet another contest, this time for the oldest aluminum-tub washer. Twelve million had been made between 1919 and 1983.

In another promotional stunt, dealers began putting a Maytag washer in the front window of their store, intending to keep it running continuously until it failed. This promotion self-destructed as both dealers and customers grew tired of watching long before the Maytag faltered.

* Records show that in 1943, Maytag found a 1911 washer in Grand Island, Nebraska. Its owner, Agnes Smentowski, refused to sell it to the company because it did her weekly wash, and she couldn't get another until the war was over.

The success of the dependability campaign indicated that Maytag washers had met and exceeded customers' expectations of quality. Although neither Maytag nor Leo Burnett knew it at the time, the fact that Maytag was successfully meeting and exceeding customer-driven concepts of dependability would later explain the general public's instant acceptance of Old Lonely.

Another "lesson learned" by Maytag's advertising effort was that the testimonial approach was never as effective on television as it was in print. Real people on television weren't as engaging and entertaining as they were in a black-and-white photograph. Posing for still photographs doesn't require the ability to act. People who looked believable in a family album-type photograph weren't able to convey the same message in the more professional medium of live action.

By subscribing to a good old solid-midwestern-fundamental commitment to do the best job and produce the most reliable product possible, Maytag had laid the groundwork for the tremendous advertising phenomenon that was to come. By sticking to their knitting out in Newton, Iowa, Maytaggers had established a benchmark in quality that has yet to be supplanted in the home appliance industry. How deeply this enduring culture of quality had

January 5, 1987

Gentlemen:

I was cleaning my desk yesterday, when I ran across the sales receipt on my Maytag automatic washing machine. I remembered buying it years ago, but I was surprised to see it was way back in 1970. The amazing thing is, I have never had a service call on it.

We have worked it hard, "three children hard," and moved four times, so it hasn't been pampered. In fact, the last four years it has washed the uniforms of the local high school cross country and track team. Our son is the coach.

I just wanted to let you know your TV ad (the bored repairman) isn't exaggerating a bit. You do make an exceptional appliance.

A satisfied customer,

Mary Nesheim

P.S.: I enclose a copy of the sales slip.

Figure 1-11. An example of an unsolicited testimonial letter, and...

12-year-old Maytag outruns high school track team.

A high school track team can really keep a washing machine on the run. And it could mean an early finish for most. But to Mrs. Nesheim's Maytag, the challenge was no sweat.

After keeping the Nesheim family in clean clothes for 12 years, their Maytag took on the added load of a busy track team. Yet even that didn't slow her machine down. In fact, the last we heard, their Maytag was still going strong.

That's an exceptional record for any machine. But it's no rare feat when the contestant is a Maytag. We've been building our washers to last longer and need fewer repairs since 1907. So hearing from satisfied customers like the Nesheims, only proves what we've known all along—practice does make perfect.

MAYTAG
THE DEPENDABILITY PEOPLE

One last reason to buy a Maytag washer: a free $50 savings bond on select models. But see your dealer now, this offer is limited.

Figure 1-12. ...the ad it inspired. © Leo Burnett.

penetrated consumers' minds was to become evident by the mid-1960s. By the time Old Lonely arrived on the scene in 1967, Maytag customers had already been conditioned, through generations of experience, to accept his no-repairs dilemma.

But Who Gets Credit?

Nobody knows precisely where the idea for Old Lonely originated. Some maintain that the idea was first seen in a Maytag advertisement carried in a trade publication. Another theory credits a Canadian radio show featuring a local appliance repairman answering listeners' questions, not unlike the Frick-and-Frack Tappet Brothers auto know-it-alls on public radio. Others claim that one of the testimonial ads run in Salt Lake City inspired the campaign. Of course, several former Burnett employees modestly lay claim to the idea.

But the real reason nobody can lay legitimate claim to Old Lonely is that a number of people, unaware of one another, contributed. The man closest to the campaign was Leo Burnett account executive Chuck Jones, who spent the 10 years between 1958 and 1968 on the account. According to Jones, the genesis of the idea came from John Held Jr., a retired cartoonist for *The New Yorker* magazine who occasionally worked for Burnett as a creative consultant. Held was part of the creative team that developed the dependability ideas during the 1960 brainstorm. His approach to the assignment was to interview some Maytag dealers. One dealer told him prophetically:

> I not only sell Maytags, I service them too. But if I had to make my living fixing them, I'd starve.

The dealer's comment struck a nerve in Held, who put the idea on paper. It became one of the 127 ad ideas of 1960. Although the idea was there, the follow up treatment was uninspiring. Even though Chuck Jones was intrigued by the concept, he followed instructions when the agency's creative head said, "Don't sell it." The vicissitudes of disobeying the agency's creative director were still fresh in Jones's mind when he sabotaged his own preference. "It's not good enough for you," he told Maytag executives in 1960 when he briefly pitched the starving repairman idea along with many others. Three or four years later, the starving repairman became the basis for a trade ad.

Jones credits Claire Ely, Maytag marketing vice president, with a stake in creating Old Lonely. Ely had asked Jones, "What if we run a line at the bottom of our ads saying 'The Most Dependable Automatics Made'?" From that discussion, the line "The Dependable Automatics" came to be used in print ads.

In 1967, while getting ready for a client presentation, Jones wandered into the office of Peter Horst, associate creative director working on the Maytag account. Drawing on the original print ad idea and trade version, Horst had worked up a storyboard about a lonely repairman. Jones asked if he could present it to the client. Horst hesitated. Not only was the concept unfinished, but it had yet to receive the requisite blessing of the creative review board before being shown to a client. Flirting with the creative director's wrath once again, Jones had the storyboard in his portfolio as he headed for his meeting.

Discussing overall concepts and showing storyboards of new television ideas was a semiannual ritual. At this particular session, Ralph Nunn, then Maytag advertising director, was not very excited about what Chuck Jones and the agency had prepared. Sensing his ennui, Jones drew his presentation to a close and began putting away his materials. In doing so he mentioned casually that he had one last storyboard, but it was still in the process of development. Nunn insisted that Jones give him a peek. It was the now-famous drill instructor scenario (look back to Figure 1-3). Nunn was so taken with the idea that he immediately ordered a single commercial to be made.

When Jones got back to Chicago, he was promptly called on the carpet for showing, and worse yet selling, the "unanointed" idea. When Jones was called before the agency's creative director, Draper Daniels, and the president, he fully expected to have his head handed to him. Standing before this final tribunal, Ed Thiele, president of the company now that Leo Burnett himself had become chairman, Jones was asked, simply, "Did Maytag buy it?" "Yes," he replied. The final judgment was swift and pragmatic: "Then that's that."

The Jesse White Years

As a veteran actor, playing the role of the drill instructor was just another afternoon's work for Jesse White. Neither he nor anyone else associated with the commercial, including the Maytag people, had any idea what was about to happen. Had White not been available and had the agency's second choice, Phil Silvers, done the part, Old Lonely might very well have taken a different tack.

Despite his long-running television series on *The Ann Sothern Show* and hundreds of movie roles, White was proudest of his role in the Broadway play *Harvey*. It was his success in *Harvey*, including the chance to re-create his Broadway role in the motion picture version opposite Jimmy Stewart, that kept him from abandoning show business altogether and returning home to Akron, Ohio, to run the family business.

In any case, Jesse White turned out to be quite a bonanza for Maytag, off the screen as well. He enthralled countless after-dinner audiences with his stories of life over the years in theater, film, and television. His proclivity to revive his burlesque routine and launch into off-color stories kept his Maytag handlers ever wary. Old Lonely was never lonely around Maytag people. White was in great demand to address dealer groups and made a tremendous impression on Maytag employees in the plants and offices, as well as on the citizens of little Newton, Iowa, whenever the company brought him to town (see Figure 1-13).

Old Lonely quickly became part of Maytag culture and an honored member of the Maytag family. More than folksy, he was friendly as he roamed the factories, shaking hands with the men and kissing the women. His down-home humor would keep the assembly line buzzing for weeks after a visit. He could cause momentary mayhem. "My god, you weigh a ton!" shrieked Maytag public relations secretary Gerry Slebiska when White once came around her desk and plopped himself onto her lap. He always left a sense of legend and memories whenever he visited the company.

Figure 1-13. Jesse White was very generous with his time and his image.

White's wryness never failed to come through, even as he slept through commercial after commercial. And he paid a double dividend for Maytag as he became a common denominator for white collar, blue collar, and the community. Everybody in Newton loved Jesse White and understood that his role as Old Lonely was possible only because consumers believed in the dependability of the products manufactured there.

Maytag periodically sent White on personal appearance tours that generated extensive press coverage. He was seldom seen without his Maytag service uniform and never was without his Maytag hat. His chutzpa charmed television interviewers into allowing much stronger Maytag mentions than could normally be expected during noncommercial appearances. White never ceased to be amazed that more people saw him as Old Lonely than saw him in all of his stage, television, and motion picture roles combined.

Old Lonely II

While nobody at Maytag ever succeeded in learning White's true age, it is believed that he was in his early seventies in 1989 when Leo Burnett, looking ahead to the introduction of refrigeration to the Maytag line of appliances, began searching for a successor. It wasn't easy. By now Old Lonely had become an institution in American pop culture. Finally, Maytag and the Leo Burnett agency settled on Gordon Jump, the erstwhile befuddled station manager of *WKRP in Cincinnati.* Maytag and Leo Burnett were pleasantly surprised that when Jump donned the Maytag repairman's uniform, the public seemed to immediately accept him as Old Lonely. Without taking anything away from Jesse White's illustrious acting career and dynamic personality, it seems that the Old Lonely character had developed an identity of its own that transcended the actor playing the role—additional testimony to Maytag's Old Lonely-as-proof-of-credibility position.

"Things come to an end sometime," White commented at the parting. "It's better than dying." White joked that someone could be lonely just so long. "How much can you take?" he concluded. "I get so lonely, I go to the airport just to get searched." (See Figure 1-14.)

Old Lonely never abandons his bassetlike pose to endorse a product. He is never a pitchman. His face is more like the *Good Housekeeping* seal of approval. A paragraph from a recent Maytag refrigerator brochure sums up what the consumer can expect:

> What best sets these refrigerators apart from others is famous Maytag dependability. While we cannot guarantee that our lonely repairman will never visit your home, we still feel your best chance of seeing him is in our television commercials.

Figure 1-14. The "Loneliness Hall of Fame," (left to right): *Le reparateur qui s'ennui,* French-speaking Canada's Serge Christiaenssens; Jesse White; Gordon Jump.

A Pop Culture Icon

In addition to his place in every American's heart, Old Lonely has also become a part of the American landscape. A large sign erected in Dallas by Cowboy football fans prior to a home game against the Chicago Bears played on the nickname of Chicago defensive lineman William Perry: "Wake up the Maytag repairman—the Refrigerator's going to need service."

Further to the south, Houston Oilers punter Greg Montgomery was dubbed "the Maytag repairman" by local sportswriters and football fans during a season in the eighties in which he punted only 11 times in eight games. And in Boston, a *Globe* reporter once crowed, "The Red Sox bullpen is filled with Maytag repairmen," because the starting pitchers had made it to the seventh inning for 12 games in a row.

Old Lonely comparisons are common in the political arena as well. Former California governor George Deukmejian (Republican) described former Los Angeles mayor Tom Bradley (Democrat) as being "lonelier than the Maytag repairman" when the mayor opposed a ballot initiative that had overwhelming voter support. During the 1988 presidential primary campaign, Senator Bob Dole said of his opponent George Bush, "Something's bothering Bush. Maybe it's being vice president too long. He's like the Maytag repairman—waiting for years and nobody calls."

When Bush's popularity skyrocketed following the 1991 Persian Gulf War, a *Washington Post* pundit penned, "These days, national Democratic consultants are the political equivalent of the Maytag repairman—all dressed up with no place to go." And during the Gulf War itself, seven Canadian jet-fighter technicians became known as "the Maytag repairmen" because the CF-18 fighters the Canadians were flying never broke down.

Ralph Nunn recently recalled that during a trip to Toronto, he heard Old Lonely comments from the ticket agent at the Des Moines airport, the person he sat beside on the flight to Chicago, the ticket agent in Chicago, a Canadian couple seated next to him on the Toronto flight, the customs agent, the taxi driver, and the hotel clerk. All Nunn did was identify himself as a Maytagger.

None of the comments Nunn heard that day about Old Lonely were solicited. In fact, Maytag never solicits any of the references to Old Lonely that are heard or seen daily throughout the world. It's difficult to find fault with a customer-driven advertising campaign that becomes part of international business language. Threads of Maytag corporate culture are found woven into the fabric of social cultures. It's equally difficult to argue that consumers, over multiple generations, don't truly recognize quality when they experience it. In the end, the evidence indicates that the Maytag culture of superior performance and reliability, started by F.L. Maytag in 1893, is genuine and enduring.

Old Lonely as Metaphor

Old Lonely has become the metaphor for Maytag dependability. It's not the cleverness of the character or how well he is played that makes the consumer believe. The fact that Old Lonely is the human manifestation of what the public already believes is a well-made product has carried the character for a quarter-century and could carry him for many years to come. Positioned against other advertising campaigns that attempt to create an image for a product, clearly Old Lonely is an example of a quality product *creating the climate* for the advertisement.

The ubiquitous comment "My mother had a Maytag" usually referred to the traditional Maytag wringer washer prior to World War II. Nevertheless, the reference to overall quality was inescapable. Over time, Maytaggers report hearing less of the reference to mother's washer and more comments related to Old Lonely. A company couldn't ask for more. The public's embrace of Old Lonely is testimony to the power and effectiveness of advertising made credible by the value and dependability of the product itself.

2

Maytag's Unwritten Credo

Complete Customer Satisfaction (An Intricate Endeavor)

Those who set policy at Maytag continue to focus on customer-driven quality and dependability. Research and company history indicate that more than anything else, consumers associate Maytag with dependable, quality products. Management preaches quality—largely to the already-saved. Workers take pride in it, and the public experiences it. The unique challenge for Maytag is to achieve the same legendary quality in other products and brands as it has in washing machines. As the corporation expands and the diversity of Maytag products broadens, the company's reputation continues to be based on *complete customer satisfaction,* which goes beyond how well a product is made to include how a dealer services it, the availability of parts, and other criteria.

Company insiders ascribe the Maytag magic to a total commitment by top management to place complete customer satisfaction ahead of all other considerations. After all, that's how F.L. Maytag managed to stay in business back in the 1890s. This customer-satisfaction-driven policy is strengthened by the fact that it has been over the years unwritten and is thus interpreted by every manager and employee in her or his own terms. No new quality religion would likely produce the same level of enduring commitment to customer satisfaction that the Maytag culture has engendered for the past 100 years. Following a concept rather than a written directive personalizes the commitment and reduces any temptation to compromise. The Maytag unwritten credo eliminates the need for synthetic "controls" in the total quality management (TQM) sense of the word.

Maytag Believes...

Although the Maytag credo has remained unwritten for nearly a century and therefore has not been limited by language, the company recently wrote down some of its beliefs for internal consumption—apparently sensing that the influx of younger management, precipitated by the expanding corporation, needed a crib sheet. Many career Maytaggers have been called upon to act as cadre—a nucleus of trained professionals—for acquired companies, while many newcomers are now staffing company and corporate ranks. The written words remain largely unchanged from F.L. Maytag's original ideas.

Figure 2-1, from a recent Maytag pamphlet, shows both Maytag's mission statement and a set of beliefs essential to achieving that mission. At the end of the Maytag pamphlet is the tag, "The Dependability People."

Any company can put words to paper. The question remains, "Does this company really practice what it preaches?" One way that Maytag implements its beliefs is evident in how the company stresses the value of "environment." In its pamphlet Maytag chose the words "...an environment that nurtures pride, mutual dignity, integrity, trust, and safety." In the absence of such a working environment, no quality program, no matter how logical or well conceived, will effect long-term improvement. Companies often hire consultants, send their people to quality college, and adopt all kinds of quality systems, only to be disappointed at how little things change over the long term. What these quality programs seem to miss is the primary value of environment.

Maytag employs many quality-oriented programs that will be described in following chapters. However, the Maytag programs, whether internally developed or adopted from the outside, are all tempered by the Maytag environment and not the other way around.

"We exist to serve our customers by meeting their demands..." Customer-defined quality is a way of life at Maytag. F.L. Maytag discovered that in the days of the threshing crews.

Leadership's Commitment—From Founding to the Present

The reputation that allowed Old Lonely a quarter-century of repose was forged almost from the very beginning. It resulted from a conscious management decision to be the best, coupled with the persistence to stick to that decision, come what may. The foreword in a 1921 Maytag catalog contained these words from then company president, L.B. (Bud) Maytag:

> A way back in 1893, when this business was first established, we determined to attain and maintain a reputation for quality, satisfaction, and service. That we succeeded is evidenced by our growth and present capacity.

The Maytag Mission

To provide our customers with products of unsurpassed performance that *last longer, need fewer repairs,* and are produced at the *lowest possible cost.*

Maytag Beliefs

To achieve our mission, we will be guided by these basic beliefs:

Customers: We exist to serve our customers by meeting their demands for long-lasting, dependable products. Customer satisfaction is our most important commitment.

Quality: Quality products manufactured and marketed by quality people has been our formula for success since our company's beginnings. Quality is the responsibility of every employee and a continuing vigil is necessary to maintain it at the highest levels.

Employees: Competent, committed employees are our most valuable resource and fundamental to our success. People will make their greatest contribution in an environment that nurtures pride, mutual dignity, integrity, trust and safety.

Profitability: For the long-range survival of our company and our individual jobs, we must maintain profit levels that provide for the continuing renewal of equipment and facilities with an attractive return to the shareowner.

Strategy: To maintain our competitive superiority, we must produce reliable, top-quality products at the lowest possible cost. (There is always a better, more cost-effective way.)

Figure 2-1. Maytag mission and belief statements.

In the threshing machinery industry we are pioneers—and leaders. We were the first to build a successful feeder, first to build a swinging carrier and first to build a husker and shredder with combination husking and snapping rolls. The cost and development of these ideas was considerable, but the whole determination of this company has always been to sell nothing until theory was converted into certainty.

The name Maytag stands for *quality.* It stands for the best in its line in the best sense of the word *best.* It stands for high-grade materials rightly used; expert workmanship thoroughly organized; skill specialized; talent responsive to business impulses; extensive equipment of the latest type and ample capacity.

Over 70 years later, Maytaggers still endeavor to sustain Bud Maytag's vision of the company. These words are not carved in marble in the lobby of the headquarters building. They're not even posted in employee break areas. Yet they seem to be etched in the conscience of every employee.

Of course many changes have occurred at Maytag in 100 years— changes that early management could not have foreseen in its wildest dreams. In 1992, Maytag Company president Richard Haines told his management group:

> In our ongoing quest to preserve our dependability franchise, we share the belief that we exist to serve our customers by meeting their demands for long-lasting, dependable products. Customer satisfaction is our most important commitment. Remember, customers don't buy quality, they buy satisfaction!
>
> Quality has been redefined for the 1990s. Products and services must not only be free of defects, but they must also *meet* and *exceed* the needs and expectations of customers.

Two years earlier, Haines had told the same group:

> Our ongoing drive to be the quality leader must continually be refined in order for us to stay one jump ahead of our competition. If we ever feel we're as good as we can get, we're in trouble. Every day, as we start to work, we have to earn the right to be called The Dependability People all over again. We know that quality will always be the foundation of our profitability. We will not undermine quality in our strategic plan to increase profits.

To paraphrase Haines, Maytag has no intention of killing the goose that laid the golden egg. The Malcolm Baldrige National Quality Award has incorporated some Maytag philosophy that evolved before Malcolm was out of knickers. "Commitment of leadership" and "customer orientation" are pillars of the Baldrige total quality thinking. Leadership commitment is also a fundamental tenet of W. Edwards Deming's approach to quality.

Quality at the corporate level was discussed at that same 1990 meeting of Maytag Company management. In 1986, then corporate CEO Dan Krumm continued to expand Maytag's horizons through a series of major acquisitions, beginning with Magic Chef, a full-line manufacturer. The Maytag Corporation was formed to encompass the enlarged empire, and the original Maytag Company became the flagship of the growing list of companies within the corporation. In his first report to management following the 1989 acquisition of Hoover, the vacuum cleaner and European appliance company, Krumm said:

Quality must be the foundation of our corporate culture. It must permeate not only what we build into our products, but all of our manufacturing, marketing, distribution and service functions.

In products, we must insist upon the same high quality across the board, not just in the top-of-the-line. The differences among our products should lie only in the market segments they serve and we must always give the customer sound value, reliability, and performance as promised.

Our emphasis on quality also extends to our people and we will provide compensation and benefit levels that are competitive and rewarding. People, after all, make quality happen and employee pride is a better guarantee of quality than rigid inspection.[1] Quality, of course, ties in other elements of our strategic plan. For example, quality will always be the foundation of our profitability and we will not undermine quality in our strategic plan to increase profits. However, increasing profitability is essential to providing long-term benefits to shareholders and employees. Our objective is to be the profitability leader in the industry for each product line we manufacture. We intend to outperform the competition in return on sales, equity and assets, and on earnings growth.

Krumm seems to be giving his executives good news and bad news. At least it would sound that way to executives from most other firms. On the one hand, he is saying that profitability must take a back seat to perpetuating Maytag's reputation for quality. On the other hand he's saying that Maytag stockholders are expecting leadership in profitability as well. Profitability and quality may seem to be mutually exclusive goals. However, the "long view" at Maytag ties the two together.

Krumm's comments embrace the human element in goal attainment. Whereas most firms would consider a corporate culture based upon no less than complete quality and customer satisfaction a "stretch goal," Maytaggers, from the factory floor to the executive conference room, assume it.[2]

---

[1] Krumm identifies another secret behind Maytag's successful cultivation of a quality culture. Latter-day attempts to impose quality discipline in companies without a preexisting and pervasive commitment to corporate pride are tenuous at best.

[2] Maytag's management philosophy and its reputation for quality and dependability have resulted in a great deal of recognition over the years. In 1983, Iowa Governor Terry Branstad helped hoist the quality banner to the top of the Maytag flagpole when *Quality Magazine* presented the company with its annual Quality Recognition award.

In 1982, Maytag was ranked as one of the 40 best-run companies in America by Tom Peters and Robert Waterman in their bestseller, *In Search of Excellence*. Waterman included Maytag again in his sequel, *The Renewal Factor*. Many of the companies originally named by Peters and Waterman in *In Search of Excellence* didn't make it to the second book. Milton Moskowitz named Maytag as one of the 100 best companies to work for in America. *Dun's Business Month* called Maytag one of the five best-managed companies in 1985. Other favorable mentions included references in *The Branding of America* by Ronald Hambleton and a CNN feature segment on Dan Krumm in 1987 for the network's *Pinnacle* series.

Mottoes Past and Present

"Quality is remembered long after price is forgotten," was the incantation of the old-time wringer washer salesman. Contemporary engineers reject the management maxim "If it ain't broke, don't fix it." The concept behind TQM's "kaizen," (from the Japanese expression for "continuous improvement") has been part and parcel of Maytag philosophy since the early days of Howard Snyder, Maytag's inventive genius. Maytag has rarely been the first to introduce a product. However, it has always invested the most to refine and improve the products it sells.

Following World War II, third-generation company head Fred Maytag II set out to build a bridge between the prewar family entrepreneurship and a postwar professional management style. Demanding flexibility and professionalism as he groomed postwar management to run the company, Fred espoused two concepts that were seminal to Maytag's management philosophy: enlightened self-interest and divine discontent.

Being Best Beats Being First

To Fred Maytag II, enlightened self-interest referred to everything from the company's altruism and community leadership to its refusal to compromise in favor of achieving short-term goals. The appliance industry is as competitive as any market, and the pressure to show impressive financial performance is intense. An historical examination of Maytag indicates that the company never caved in to any pressure that favored short-term benefits at the expense of long-term benefits. Many of Fred Maytag II's decisions cost the company more in the short run, yet kept the focus on quality and dependability, resulting in long-term profitability. Fred II, his father Elmer, uncle Bud, and grandfather F.L. all demonstrated similar abilities to patiently take the long view.

For example, Fred delayed Maytag's entrance into the automatic washer market following World War II until Maytag had a design that performed as reliably and cleaned clothes as well as the Maytag wringer washer that set the benchmark in quality and performance for the industry. Watching competing washing machine manufacturers get automatics on the market before Maytag must have driven young executives crazy. Yet Fred's priorities were rigid, and sweating through the meticulous development of the Maytag automatic etched an indelible message into each Maytagger's consciousness. In this way, patience and the long view crossed the bridge between prewar family entrepreneurship and nonfamily leadership in the years to come.

Fred Maytag II didn't allow himself or the company to be seduced by the temptation to be first just for the sake of it. While other manufacturers rushed to get their automatic washers on the market following the war, Maytag waited until it could achieve its design objective. It took four years, but the first Maytag automatic washer got clothes clean—unlike the tattle-tale gray results that other manufacturers accepted as a trade-off for automation.

Maytag planned then, as it still does, to be around as long as consumers value quality and dependability. The long view grants the permission to be the best at the cost of being first. Few if any contemporary consumers have any idea who brought out the first automatic washing machine. However, few if any would name anyone but Maytag if asked who makes the *best* automatic washer. Maytag's enlightened self-interest ultimately works in the best interest of the company and consumers.[3]

Tinkering All the Way to the Bank

Divine discontent was Fred II's way of describing the constant search for new and better ways that he hoped would characterize Maytaggers— especially the design engineers. Now, as in the beginning, the emphasis at Maytag is almost entirely on product development—that is, making existing products better rather than researching new and different products for the sake of being new and different. Maytag is known as a leader in innovation despite the fact that it seldom invents anything. Maytag's impressive list of patents results from making continuous refinements to existing products.

Divine discontent at Maytag propels innovation and continuous improvement in all phases of the business. TQM advocates refer to "process orientation" as a focus on customer behavior and solving customer problems rather than a focus on profitability and/or production quotas. With his divine discontent, Fred II implies that the same focus has existed at Maytag from the beginning. Without neglecting fiscal responsibility and marketing objectives, Maytag concentrates on cleaning clothes better than anyone else in a machine that lasts longer and needs fewer repairs. The profits take care of themselves. As current Maytag CEO Leonard Hadley sums it up: "Our future lies with the past."

---

[3] As Krumm and Haines both implied in their remarks to management, the long view might appear as an expensive luxury to tightwad bean counters or as competitive doom to short-sighted and overly zealous marketing folks. However, Maytag has successfully proved that the long view, as enlightened self-interest, is money in the bank.

Maytag on the "Make or Buy" Debate

Capital investment plays a significant role in Maytag's quality story. The company has an ongoing record of reinvesting in state-of-the-art capital equipment. Much of this equipment is used for vertical or backward integration, otherwise known as in-house production of components. Historically, Maytag has manufactured more of its own components than anyone else in the business.[4] Maytag quality standards leave the company no alternative but to make, rather than buy, the most critical components in its products (see Figure 2-2). Many components available from outside suppliers simply don't meet Maytag's quality standards.

Some would-be suppliers can't comprehend the core level of Maytag's cultural commitment to quality. Maytag has always had too much at stake to allow mediocre quality from a supplier to become the Achilles heel of its

---

Do-It-Yourself Rubber Parts

In preparation for the introduction of its automatic washer, Maytag began fabricating its own rubber parts because an outside vendor capable of meeting the company's strict specifications could not be found. The boot seal keeps the wash tub from leaking while permitting the driveshaft to connect the agitator above to the transmission below the tub. A carbon ring mates with a Teflon (formerly stainless steel) ring. A human hair between the two would be enough to cause the tub to leak.

Raw rubber and various ingredients are compounded on a rubber mill, then samples are tested in the process control laboratory before the batch is released for production. Each finished part is inspected and the seal gets a vacuum check for leaks after it is installed in the tub.

Another rubber part fabricated by Maytag is the rear drum support on its dryers: basically a rubber tire bonded to a plastic wheel. Like every Maytag component, the drum support has to undergo a life test in the manufacturing engineering lab. It is operated through 10,000 dryer cycles, or 200 million revolutions, the equivalent of rolling for a distance greater than the circumference of the earth at the equator.

Figure 2-2. Taking the extra step in the name of quality.

---

[4] Maytag purchases only two main categories of components from the outside: electrical and decorative. Over the years, a major competitor, General Electric, was also a major supplier of electric motors. More recently, GE has supplied plastic raw materials. One of the more notable episodes in Maytag's historical relationship with GE took place in 1921. In the second calendar quarter of that year, a low period in Maytag's fortunes, GE took Maytag's 7 percent preferred stock, rather than money, in exchange for its motors.

products. A secondary benefit of backward integration has been the economy generated by internalizing the profit that otherwise would have gone to outside suppliers.

Testing to Double Life Expectancy

Similar to the absence of "designed obsolescence" at Maytag is the absence of certain quality assurance terms such as "acceptable quality level." The Maytag alternative is complete customer satisfaction. While many companies strive for "zero defects" in their manufacturing, Maytag's universe goes beyond how well the product is assembled as it leaves the factory to how well the product will perform for the consumer over time.

Reliability testing at Maytag is designed to expose a product to at least twice its life expectancy, usually at triple its overload capacity. Components that can pass such an extreme test are expected to perform to the standards articulated by Fred Maytag II. He wanted to see a Maytag washer run in the home for 10 years before needing a major repair. Hence the reliability test for twice that time.

Accelerated life tests are difficult to design. It isn't good enough just to turn the washer on and let it run. Driving it around a test track continuously for 100,000 miles, so to speak, doesn't account for the starting, stopping, cool down, and other factors that accurately replicate the type of use the product can be expected to experience in the field. Therefore Maytag testing procedures reproduce realistic conditions while at the same time condensing the equivalent of 20 years' use into a few months.

An Unusual and Exacting Exercise in Quality

If and when a Maytag component fails in the field, the same testing lab recovers the part and inspects it to determine the cause of the failure. In an unusual industry practice, Maytag field service organizations are given credit for returning failed parts. Maytag is particularly anxious to see failed electrical parts, such as timers and motors. Dealers prepay freight on returned parts and are given credit for the part *plus* a handling fee. In effect, Maytag buys back whatever doesn't work to put it under the microscope.

The Maytag lab also tests crated appliances on their ability to resist shipping damage, using devices that simulate a rough ride on the railroad or a quick-stopping semi. While some competitors turn to a container company for packaging design, fashioning their own edition of "product certification," Maytag even sets its own standards for product packaging and then

sends the specifications to the container supplier to manufacture, preferring to invest Maytag dollars in the product rather than in unnecessary dis-
posable packaging. Container suppliers, eager for Maytag business,
manufacture to Maytag's specifications and design standards that provide
more efficient packaging.

We're Not the "Quality Police"

Maytag's quality control and inspection department makes sure that best-
laid plans do not go awry on the plant floor. To maximize efficiency, the
quality inspector, operator, and supervisor work in concert, enabling each
operator to inspect his or her own work. G.H. Weaver, Maytag's director of
quality and reliability, reports that operators are generally enthusiastic
about taking on the inspection job. "They are interested in doing a good
job and take pride in their work," he says.

According to Weaver, instead of just playing the role of quality police,
Maytag quality inspectors are prevention specialists who help operators
anticipate and correct problems. Special training is required for self-
inspecting operators, particularly where statistical process control (SPC), a
method of statistically analyzing defect rates, is employed. Despite the additional expense, Maytag SPC is an important tool in fixing problems quickly
as well as preventing problems before they occur.

For Every Unit: A Ride
on the Merry-Go-Round

Each and every Maytag washer and dryer gets a ride on the quality control
department's merry-go-round before it can be crated for shipment. Besides
giving both the appliance and the inspector a ride, the merry-go-round fix-
ture permits testing procedures without disrupting the pace of the assembly line. A row of washers or dryers leaves the circle and a new row is added
every few seconds. Meanwhile, the rest of the riding products continue
their several-minute trip, having their innards checked; the assembly line,
fed with tested appliances, never misses a beat. There is a siding spur on the
line to receive any unfortunate washers or dryers that flunk the merry-go-
round exam. After corrections are made, these appliances must run the
gauntlet once again before resuming their journey to be crated and carried
to the warehouse.

During its ride, each dryer is connected for operation and subjected to a
series of tests for possible problem areas, such as wires, belts, thermostats,
tumblers, timers, and scratches. A washer gets its current draw monitored
as water is pumped in and spun out again. As a result, there is a trace of

water in every Maytag washer as it leaves the factory. Rumor has it that a competitor has been known to splash its washers with water prior to crating, creating the illusion that they, too, have been run through a complete cycle. The truth is that even if a competitor's machine arrives at the dealer wet, Maytag is the only major washer manufacturer in the world that subjects every washer to a complete testing cycle before shipping (see Figure 2-3).

What a Difference a Day Makes

Working on the Maytag merry-go-round reportedly gives inspectors a feeling of pride, knowing that they have played a vital role in preserving the quality of Maytag appliances.

> There are very few things that get past us up there. I like being an inspector. You feel, when you leave at the end of the day, that you've caught rejects. There's a lot of responsibility there. You feel like you're doing something [important], and when those dryers go off the merry-go-round, you feel like it's a good product.

Just before crating, 20 washers and 20 dryers are randomly selected each day for still further testing. Each gets a thorough inspection, then is operated for 24 hours, which is the equivalent of a month's use in the average home. Similar tests are performed on the other products.

Figure 2-3. Every washer is tested on the merry-go-round.

Attacking Quality Problems at the Source

Maytag quality inspectors' authority to identify and deal with problems is more than mere window dressing. One day in 1959, at a time when the company was faced with a large backlog of orders, Charlie Gecan, head of quality control, placed an embargo on all shipments in the warehouse and stopped production. Gecan, not much higher than wide, and with a face that could have played Old Lonely, was a bulldog when it came to quality.

He later explained:

> A high wattage reading was being taken in final inspection on one of our products and the cause was not immediately apparent. With my superiors not available [at that moment], we had to make the difficult decision whether or not to shut down production and stop all shipments. I must admit that at the time, it looked like it might be easier to compromise and hope that there weren't any units that would cause trouble. I knew, however, that this wasn't the Maytag way of doing business. The production lines were ordered shut down and we were able to isolate the problem within 24 hours.

Gecan made his neck-stretching decision at a time when a Maytag (Fred II) still occupied the front office. The head of quality control was greatly relieved to learn later that both Maytag and financial whipcracker George Umbreit fully supported his decision. In retrospect, it was the Maytag culture of quality, the unwritten credo, that informed Gecan's decision. In light of the company's heritage, it would have been unthinkable for anyone to have suggested that profit and production output should take precedence over product dependability. As with other Maytaggers, the threads of quality and customer service were woven into Charlie's professional fabric.

Buying Quality at Maytag

Quality is just as critical when purchasing raw materials and components as when fabricating. Selecting the right vendor is also important, according to Dean M. Ward, former head of purchasing for Maytag and later in charge of purchasing for the entire corporation. "I believe that developing long-term relationships with vendors is an important aspect of quality. I see no advantage in jumping from company A to company B and then back to company A."

Most Maytag vendors have supplied components and materials for many years, some starting as far back as the 1930s and 1940s. Nevertheless, Ward is quick to add, "We're always interested in new materials and new technologies." If Maytag is seriously interested in a new vendor, Ward or an associate will visit the factory.

> We talk with the company's management, look at the plant, check out the housekeeping, see how people are working. All this helps us to determine if the company is running an efficient operation. We can tell if a company is truly interested in providing quality components or materials.

Just-In-Time, Iowa-Style

Maytag has added new vendors in recent years, several of them in Iowa—ideal for a just-in-time (JIT) arrangement. One example is a supplier of wooden shipping crate bottoms. These are bulky items, and one is required for each appliance. This vendor, located in Newton, is part of a just-in-time program that schedules deliveries to coincide with particular product needs. JIT works for other nearby suppliers, particularly those with bulky products, such as a carton producer in Cedar Rapids, 90 miles to the east. Ward adds: "Some vendors tell me that [other] users of components and materials are backing off of JIT. The cost of expediting JIT on the part of the user exceeds that of maintaining inventories."

Receiving Inspection

Despite the fact that inspection is becoming outmoded in the quality crusade, Maytag still inspects every part from a new vendor. Timers, for example, are run through their entire cycle. After a specified quality level has been established, the inspection is cut to a sampling. Defective parts from the field, following analysis in the manufacturing engineering lab, provide the purchasing department with ammunition in discussions with vendors. Another quality check involves having the vendor send a sample of plastic material ahead for testing before the carload arrives for unloading, to ensure the material meets specifications.

Supplier partnerships are vital to Maytag's continued success. Maytag expects its products to last longer and need fewer repairs. In real terms, neither Philip Crosby's zero-defects approach nor W. Edwards Deming's reliance on probabilities for superior product performance can fully account for the type of long-term dependability Maytag engineers into its products. Maytag seems to have succeeded in establishing a sense of partnership with both suppliers and employees. Workers on the factory floor acknowledge that the long-term performance of Maytag products is their number one concern, and to that end, they're all participants in product inspection.

Single suppliers linked to companies through a common TQM program and client certification is becoming a familiar arrangement in American industry, and Maytag too has abandoned its former policy of requiring more than a single source.

Steel is the principal raw material in major home appliances, but Maytag has turned steel procurement over to a corporate committee that negotiates with a single supplier for the whole corporation.

However, Maytag supplier specs are no less rigorous than before. Even in times of steel shortages, when Maytag has been unable to get delivery on the zinc-coated steel[5] it uses in washer and dryer cabinets to eliminate rust, Maytag executives consistently resisted the temptation to substitute the less expensive sheet steel that other appliance manufacturers regularly use in their products (see Figure 2-4).

The first executive to say no to substitute steel was Fred Maytag II. Even though inventory was low at the time and his hard line against compromising on components threatened to interrupt production, the fact that the president himself stood firm empowered many executives who followed him to make similar tough decisions in favor of quality versus compromise.

The Role of Quality in the Service Department

Just as quality control monitors manufacturing performance, the service department supports the marketing effort, not only in the traditional role of dealer training and parts availability, but also as the early-warning system constantly monitoring Maytag quality in the field. Maytag learned early on that it is cheaper to fix a product in the factory than in the field. It isn't enough to keep customers happy by ensuring prompt repairs. Maytag wants to know what went wrong and how to prevent it from happening again. The historical record of having the lowest service incidence in the industry apparently hasn't kept Maytag from striving to eliminate service complaints altogether.

[5] Around 1950, when the first Maytag automatic washers reached coastal areas, like Florida, with high exposure to salt-water environments, the need, as with automobile bodies, to protect washer cabinets from rusting out became evident. That was when zinc-coated steel was first introduced. Over time, a scratch in zinc-coated steel will literally heal itself. The zinc coating proved so reliable that a five-year warranty against cabinet rust was issued.

Figure 2-4. A few months at the bottom of a river in Ontario—dramatizing the rust-resistant qualities of Maytag appliance cabinets, made from zinc-coated steel.

In addition to issuing credit to dealers for returning parts that fail in the field, Maytag engineers and production people go into the field to accompany service people on service calls. Maytaggers seem eager to observe first-hand how Maytag products perform in the user's home.

Defining Warranty: A Promise of Customer Satisfaction

Because Maytag has such a firm handle on its service incidence and warranty expense, it is able to turn its good record into a marketing tool by extending warranties. The 10-year warranty on the new transmission (see below, p. 51) is not the only example of warranty extension. Any warranty is a legal document, and it is scrutinized by attorneys to minimize exposure. With Maytag, however, interpretation of obligations to consumers have traditionally been liberal. Maytag views the objective of warranties not as antecedents to winning lawsuits, but rather as promises of customer satisfaction.

Extending Parts Availability

A sure way to offend customers is to effectively obsolete their appliance through unavailability of parts after a short time. Not only does Maytag want its washers to work for 10 years before needing a major repair; it expects those washers to keep operating for 25 years or more. Parts availability is maintained for all models so long as there is a reasonable expectation that parts might be needed. For Maytag, a reasonable expectation is 25 years on all products.

Not only are parts kept around for a long time, but they are made very accessible both to servicing dealers directly and through parts distributors. Over 100 parts warehouses located around the United States and Canada supplement the central Maycor (see Chapter 11) parts warehouse in Milan, Tennessee.

From a modern TQM perspective, "zero defects" refers to products being manufactured and delivered defect-free. Maytag is obviously a world leader in this caliber of manufacturing. However, TQM vernacular has yet to coin verbiage to project performance expectation over two and one-half decades the way that Maytag does.

Red Carpet Service

Factory service schools are a routine part of Maytag training. The company also holds service training sessions at the dealer level. Major cities often are serviced by a central service agency covering the whole market. Such agencies can be independent or company owned. Dealers in those markets have the option to perform their own service or contract with a central agency.

All Maytag dealers are required to provide service, either from their own department or from a central service agency. Maytag Red Carpet Service was developed in the early 1970s to ensure Maytag owners that a Maytag service representative would respond to their call within 24 hours. The Maytag technician wears a uniform just like Old Lonely's, complete with cap and red bowtie. The technician carries a white toolbox and two "red carpets," large red cloths to be spread over the appliance to prevent scratches (see Figure 2-5). The Red Carpet technician gives each customer a postage-paid return card on which to report his or her level of satisfaction with the service call. In addition to the fast response, technicians' trucks are stocked with a large parts inventory to minimize callbacks.

Figure 2-5. Red Carpet Service, another aspect of Maytag's commitment to its customers.

Since the Maytag Corporation consolidated parts and service under the name Maycor in 1987, the Red Carpet program has come under the control of the sales department and is a component of Maytag Home Appliance Centers—specially licensed dealers who carry only Maytag products.

Work Simplification: The Employee as Change Agent

Maytag has the type of fully committed, well-trained, and involved work force that Baldrige Award examiners look for. Everyone at Maytag, from top to bottom, is involved with continuous improvement and achieving quality and dependability objectives. This full participation is not new to Maytag. Although it has existed in one form or another from the turn of the century, it became a formal training policy shortly after World War II.

After hearing consultant Allan Mogensen outline his work simplification concept in 1947, Maytag executives quickly began formal training of engineers and supervisors in those principles[6]

---

[6] Mogensen operated a school for work simplification in New York State. Many companies, including Maytag, sent their engineers and other employees to study under Mogensen over the years.

It took a 10-hour presentation to suspicious union leaders in 1948 before all production employees began work simplification training.

Building Employee Awareness

Maytag established three goals, all stressing teamwork between employees and management. The first goal was to develop employee awareness of and input into management problems and to acknowledge employee contributions by personal recognition and cash awards. An employee could earn half the net savings of his or her idea for the first six months, up to $5000, later increased to $7500.

Creating an Interchange of Ideas

The second goal was to develop and encourage a friendly, cooperative interchange of ideas among employees, their supervisors, and staff departments through the discussion and solution of common problems. The employee's immediate supervisor and then a member of the engineering staff are involved in helping refine the idea, which must be submitted on a standardized form, including an estimate of cost reduction. All submissions in the work simplification program must involve cost reductions. The interface between employees, supervisors, and engineers forms a miniature version of a quality circle—sort of a "quality dot." Nobody knew what a quality circle was in 1947, but the quality dots seemed like a good idea at the time.

Overcoming Resistance to Change

The third and perhaps most important goal focused on working to overcome traditional resistance to change by giving employees the opportunity to initiate changes and to participate in changes made by management.

Before being eligible to participate in the program, employees must complete a two-and-a-half-hour training session. Most employees respond favorably and the participation level is high. After 40 years, Maytag's work simplification program continues to produce record numbers of ideas, both submitted and installed[7]

Factory supervisors receive 16 hours of training and have their own program, but without the cash carrot attached. They also receive recognition

---

[7] Maytag earned the National Association of Suggestion Systems' Performance Excellence award in 1991 for the nineteenth time in 21 years. In 1991 alone, a total of $239,174 was paid to Maytag production workers for their ideas, an average of $79.17 per installed idea. Overall, 6098 suggestions were turned in that year.

for the efforts of their employees and are honored at an annual dinner. Since their inception, more than $92 million has been generated in cost savings by the combined programs. Although work simplification presaged the modern quality revolution, many aspects of the concept parallel TQM goals, teamwork and employee involvement foremost among them.

A companion program was introduced at the 1991 work simplification dinner. The new quality bonus program pays employees cash bonuses of between $25 and $500 for ideas that improve quality but don't necessarily decrease costs.[8]

What Price Quality?

To the uninitiated, the assumption may be that a quality product is an expensive product. While it's true that quality can add cost, as in the case of using zinc-coated steel to eliminate rust, far more often the most reliable component is also the least expensive. Poor engineering tends to use solenoids, switches, widgets and bailing wire in a Rube Goldberg effort to get the job done. All this just adds cost to the product as well as making it more likely to fail and harder to repair.

By contrast, good engineering and design finds a simpler way to get the job done, using fewer parts and making the component more reliable and less costly to produce.

Breakthrough! The Revolutionary Helical Drive—1956

The Maytag automatic washer provides some classic examples. The original Maytag automatic, introduced in 1949, was built like a battleship and cost almost as much. It accomplished the assignment of getting clothes as clean as a Maytag wringer washer, but it was overbuilt in the process.

Among the many refinements that followed was a revolutionary trans-mission, introduced in 1956. The Maytag *Helical Drive* used the helix prin-ciple to change oscillation (agitation) to spin with a reversible motor (see Figure 2-6). The new drive eliminated over one-third of the moving parts used in previous models, resulting in a far simpler and less costly design that greatly improved reliability. Ever-cautious with its reputation, Maytag installed the Helical Drive in a new, lower-priced washer called the High-lander before incorporating it into the entire washer line.

---

[8] The work simplification program pays the employee 50 percent of the cost savings for the first six months. The quality bonus program encourages quality improvement suggestions even when there are no cost savings involved.

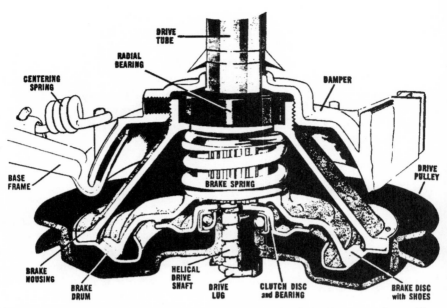

Figure 2-6. Helical Drive transmission—fewer parts, simpler design, lower cost, longer life—and basis for the nickname "gutless wonders" given to Maytag machines that featured it.

Breakthrough! The 1989 Dependable Drive— Improving on Revolutionary

The Helical Drive caused Maytag washers to be called "gutless wonders" by service people because there was so little to see when the front panel was removed. It remained the delight of dealers and the bane of Old Lonely for a generation. But eventually Maytag's eternally tinkering engineers found an even better way and, in 1989, introduced the *Dependable Drive.* If the Helical Drive was revolutionary, the Dependable Drive was little short of incredible (see Figure 2-7). Based on the principle of orbital drive, it reduced components by another 40 percent, ending up with only three moving parts.

The notion of tampering with proven features never completely escapes resistance. John Mellinger, head of Maytag R&D in 1989, recounts, "If there was one thing that people in the field told us not to change in our automatic washers, it was the transmission." But the potential of the new design led the company to move from mock-up to installing the transmission into production models. It was the first time that manufacturing was part of the process because one objective for the Dependable Drive was to increase manufacturing efficiency. Initially, limited tooling was produced and the product was test marketed in the Chicago area, not so much to prove reliability, but to satisfy management

Figure 2-7. Dependable Drive, 1989. Count 'em, only three movable parts.

that it wasn't tampering with something so fundamental to the Maytag washer that it dare not attempt the change.

After 18 months of field testing, in both household and commercial washers, the company was convinced it could proceed with the new design. Of the 30,000 units placed in the field, just 40 were returned and only 9 of those for so-called design defects. And even those 9 defects were related to preliminary assembly procedures that would not be used in the final assembly process. "We were really excited about the reliability, even more so than we had been earlier," Mellinger added. Following the results of the Chicago test, the warranty on the new transmission was extended to 10 years, up from the 5-year warranty on the Helical Drive. The move assured customers and dealers that the new transmission represented a genuine improvement that Maytag would stand behind (see Figure 2-8).

Job Enlargement: Fostering a Sense of Ownership

Job enlargement is another employee program administered by Maytag's industrial engineering department. Job enlargement entails job stations

---

Still Running After 181 Years

In April 1990, Maytag reliability engineers began running three of the new transmissions through continual agitation tests until the units eventually broke down. The first of the three failed after operating for the equivalent of 150 years of normal operation. The second unit lasted even longer and three months later, after the equivalent of over 180 years of operation, the third was still running and Old Lonely was still snoring.

Figure 2-8. Testing to failure—a long-term proposition.

being rearranged to permit an employee to produce a complete part or assembly instead of performing only a small function in a subassembly group. Maytag found out early that employees like the idea of being responsible for a completed part or assembly, including inspection. The job becomes more challenging and less repetitious. Frequently, the employee is able to mark the part with his or her name or number. The operator derives a sense of ownership from the arrangement and becomes more personally responsible for the part, all of which results in improved quality.

The word *quality* has more than one meaning on the Maytag factory floor. In addition to a "quality product" as the consumer defines it, the word also refers to fewer rejects, less scrap, and increased efficiency, all of which reduce the cost of producing the quality product, since there is less chance of a faulty part or assembly getting into the system.

The company benefits from elimination of bottleneck sub-assemblies that once depended on the pace maintained by a group of employees on a conveyor line. Under job enlargement, several employees, working at their individual work stations, produce such things as power units, control panels and water pumps for automatic washers.

The Maytag "Incentitive" System

The Maytag incentive system has its roots in a piecework system installed in 1908 by John E. Herbst, a consultant from Chicago Engineering Company, who stayed on at Maytag as head of the machine shop after installing his system in the foundry, blacksmith shop, machine shop and woodworking department. At the time, all departments were primarily involved with farm implement production. The Maytag Pastime washer was barely a year old.

Administering the company's incentive system is the traditional role of the industrial engineering department. Engineers establish standards for each measurable job and employees can earn additional money by producing above 100 percent of that standard.

Standards also provide the operator with needed information concerning important job characteristics and the work elements required to produce a quality part. Because it's more difficult to apply standards to automated processes, special incentive programs have been developed that provide a premium for quality. If operators reduce their defect rates below the established standard, they are paid a premium.

The incentive system continues to be popular with employees and has survived numerous attempts to scuttle it, first by the United Electrical Workers and later by the United Auto Workers. The idea that workers should be paid according to their individual productivity has always been anathema to organized labor, for whom fairness means absolute equality, regardless of individual incentive or contribution. The program has also survived the failure of many participants to properly pronounce it. Discussions on the shop floor often deal with "incentitives."

HPWTs and Other State-of-the-Art Organizational Techniques and Work Practices

When Maytag built a new factory in Tennessee to manufacture an entirely new dishwasher design, the company seized the unique opportunity to install a new management concept. Dishwashers were originally built in Newton. When a new series design featuring a plastic tub replaced the older porcelain enamel tub, it made sense to start fresh with a new factory. The new facility would eventually make dishwashers for several brands under the Maytag corporate umbrella. The plant opened in mid-1992.

Consultant Bob Huffman, with a Procter & Gamble background, was instrumental in developing the new approach. High-performance work teams (HPWTs) are created in place of a customary vertical management structure. Employees are carefully selected to create a team atmosphere. Successful candidates undergo three sets of interviews and a two-week orientation.

The organization chart is flattened and management and staff support is thin. There are no craft restrictions. Employees are nonexempt weekly salaried and pay levels are based on knowledge, starting at level one and progressing to at least level three within 18 to 30 months. Everyone is cross-trained and flexible. Employees are called "associates," and "coordinators" replace supervisors. There are no neckties. There is no reserved parking.

Team meetings are held one hour per week on company time. Some are all-plant meetings, and some are smaller groups. The goal is to share much more information than a customary "need to know" system. Training is continuous and everyone is aware of the company's business plan. Although transforming other, more traditional work locations will take substantially longer, Maytag is implementing selected elements of the new concept wherever possible. Over 100 Newton employees have already participated in a training program on world-class manufacturing offered by the Des Moines Area Community College. Another implementation of the flat organization involves combining manufacturing and R&D personnel in various task forces.

The Dependability People

When Maytag's Newton plants shut down for two weeks each summer, employees scramble to the far corners of North America for their vacations. For a number of years their car and camper bumpers have carried a Newton message, changing from time to time but always including the words "The Dependability People." For them, Old Lonely represents not just the product but the people who make those washers so dependable. Research indicates that pride of craftsmanship has always been a part of the Maytagger. It may relate to the amazing longevity of employment. Many present-day workers represent the second and third generations of Maytag families, whose parents and grandparents put in from 25 to 40 years at Maytag before retiring.

Maytag employees take pride in being The Dependability People. A regular feature in the weekly employee publication pictures employees in the plants and is headlined: "On the Job With the Dependability People." The issue of quality has never been raised in labor negotiations. Quality is as important to the union at Maytag as it is to management. In a meeting between union and management negotiators that forged the most recent Maytag contract, Maytag Company President Dick Haines told the group:

> We have always believed that our work force is the best in the business, and we still believe that the people you represent take pride in building the highest quality products that money can buy. I ask you to look to the needs of those employees and remember that their needs and the company's needs are one and the same. Neither can exist without the other.

Team Maytag

From the earliest days of Howard Snyder's innovations and F.L. Maytag's hands-on knowledge of the farm implement business, teamwork has been a mainstay at Maytag. Following an increasingly popular practice in American business, Maytag has embarked on a cross-training program that institutionalizes job swapping. Two of the first graduates of the three-month cross-training program at Maytag in 1992 were Mike Hamand, a materials development engineer in the research and development department, and Lorraine Williams, a process engineer specializing in organic finishes (see Figure 2-9).

Both employees reported that the team atmosphere at Maytag gave the Maytag cross-training program a running start. As program advocates anticipated, learning the ins and outs of each other's jobs improved communications between entire departments. It's long been accepted that an effective way to master a subject is to teach it to someone else. The cross-training experience accomplishes just that. More important, cross-training tends to promote the world-class manufacturing concept and reduce craft restrictions.

A Maytag internal employee publication extols the new cross-training program as another example of the company's never-ending commitment to continuous improvement. In their words, "The best just keeps getting better." Williams not only was exposed to Hamand's specific job responsibilities but also interacted with other employees in Hamand's research

Figure 2-9. Mike Hamand and Lorraine Williams are graduates of a cross-training program designed to enhance job flexibility.

department universe. While visiting an injection molding facility, she helped a tool engineer, a designer, and a reliability engineer solve a molding problem.

Perhaps the unwritten credo at Maytag has been most successful over the years in helping everyone in the organization to maintain a sense of the big picture. As a direct result of his cross-training experience, Hamand came face to face with the ghost of Howard Snyder, and perhaps F.L. Maytag too. As Hamand describes it, cross-training taught him that his own thinking was too limited. "I believed that only limited objectives could be achieved." After crossing over into another discipline for three months, he was able, for the first time, to fully appreciate "the effects of my decisions on production, and what was required to produce a Maytag washer and dryer."

3

Quality Is Flesh and Blood

Flashback: The Origins of Maytag's Customer Orientation

Total commitment to quality can come only from within. All the modern industrial quality paradigms notwithstanding, unless an individual and, in turn, an organization full of individuals truly internalize the ultimate value of quality, the concept will not endure. Granted, not everyone within an organization can work with customers directly and personally experience their positive or negative responses to a product or service. So where does "customer orientation" in the total quality management sense of the term come from?

In a well-run company, everyone has a "customer." Those who don't deal directly with users of the product or service *do* deal directly with others inside the organization, and the quality of internal service contributes to the overall result. Just as Mike Hamand learned through the Maytag cross-training program, everyone in the organization is part of a system and, therefore, affects the quality of the company's final product or service.

There is a direct relationship between how satisfied the internal customer feels and the satisfaction the end user feels. The quality of the relationship between the company and its customers is equal to the quality of the internal relationships within the organization at all levels. The cumulative corporate attitude produces synergy and, ultimately, customer satisfaction.

Over time, a well-managed company must weave a fabric of customer orientation that every employee's garment is sewn from. This is how a *culture of quality* evolves, and customer orientation is implanted into every employee's belief system. This companywide commitment to quality won't happen unless top management is totally devoted to the quality culture and able to transmit that commitment throughout the organization. Such a commitment to quality can proceed either from an immediate need to turn a company around or from a fierce and abiding faith in the vision of those who went before.

Inasmuch as Maytag is considered by many to be one of America's premier examples of a quality culture, let's take a look at the origins of the company's quality imperative. Who was responsible for setting the company on that track, and why? Who was the person that went before? What social climate did that person live and work in? What social and cultural constructs informed that individual's decisions?

For the Maytag Company, and now the Maytag Corporation, the first person—the flesh and blood—was Frederick Louis Maytag. A brief journey into F.L. Maytag's history reveals much about the man and the culture of the company that bears his name. The culture of quality at Maytag was born long before the company's washing machine was ever invented. History and nostalgia buffs—not to mention sentimentalists—should enjoy this journey back into the past.

Introducing a Hundred Years of Leadership

In light of Maytag's success, an argument can be made that the element of leadership in the quality equation is not only the most important but, in a large sense, the only element necessary to achieving quality goals. Conversely, quality goals can't be reached in the absence of effective leadership.

Leadership embodies the ultimate commitment to do whatever is needed to achieve success. That commitment must be total and undiluted, unswerving, single-minded, not-to-be-dissuaded. It refuses to be sidetracked and must focus on the *long view*. This long-range outlook—or as the Malcolm Baldrige organization calls it, "future orientation"—never loses sight of the ultimate objective and refuses to compromise for short-term gain. Taking the long view means dedication to the big picture.

It's not enough that leadership understand and fully subscribe to the long view. To be effective, the long view and long-term goals must be transfused to the entire organization. Nor can this be accomplished on a need-to-know basis. Therefore, leadership must also possess the ability to infect others with the long-term dedication bug. This infectious quality, call it charisma if you like, is the defining element in those generally considered to be great leaders. However, tremendous charisma isn't required so long as there is a genuine commitment on the part of the leader to bring everyone on board the long-term-vision team.

Quiet but dedicated leaders can be as effective, if not more effective, as charismatic types. The qualities of effective leadership can be learned and cultivated, particularly in the proper climate. One key ingredient seems to be hunger. Hunger often appears to be the motivation that drives the extraordinary effort that effective leadership requires. Those who have led the Maytag Company for the first 100 years represent a broad diversity of temperament and personality. Yet they have all shared a hunger for customer satisfaction. Studying the commonality of purpose and dedication in these people is an important key to understanding Maytag's success.

Of the four Maytag family CEOs, shown in Figure 3-1, founder F.L. Maytag was the most outgoing, flamboyant, articulate, and optimistic. He had sufficient enthusiasm for entrepreneurism. He was the ideal founder. His son Bud Maytag had a similar, albeit more sophisticated personality, but lacked the fire to survive the inevitable generational struggle with his father. However, sharing his father's long-view perspective, Bud made significant contributions to the company's marketing strategy during his brief tenure.

F.L.'s other son, Elmer, was more conservative and quieter than either his father or brother. Elmer's personality balanced F.L. and Bud's shoot-from-the-hip approach. Elmer's sensible controls helped build a solid financial structure for Maytag that probably wouldn't have existed were it not for his involvement.

Elmer's son, Fred Maytag II, brought a combination of entrepreneurial enthusiasm and sound judgment to the job and was the most charismatic Maytag CEO since his grandfather, F.L. Fred Maytag II and his successor, George Umbreit, made a good team during their time together. Each man balanced the other's strengths. Fred painted with a broad brush and Umbreit worked meticulously on the fine details. As the last CEO from the Maytag family, Fred could make decisions with the confidence that it was largely his own money he was placing at risk.

Of the four professional managers who have headed the company since Fred Maytag's untimely death in 1962 (See Figure 3-2), the first two, George Umbreit and E.G. Higdon, could be considered caretakers and no doubt saw themselves in that role.[1] Both men had worked closely with Fred, Bud, Elmer, and F.L. for most of their careers. Neither had aspirations toward leadership, and both were aware of their shortcomings in the CEO position. Despite their lack of leadership grooming and narrow financial focus, they were both able to broaden their horizons and function as total managers.

The next CEO was an architect of major change during his 18 years at the helm of Maytag. Dan Krumm may well be remembered as the first great leader at Maytag outside of the family. Like his family and nonfamily predecessors, Krumm learned fast in a changing business climate while maintaining an unyielding dedication to the unwritten Maytag credo.

---

[1] If Fred Maytag II had not died of cancer at the age of 51, neither Umbreit nor Higdon would have assumed leadership of the company. Fred Maytag II was younger than the other two and, had he lived longer, probably wouldn't have retired until well into the Krumm era of the 1970s and 1980s.

Figure 3-1. Maytag family leadership (1893-1962). (Top left) Maytag company founder F.L. Maytag. (Top right) L.B. (Bud) Maytag, younger son of F.L. (Lower left) E.H. (Elmer) Maytag, F.L.'s older son. (Lower right) Fred Maytag II, Elmer's son, the third and last generation of family leadership.

Figure 3-2. The era of professional management. (Top left) George Umbreit (1962–1966). (Top right) E.G. Higdon (1966–1974). (Lower left) Dan Krumm (1974–1992). (Lower right) Current CEO Leonard Hadley.

Present CEO, Leonard Hadley, took over from Krumm in 1992, and the most significant marks his leadership will etch in Maytag history have yet to be made. An Iowa-born, small-town-reared fellow, well-versed in Maytag lore, Hadley possesses a sense of dedication that skates right up to stubbornness and appears to have all the makings of a Maytag CEO. In all likelihood, Hadley will be the last Maytag CEO to have known or worked for a member of the Maytag family.

Each of these Maytag leaders played a significant role in the evolution of Maytag during the company's first 100 years. However, quality first became a part of Maytag culture during the reign of F.L. and long before the Maytag name became synonymous with washing machines.

The World in Which F.L. Maytag Came of Age

Frederick Louis Maytag was born on a farm near Elgin, Illinois, now a Chicago suburb, on July 14, 1857. His parents were born in Prussia and emigrated to the United States as teenagers. His father, Daniel W. Maytag, declined to follow his hereditary vocation as a teacher and learned carpentry instead. He arrived in America in 1849 aboard what his obituary said was the first steamship to cross the Atlantic. Actually, the steamship Great Western made the crossing in 1838 and scheduled service was begun in 1840. He took up his trade in Chicago. After a year, he moved west and found work in Independence, Iowa.

F.L.'s mother, Amelia Toenebohn, was born in Hannover and came to America in 1850 with her family aboard a sailing vessel that docked in New Orleans after a 13-week passage. Her family also settled in Independence. Amelia married Daniel Maytag in 1856, and they moved to a farm in Cook County, Illinois, where F.L. was born the following year.

After a few years there and downstate on another farm in Clay County, the family moved to Mattoon, Illinois, in 1865 and established a grocery in their home. Eight-year-old F.L. worked as a delivery boy for the business. By now, there were five Maytag children.

When the opportunity presented itself, Daniel traded his Mattoon property for a quarter-section of prairie in Marshall County, Iowa. In October 1866, he and the sons moved to Iowa by covered wagon, with the family milk cow trailing behind. Amelia and the girls came later by train. F.L.'s father and the boys built a small house that protected the family from their first Iowa blizzard that winter.

Daniel moved his family one more time. He sold his 160 acres at $12.50 an acre and bought a half-section at half that price near the town of Laurel, Iowa, midway between Newton and Marshalltown to the north. There the

Prussian carpenter built yet another home, which still stands. All together, Daniel and Amelia had 10 children, one of whom died at the age of 5.

An Entrepreneur From the Start

As the eldest son, F.L. learned to run the farm and generally take charge of things while his father was off building houses, barns, schools, and churches. Before his tenth birthday, young F.L. had broken 80 acres of prairie sod to the plow—an impressive achievement for an adult, much less a young boy. At the age of 13 he had mastered the full scope of general farm work. By 15, F.L. Maytag was harvesting like a veteran. As an adolescent, he once husked and cribbed 120 bushels of corn in a single day—an accomplishment any farmer would be proud of.

F.L. attended school a total of 22 months by his own account. It was said that he found schoolwork difficult. When he was 16, he persuaded his father to send him out with a threshing machine to do contract work for other farmers. He solicited jobs, operated the equipment, and settled accounts with farm customers for the next seven seasons. When he reached 21, his father gave him a team of young horses. F.L. bought a new wagon on time and secured a contract to supply coal for the winter to the schoolhouses in his township. He hauled the coal from mines several miles south of Newton. On delivery days he left home for the 20-mile journey early enough to reach the mines by daylight and often did not return home until after dark. On one early winter trip he hadn't gone a mile before one horse stepped into a deep rut in the dark and broke its leg. The profit F.L. had hoped for that winter vanished in an instant. Like most young men of his day, especially in middle America, Maytag was no stranger to hard work and occasional disappointments. However, the dream of financial success drove him onward, just as the same dream fuels the efforts of entrepreneurs in the 1990s.

The Siren's Song of Farm Implements

Daniel Maytag prospered as a carpenter, in large part owing to F.L.'s success in managing the family farm. Not surprisingly, the senior Maytag was reluctant to see F.L. leave the farm for a business career. He offered his son an 80-acre tract complete with a house as an enticement to stay on the land, but F.L.'s sights were already fixed on the world of business.

In January 1880, F.L. was offered employment as a salesman for a farm implement dealer in Newton, Iowa, for $50 a month. He accepted, and in March, at age 23, he went to work for McKinley & Bergman. F.L. later confessed that he was initially unsure of his own sales ability, but he was rehired for a second season, although no mention is made of a raise in salary.

In the fall of 1881, the senior partner in the farm implement firm put his share of the business up for sale. By that time F.L. had saved $800. He convinced his father to loan him an additional $2700 so he could purchase a half-interest in the firm, which was renamed Maytag & Bergman. Thus did F.L. become a full-fledged entrepreneur by the age of 24.

Dena Bergman: Reinforcing the Business Link With a Marital Link

F.L.'s new partner, W.C. Bergman, was two years older and had grown up on a farm north of Newton. W.C.'s father had emigrated from Germany about the same time as Daniel Maytag. The year after the Spirit Lake Indian massacre of 1856, the elder Bergman moved to that Iowa village where his daughter, Dena, was born in 1859. The Minnesota massacre of 1862 again brought tragedy to within 20 miles of Spirit Lake, and Bergman elected to return to the safety of central Iowa, settling on the farm 8 miles north of Newton, where W.C. and his sister Dena grew up.

As a young woman, Dena kept house for a bachelor brother on one of the farms where young F.L. helped out with the fall harvesting. On October 21, 1882, Fred and Dena were married, setting up housekeeping in a $1200 Newton home with an $800 mortgage (see Figure 3-3). Eventually, their two sons and two daughters would all play a role in the Maytag company.

Newton, Iowa: Eventual Home of Maytag the Man and the Company

Jasper County, Iowa, had been organized and the city of Newton established as the county seat just 36 years before F.L. and Dena married. It was 1846, the year Iowa was admitted to the union. Lots were sold and the first building went up. A church was started. A postmaster was named the following year, and in 1850, the stagecoach replaced riders carrying the mail. In the winter of 1856–57 some 3000 Mormons passed through Newton on their migration westward. In 1857, the year F.L. was born, Newton was incorporated and elected its first mayor, Hugh Newell. In the next few years a library association was formed, and a school district was begun. In 1866, the year the Maytag family moved to Iowa, Newton had 30 stores, 8 lawyers, 8 doctors, 3 hotels, 2 newspapers, and 2 dentists. Store hours were 7 a.m. to 10 p.m.

The railroad arrived in 1867. The following year the first bank was established after the infamous Reno gang, a contemporary of the James and

Figure 3-3. Wedding photo of F.L. Maytag and Dena Bergman.

Younger boys, blew the county safe and made off with $3500 of the taxpayers' money.[2] Newton's first town marshall, Cyrus Axtell, wasn't hired until 1875. A fire engine was purchased in 1879, an electric light plant was built in 1883, and the first telephone arrived a year later. In 1886 a city hall was built, and 29-year-old F.L. Maytag was elected to the city council as Second Ward alderman, defeating August Wendt 176 to 28. F.L. was reelected twice, but the winning margin shrank each time.

A Second Venture, This Time in Lumber

By 1890, Newton had a population of 2564 and new street lights. In February of that year F.L. sold his interest in the farm implement store to his brother-in-law partner and to M.A. McKinley. In April he purchased the W.R. Manning lumberyards in Newton, in Colfax, 10 miles to the west, and Reasnor, 10 miles to the south. In 1894 F.L. took on A.K. Emerson as his partner in what became the Maytag & Emerson Lumber Company. The business prospered. When the firm won the contract to supply coal for the city of Newton in 1898, F.L. no longer had to rise before dawn to drive the horse-drawn wagon. Maytag sold his interest in the lumber company in 1904 to W.E. Denniston. The Newton yard stayed in Denniston family hands until it was sold in 1990.

The Parsons Band Cutter and Self-Feeder

F.L. Maytag was already a successful retail businessman and knowledgeable farmer at the age of 38. But his education in the world of manufacturing and marketing, taught in large part by Mother Nature, was just beginning. The lessons F.L. learned in the years that followed became the backbone of a Maytag Company management philosophy that is now nearly a century old and still in practice.

In the fall of 1892, F.L., still a lumber merchant, and two of his Bergman brothers-in-law witnessed the demonstration of a remarkable new product—a first of its kind. The demonstration took place on the Henry Hoerling farm about eight miles north of Newton. The inventor was George W. Parsons, a farmer and thresherman who lived near Newton. The invention was a band cutter and self-feeder attachment for a threshing machine.

[2] The Reno gang, a large group of bandits, robbed and safecracked their way through the Midwest during the 1860s. Pinkerton agents brought them to justice soon after the Newton event.

F.L. later documented the 1892 Parsons band cutter and self-feeder demonstration.

> He had acquainted me with his enterprise and kept me advised as to his progress and, having been myself a practical thresherman as well as a dealer in threshing machines, I became intensely interested.

When Parsons was ready to test the invention, F.L. volunteered to help him attach it to the separator, writing later:

> I realized the great need of such an improvement and, [although] many others had worked on the problem and failed, I believed there was a solution and that Mr. Parsons might at last have found the key to it.

That first crude attachment was the beginning of the solution to the problem of feeding a threshing separator, doing away with several dangerous jobs on the threshing crew and speeding up the separating process. F.L. was so impressed with the potential of Parsons' invention that he enthusiastically accepted Parsons' invitation the following spring, along with in-laws W.C. and A.H. Bergman, to participate in the development and marketing of the band cutter and self feeder.

The Origins of Maytag's Unwritten Credo

In March of 1893 the Parsons Band Cutter and Self-Feeder Company was incorporated. F.L. and the Bergman brothers each invested $800 and George Parsons contributed his invention. Each held 25 percent of the stock. The elder Bergman was elected president and manager. A.H. Bergman, W.C.'s brother, was vice president, and F.L. was named secretary. Parsons directed production. The new firm immediately contracted with Skow Brothers Foundry in Newton to manufacture 150 attachments.

By July 1 they had sold most of the first lot and placed an order for an additional 50. F.L. later made a distinction between sold and satisfied:

> I say *sold* in a then commonly accepted sense of the word. But right there we four learned that nothing is actually sold until it is in the hands of a satisfied user, no matter if it has been paid for. About 65 or 70 of those machines were paid for, leaving about a hundred that were condemned or discarded by the users as unsatisfactory.
>
> How many of the machines paid for were satisfactory, actually sold, and became boosters for the band cutter and feeder industry and how many were unsatisfactory and were so many hammers knocking the business, I never knew.

I do know that the season was one of hard work and anxiety and ended in serious financial loss for a $2400 concern. How much the loss was we did not attempt to determine. We were afraid to look an inventory in the face. Thus we ended the first year's venture and immediately began to consider the campaign for another season.

Giving the Enterprise Undivided Attention

After about three weeks of discussion and counsel, it was decided to make the necessary changes in the mechanism to overcome its initial failures. The first year, none of the owners had given his entire attention to the fledgling company's affairs. Each was busy at a regular bread-and-butter earning occupation and was thus obliged to handle his part of the new enterprise as a sideline.

"As the result of careful study and planning," F.L. wrote, "it fell to my lot to arrange my business affairs so that I could give my entire time to the management of the business." How very fortunate for F.L. If the operational responsibility had fallen to any of the others, the Maytag name would probably be unknown and the Maytag fortune unmade.

In the following autobiographical record, there is evidence of how F.L. increasingly became part of the company and how the company increasingly became part of F.L.:

> And now I come up to the real beginning, January 1894, when we rented an honest-to-goodness office in the opera house block and leased the old Newton Stove Works, a 30 by 40 foot building with a caved-in roof and without windows and doors.
>
> We repaired it, installed woodworking machinery, contracted for lumber and supplies, and engaged Skow Brothers to furnish the finished castings and shafting. All the operations of woodworking, assembling, painting and finishing were done in this little shop and a small frame shed.
>
> As secretary, I was supposed to be an office man, but in those days the line was not so strictly drawn between office force and factory workers, so I made free to spend my spare time as a hand in the shop.

Kaizen, the 1895 Version

The struggling enterprise built, sold, and delivered 285 machines, most of them paid for, in the first year under F.L.'s leadership. The previous year's losses were made good and the future brightened.

Even though the improved machines produced greater customer satisfaction, further changes and improvements were needed. A machine with the improvements was shipped to the farm of W.D. Cotrell at Laurens, Iowa. Parsons and F.L. followed it around for two weeks while it harvested different types of grain, and they came away delighted with its performance.

Panic

In March 1895, an office building was constructed near the factory and in F.L.'s words, "we began to feel that we were a genuinely established industry." Things went smoothly for two months. Then a financial crisis struck Maytag and the Midwest in general. Credit was cut off suddenly and completely. The Panic of 1893 had finally arrived in the agricultural heartland—two years late, but devastating nonetheless.

It was a period of unprecedented failures. Established concerns, great and small, and new and promising ventures everywhere were failing. Discontent was rampant throughout the nation. The approaching U.S. Presidential campaign pitted soft-currency advocates against hard-currency advocates. The whole country was scared stiff, and the great eastern money centers had refused rediscount accommodation to western bankers, including the Parsons Band Cutter and Self-Feeder Company's banking connections.   Faced with impending doom, the owners of the Parsons feeder reasoned this way: "Whether banks fail or factories close, and no matter who wins the election, people must eat. Therefore grain crops must be harvested and threshed."

Arguing that their enterprise was part of the fundamental business of producing bread, they managed to talk the banker into an additional $1000 in credit and cadged small loans from friends. F.L. parted with his last personal negotiable asset, a $5600 mortgage note, to weather the financial crisis. But the worst was yet to come.

Heavy Straw Almost Breaks Their Back

Reports of trouble began to arrive from the field. Heavy rains throughout the Northwest had produced unusually heavy straw growth that was overloading the machines, causing serious breakage, delays, and tremendous customer aggravation. The lights burned long into the night in the little Newton office as complaints poured in by mail and by telegram. It became necessary to dispatch every hand they could muster to the field with extra parts and means of repairing and strengthening the machines to meet the unusual conditions.

It was a lonely wagon ride to a distant field where disgruntled harvesters were waiting. F.L. and his partners had many sleepless nights before they were finally out of the woods. They sustained some serious losses, but the season ended with disaster averted and everyone focused on the need for improved quality and dependability.

Again improvements were made, this time so complete and satisfactory that F.L. proclaimed:

> We could at last claim to have solved definitely a problem on which threshing machine manufacturers and independent companies had spent tens of thousands of dollars and had failed—a reliable, workable band cutter and feeder.

F.L. and his partners stood by their product so convincingly that practically all threshing machine manufacturers—at one time 28 different concerns—purchased and resold Parsons attachments as an essential part of each separator. One of the first lessons F.L. Maytag and his partners learned was that dissatisfied customers refuse to pay for the product or, worse yet, make the manufacturer pay and pay again for poor quality.

In F.L.'s case, harvesters, irritated by machinery that broke down, would discard the feeders in the field, refusing to pay, and move on, using traditional harvesting techniques. Even when the customer's money had been collected, it was still possible to spend all the profits and then some in servicing defective products.

By the time F.L. turned his attention to washing machines, these truths regarding product quality and dependability were ingrained in his psyche. Maytaggers in the generations that followed didn't live through F.L.'s experiences. Yet company management somehow kept the lessons he learned in the consciousness of every employee. There is no statue of F.L. anywhere at Maytag. However, management decisions at the Maytag Company continue to reflect the truth he discovered about customer satisfaction a century ago.

Howard Snyder: A Remarkable Innovation Story Begins

A little informal market analysis in the three-year-old company resulted in F.L. finding and hiring an incredibly prolific innovator who found ways to improve company products for a generation. F.L. noticed that although many units were sold around Austin, Minnesota, few calls for factory service came from customers in that area. In 1896 he visited the territory and discovered the reason.

A young local mechanic was showing such unusual aptitude for servicing Parsons feeders that there was no need to call for a factory representative. His name was Howard Snyder and he had some ideas for improving the machine. After sharing some of his ideas with F.L., he was hired as a field representative and salesman at $50 a month. He came to Newton in 1898, became head of the experimental department in 1912,[3] was plant superintendent during World War I, and served as a vice president from 1921 until his death in 1927. Although his major contributions were to come later, Snyder made his presence felt almost immediately (see Figure 3-4).

Parsons Spins Off

In 1896, George Parsons was seriously injured while working on an experimental machine. He decided to sell his interest in the company to F.L. in 1898. Parsons and a new partner then purchased the Brown Foundry in Newton and formed Parsons, Rich & Company to run the Parsons Hawkeye Feeder Works. Parsons bought out Rich in 1901. Nearly a thousand feeders were produced in 1903 before the plant burned to the ground. The plant was rebuilt on East Main Street and later was designated as the East Feeder Works after F.L. and W.C. Bergman bought controlling interest in 1904. The businesses maintained separate identities even though they were now under the same management.

Competition Leads to Some Early Benchmarking

Shortly after the turn of the century, Parsons people began to hear about a competitor with a better product. A company in Halstead, Kansas, was producing the Ruth self-feeder. It seems a Mr. Ruth had purchased an early Parsons machine and found ways to improve it. F.L. wrote:

> I determined to investigate the workings of the machine in the field and, accordingly, Howard Snyder and myself spent 10 or 15 days in the threshing fields of Kansas, Minnesota, and the Dakotas, watching the operations of this competitor. The more we saw of it the more we became convinced that it was not only as good, but better than the Parsons (see Figure 3-5). Of course, we did not openly admit its actual superiority—not yet—but we determined to find out immediately what the prospects were for buying it up.

Investigation proved conditions to be favorable. Stock in the Ruth feeder was owned by farmers living near Halstead. The company was operating on limited capital, and the manager, a Mr. Hegge, was in ill health. F.L. continued:

> We decided to act promptly and at once wired Mr. Hegge, asking him to come to Newton with a view to negotiating for the purchase of his com-

---

[3] Forerunner of the research and development department.

Figure 3-4. Howard Snyder, the talented Minnesota mechanic who ultimately became the inventive genius behind much of Maytag's innovative success.

Figure 3-5. The Ruth self-feeder, an early instance of bench-marking the competition.

pany's patents and business. He promptly accepted the invitation with the result that we purchased the patents, goodwill and about $2000 worth of machinery for a flat sum of $80,000 and made immediate arrangements to manufacture and market the Ruth machine in connection with the Parsons.

The Ruth was produced in Newton beginning in 1905 in a new facility built for that purpose. That year Newton boosters boasted that their city was the band cutter and self feeder capital of the United States. It would be 20 years before the community would brag about being the washing machine capital of the world.

In a 1919 booklet, F.L. said:

> The test of time and comparison confirmed our original judgment that the Ruth was really a superior device, so the manufacture of the Parsons, the original successful band cutter and feeder, was discontinued after two or three years in favor of its younger rival. The Ruth feeder is now recognized by the trade in general as the best machine in its line on the market.

Since Maytag made and marketed three different brands of band cutters and self feeders for several years, it must be assumed that they represented different price points in the marketplace, with the Ruth at the high end.

Satisfaction Guaranteed

At the same time production of the Ruth was moved to Newton, the Buffalo hay press was purchased from a Kansas City firm and brought to Newton as well. One of Howard Snyder's early tasks in Newton was to develop a corn husker and shredder, which was introduced in 1905. The new product was so much better than the competition that the company issued an incredible warranty, shown in Figure 3-6. Fourteen years later, F.L. wrote, "We have never been called upon to make good on the guaranty."

In 1907 Parsons Band Cutter and Self-Feeder Company, now known as the West Feeder Works, was termed the largest feeder factory in the world, employing 175 persons, including five representatives in Argentina. Products included the Parsons feeder, the Ruth feeder, the Success corn husker and shredder, the Buffalo hay press, and several accessories. In addition, Parsons Hawkeye Manufacturing Company, known as the East Feeder Works, made Hawkeye band cutter and self feeders, manure spreaders, grain graders and cleaners, hog waterers, and accessories. F.L. managed both the east and west facilities and ruled over a world-leading company for the first of two times in his life. Next came the seeds of the second.

Figure 3-6. The 1905 husker and shredder guarantee put into writing Maytag's confidence in the superiority of its product.

The Inauspicious Washing Machine

In November 1907, the Pastime hand-operated washing machine was added to the product line. Adding the washer met a major need for the company. Sale of farm implements was highly seasonal. Production was furious in the spring and all but stopped by fall. The plants needed something to keep them busy during the winter months. Demand for washing machines was not seasonal, and production of the washers utilized many of the craft skills and materials used to manufacture farm equipment. No one recorded who actually invented the Pastime. Other types of wooden washing machines were already in use: the One Minute washer and the Automatic Electric washer, for example, both made in Newton. That same year, Skow Brothers Foundry of Newton began manufacturing a washer for Thompson Brothers. The first washer to appear at the Iowa state fair, in 1867, was the Doty, made in Connecticut. The Pastime design might well have been Howard Snyder's version of existing washing machine technology. In any event, once the Pastime appeared, Snyder never stopped improving it, just as he had overseen continuous improvement on farm implements.

Grooming the Second Generation

F.L.'s son Elmer joined the company in 1903. After two years of study, Elmer had lost interest in the University of Illinois and completed his formal education at Quincy Business College in Quincy, Illinois. He worked six years as an expert mechanic, repairman and sales rep for his father's company and spent a winter as a South American representative before F.L. gave him the day-to-day management reins in 1909.

The grain growing season in South America being the reverse of that in the great North American wheat belt, Parsons sales reps could put winters to good use by traveling south. August Tabbert, hired by F.L. in 1903, made trips to South America in 1906, 1907, and 1908 to supervise installation of Ruth feeders. Elmer accompanied him in 1906. The original connection had been made in 1903, when an Argentinian visited Newton and ordered some Parsons machines.

E.L. Griffin was dispatched to South America in 1904 to establish the business there. He reported that he had to wear weapons constantly to protect himself from laborers who felt threatened by the labor-saving machines he was installing. Griffin designed a "South American" model for that market. A big shipment of Parsons machines went south in 1905. Argentina threatened a 25 percent tariff on imported farm equipment and repairs. Maytag enlisted the help of U.S. Senator J.P. Dolliver, who wired Secretary of State Elihu Root. There is no evidence that the tariff was ever imposed. In 1906, 300 feeders were shipped to South America, along with four employees. In 1908 one of the Parsons agents spent the summer in Europe selling feeders before going to South America for the winter.

In October 1909, having already acquired George Parsons' interest in the Parsons Band Cutter and Self-Feeder Company, 52-year-old F.L. Maytag bought the Bergman brothers' stock for $500,000, reorganized the corporation in December, incorporated in Delaware, and renamed the company after himself. After turning operations over to Elmer, he pursued other interests. F.L. later wrote:

> In June 1909, I acquired certain outside interests that appealed to me and commanded my whole time and attention, so I entrusted the management of the Maytag Company to my son, E.H. [Elmer] Maytag, who had assisted in the management for some time previous. From Jan. 1, 1910, to the latter part of 1915, nearly six years, I devoted very little time to the company's interests.

Restless Times and Restless Entrepreneurs

The early years of the twentieth century were restless times for many entrepreneurial spirits in the United States, and F.L. Maytag, like his father before him, was a restless man. The first two decades of the twentieth century spanned the time between the horse and buggy and air travel. The spirit of invention and opportunity was everywhere. There were fortunes to be made—and lost.

F.L. spent much of his time during this period in Chicago, then the second largest city in the United States and fifth largest in the world. Over a third of the nearly 2 million Chicagoans were foreign-born—more than three-quarters if those born of foreign parentage are included. The Germans, a half-million strong, were by far the dominant group. Chicago's corrupt downtown First Ward was once described by Senator Paul Douglas as the place that "gave to the city and to the Midwest the chance to privately enjoy every form of vice that was publicly condemned." Chicago was an exciting place.

Disastrous Digressions

Outside interests had always intrigued F.L. The Maytag Company itself had started out as a sideline to his lumber business. His earlier investment in his brother's Laurel store was followed by investments with friends and cronies in a Newton department store. He erected a building to house the Newton post office and, on the second floor, the Taylor-Newell shirt factory. He and two partners were granted a water franchise by the city of Newton in 1902. The water plant was later sold to the city just under cost.

Working on the Railroad

Proceeds from the sale of his lumber business in 1904 soon found a new home in an ill-fated railroad venture. P.F. Sherman, a successful implement dealer in Sioux Falls, South Dakota, who carried Parsons products, came to F.L. with a prospectus whereby each of 10 investors would make an initial contribution of $10,000 to construct a railroad between Sioux Falls and the town of Colton, 20 miles away. F.L. bought in.

Before work began on the South Dakota Central, one of the shareowners dropped out and Maytag picked up his share. It soon became apparent that additional capital would be required and each holding was assessed $6000. At this point, F.L. had $32,000 invested. Another investor was unable to continue and Maytag took over a third share, bringing his total investment to $48,000.

Sherman, who had been elected president, got into a controversy with another of the stockholders, who threatened a lawsuit. Maytag soon owned another share for a total investment of $64,000. More capital was needed and F.L. loaned the corporation another $40,000. Now he had $104,000 invested.

Two years later, it was decided to extend the line to Watertown, 80 miles away. A mortgage loan of $1 million was obtained with the assistance of F.L., by then a state senator. Before the line was completed, it was necessary for him to loan an additional $80,000. These loans subsequently were repaid.

Meanwhile P.F. Sherman was certain the railroad could be sold to one of the larger connecting roads, but negotiations were not proceeding. The investors became restless and in 1911 selected Maytag to succeed Sherman as president. Maytag acquired Sherman's interest, and after a year of effort, he secured an offer of $45 a share for controlling interest (which F.L. obviously had) but not for the balance of the stock. He urged the four remaining original syndicate members to accept the offer, which he would have prorated among them. They declined and F.L. felt it improper to desert them, so he proceeded with the operations.

Disaster Overtakes the Railroad

It became necessary to buy new equipment for the railroad. The bankers in control were requested to permit the sale of bonds to pay for it, provided a survey of the property proved satisfactory. The survey was favorable, so anticipating their approval, Maytag endorsed a company note to pay for the new equipment. However, when the board members met with the Chicago bank, they were coldly and bluntly advised that the sale of the bonds could not occur. No reason was given for the refusal. Maytag said, "I believe this was the hardest blow during my entire business experience. It almost put me to bed."

Interest on the $750,000 bond issue was soon due. Other shareowners refused to aid in meeting the payment. Inevitable foreclosure and sale resulted, and the Great Northern took over the South Dakota Central in 1914. In addition to losing his entire investment, Maytag had to pay the $60,000 he had guaranteed for the new equipment. In all F.L. would have been $400,000 better off if he had never accepted the original offer. His investment collateral was the washer business, which he bled severely on more than one occasion. Since he had no accountability, he regarded all the company's financial resources to be at his disposal.

The Maytag Motor Car

An interesting and little-known sidelight of Maytag history is that of F.L.'s involvement in the automobile business. In May of 1909 F.L. and Elmer together purchased three-fifths of the Mason Automobile Company of Des Moines, a total investment of $75,000. F.L. was elected president, Elmer, treasurer, and Edward J. Rood, secretary. Other directors were E. R. Mason and D.J. and H.L. Pattee. Designer Fred S. Duesenberg of the famous Duesenberg brothers remained as factory superintendent.

At the time the Maytags bought in, plans called for doubling the 400-car annual capacity. That July, Elmer and some cronies went to Ft. Dodge, Iowa, to meet the Glidden tourists. The Glidden tour was an annual event designed to competitively test cars under cross-country conditions. The Mason car was entered and, true to Maytag form, became the only two-cylinder car to complete the tour. It finished an hour and twenty minutes ahead of schedule. Senator Maytag and two others drove the Glidden entry from the Des Moines factory to Newton, 39 miles away, in 85 minutes (see Figure 3-7).

The Motor Car Moves to Waterloo

Late in 1909 the company was reorganized as the Maytag-Mason Motor Car Company with a new million-dollar capitalization. The company was lured to Waterloo by local industrial development boosters. The Waterloo factory employed 250 workers and operated on a 22-hour day, with plans to make 2500 cars a year. Two weeks before the Winnipeg exposition, F.L. sold his

Figure 3-7. The Maytag Mason—an obscure side-story in the history of automotive engineering. Pictured are F.L. and grandson Fred.

controlling interest in the company to William Galloway of Waterloo, and Maytag was dropped from the firm name in 1912. The automobile fiasco cost F.L. $300,000.[4]

F.L., Founder and Seed Planter

Perhaps the most revealing aspect of the automobile fiasco was the depth of pride exhibited by F.L. when, after his ship came in, he repaid by personal check the losses incurred by Newton citizens who had invested in the Maytag-Mason Motor Car Company out of confidence in him. The checks arrived Christmas morning 1923 and totaled approximately $20,000.

F.L. Maytag's history reveals that he was not the shrewdest businessperson who ever lived. Like many successful people, he struck out many more times than he hit the ball. On its hundredth birthday, the company he

---

[4] The first car, a two-cylinder model, was a performance success, earning the nickname "goat" for its hill-climbing ability. It was also financially successful. However, Buick introduced a four-cylinder car and Maytag decided to compete. The company went broke trying to design a competing model. Although F.L. sold out in 1910 to the man who had been instrumental in luring the automobile enterprise to Waterloo, he had a hard time "getting clear of the wreckage," according to his biographer who added that F.L. divested himself all right, but "not without deep dents in his financial structure."

founded is recognized around the world for a philosophy that is bigger than the founder or the three Maytags who followed in his footsteps. Even if F.L., Elmer, Bud, and Fred Maytag II never individually embodied all that the name Maytag represents in American manufacturing, F.L. planted the seeds of the reputation for dependability. The cumulative Maytag philosophies regarding quality and customer service—and accountability—indicate that through the ensuing generations, loyalty to those basic truths was never sacrificed to enhance the bottom line.

Modern corporate executives and aspiring managers can learn a great lesson from this historical perspective. A cultural dedication to quality and customer service within a corporation must become personal before it will begin to pay dividends to the company in a palpable way. More important, the subscription to a culture of quality can begin at any time. As the Maytag story unfolds, it becomes increasingly evident that a culture of quality is a cumulative thing and can't be decreed by memorandum from the executive suite or from the advertising department.

4

Applying American Ingenuity to Household Chores

Early Innovations Set Maytag on a Lifelong Course of Continuous Improvement

Divine Discontent

Continuous improvement is a special form of innovation that facilitates change and optimization. A classic example is what happened in the Japanese auto industry over the past several decades. U.S. automakers have been accused of allowing quality to slip over that period, resulting in a corresponding increase in popularity for Japanese-built automobiles.

Some U.S. automakers contend that such an assessment is not accurate. They maintain that quality in American automobiles remained about the same or improved slightly even as domestic sales of Japanese automobiles were increasing. The same auto executives do admit that while quality levels in American cars remained somewhat stagnant, the cumulative effect from continuous improvement of Japanese products caused a dramatic increase in Japanese quality and the American marketplace responded.

Just as the tortoise eventually overtook the overconfident hare in the famous fairytale race, the secret of continuous improvement is in the cumulative effect over time. Like compounding interest on a savings account, good things often happen slowly and quietly.

When Fred Maytag II said that Maytag didn't have any big secret behind its success, he could also have said that reaping the rewards of continuous improvement doesn't require genius—just persistence. The process isn't revolutionary, it's evolutionary. Corporate success through continuous improvement doesn't depend upon edicts from an ivory tower or the creations of mad scientists down in research and development. To be effective, it needs to be a pervasive attitude at all levels in the company. If everyone is constantly looking for improvements, someone will eventually find some and optimization will continue.

An important element in continuous improvement is flexibility by everyone in the organization. Everyone must be willing to accept change. Change is threatening to many businesspeople, and they expend a great deal of energy preserving the status quo. It's a tremendous leadership challenge to help people work through their fear and resistance to change.

At Maytag, the concept of continuous change began before the turn of the century and remains the basis for continuing growth and survival. Fred Maytag II gave his grandfather's commitment to continuous improvement a name—"divine discontent." According to Fred, it was divine discontent that led to the perfection of F.L. Maytag's first product, the threshing machine automatic feeder and band cutter. It also contributed to breakthroughs with the gasoline engine that later permitted Maytag to reach millions of washer customers who didn't have electricity.

Divine discontent led to improvements in the washing machine that Maytag pioneered, and it continues to drive improvements in other appliances in the Maytag family, including the dishwasher, for which an entire new factory recently was designed and built. Continuous change allows a company to pull ahead of competition, as the Japanese automakers did, and to stay ahead as competition duplicates previous improvements.

In a speech to Los Angeles security analysts in 1959, Fred Maytag II indicated that the hot breath of competition could be felt on Maytag's neck. He described how Maytag had introduced a washer three years earlier that featured cold-water washing with slower agitation and spin speeds to handle synthetics and hand washables. Within 12 months, the once exclusive Maytag concept had been copied by no less than five companies. By 1959, the features were available in *all* competitors' lines.

Innovation and invention might move a company ahead of the pack for a short time, but only continuous commitment to quality will provide staying power. Since the concept of continuous improvement at Maytag was at work long before there was a name for it, it should prove interesting to examine some of the landmarks in the company's history of innovation and divine discontent.

The First Washers

The first washing machines that appeared in the American wash house in the middle to late nineteenth century were little more than mechanized washboards. Even so, early washing machines saved time and knuckles. Previously, clothes were washed by soaking them in a tub full of soapy water and scrubbing them by hand against a corrugated metal washboard.[1] The clothes were then transferred to a tub of rinse water and wrung out by hand before being hung up to dry (see Figure 4-1). The earliest washing "machines" were wooden washtubs with some sort of hand-powered mechanism to drag clothes against a corrugation, either circuitously or by rocking them back and forth (see Figure 4-2).

How Little Newton, Iowa, Became Washing Machine Capital of the World

The Hawkeye Incubator and Brooder Company was formed in 1898 by F.L. Maytag's partner, W.C. Bergman, and Fred Bergman, a brother. The incubators hatched chicks, and brooders kept them alive long enough to fend for themselves.

In 1904, Fred Bergman and his wife saw a One Minute hand-powered washer at the Iowa state fair. It featured a corrugated wooden tub instead of a ratchet slat design.[2] Bergman arranged to manufacture the product for the inventor. Some of the Hawkeye Incubator and Brooder directors opposed the move, but Bergman finally got permission in 1905 to secure enough materials for 500 washers. Less than six months later, Hawkeye had produced nearly 3000 washing machines, which represented almost half of the company's business activity.

Twelve months after manufacturing its first One Minute washing machine, the Hawkeye operation was shipping 100 washers per day, and by 1907, it stopped manufacturing incubators altogether and upped washer production to 175 per day. That year the Automatic Electric washer was built by Skow Brothers Foundry in Newton, and the following year the Automatic Electric Washing Machine Company was organized, producing five units a day that sold for $60 each.

---

[1] Anymore, washboards are better known as musical instruments of the percussion family, played by rubbing and tapping metal spoons against the metal corrugations.

[2] The ratchet slat design moved a curved set of wooden slats back and forth over clothes in a tub with a curved bottom.

Washing the Old-Fashioned Way: A Rugged Endeavor

Washing by hand and machine washing both required wash water to be heated, often over a wood fire or in the cistern of an iron range fired with corn cobs. Then the heated water went into the washtub, along with shavings of strong yellow laundry soap whittled from the bar so they would dissolve more easily.

With the hand method, white clothes were often boiled in a copper boiler after being washed. Instructions called for half-filling the boiler with cold soft water and enough soap solution to make a light lather. A soap solution was bar soap predissolved in a small quantity of hot water. Best results were obtained when there was a large quantity of water and the boiler was but half full of clothes. Results were decidedly best when the wash water took a long time to reach the boiling point and boiled about 10 minutes. Of course, the boiler had to be over a fire. A clean stick was necessary for handling the hot clothes. According to the laundering manual, the germs that made clothes smell bad were easily killed by boiling.

> Rinsing is very important, for clothes must be free from soap before bluing, especially if you use the liquid blue. Lift the clothes slowly out of the boiler into a clean pail or dish pan and drain them to get rid of the soapy water before dropping them into the rinsing water. Use soft water for the first rinsing, then hard water if color of rainwater is not good. The first rinse water should be warm or the soap curd will harden on the clothes and it may be necessary to rub to get it off. A second and even a third rinsing water is desirable. It is careless rinsing that leaves clothes a bad color, and no amount of bluing will cover it up.

Bluing was used to make white clothes appear brighter, not unlike the optical dyes found in some detergents today. Soft water was highly prized, and rainwater was collected in a cistern—or the proverbial rain barrel—because it was soft.

Figure 4-1. Turn-of-the-century laundering techniques.

The First "Maytag" Washer: The Pastime

After F.L. Maytag bought out partner George Parsons in 1898, Parsons purchased an old foundry property and obtained financial backing to form Parsons, Rich & Company to operate the Parsons Hawkeye Feeder Works.

Figure 4-2. A view from the top of an early corrugated washing machine. The clothes were dragged against the corrugation.

In 1904, partners F.L. Maytag and W.C. Bergman bought controlling interest from George Parsons.

In November of 1907 the Pastime washing machine manufactured by Parsons Hawkeye went on the market and the now-legendary Maytag washer was inauspiciously born. The company by then also was managed by F.L. Maytag, who put the Parsons Band Cutter and Self-Feeder Company, known as the West Feeder Works, and the Parsons Hawkeye Manufacturing Company, known as the East Feeder Works, together two years later to create what has been known ever since as the Maytag Company.

Utilizing the woodworking and foundry skills of the feeder business, the washer fit well into the existing line. It also helped fill a seasonal production gap. The highly seasonal farm equipment business experienced maximum demand in spring and no demand at all after the autumn harvest. It was impractical to produce and stockpile against future demand because tying up capital in inventory and storing bulky machines were both undesirable. The washer business has a fairly flat curve, since clothes get dirty all year round.

An early illustration (see Figure 4-3) showing a boy at the crank of a Pastime washer read:

> A Pastime washing machine with a five-year-old kid attached will do your washing in twenty minutes with no more wear on the kid than would result in twenty minutes playing marbles.

Figure 4-3. The Pastime, Maytag's first washer: minimal wear-and-tear on the kid.

Although the Pastime was actually quite similar to other machines, that didn't stop the catalog copywriter, who puffed:

> The Pastime washer is constructed on lines that give it the following good qualities in a greater degree that are found in any other washer: Simplicity, Durability, Ease of Operation, Quick Work, Clean Washing.
>   We guarantee the Pastime washer to wash clothes quicker, cleaner and to operate easier than any other handpower washer on the market. We further guarantee it to be well made and of good material.

From the very first model, Maytag washing machines were designed and guaranteed to clean clothes better and need fewer repairs than competing products. From the beginning, the Maytag difference has been due in large measure to a concept that could be called "sophisticated simplicity." Simplicity in design became the trademark of Howard Snyder and his successors in Maytag research and development.

The Hired Girl

Two years later, the lever-operated Hired Girl model was introduced (see Figure 4-4). This washer could be operated by hand or by a power takeoff

Figure 4-4. The Hired Girl washer allowed attachment to an outside power source.

pulley from a gasoline engine. A wringer was added, also powered from the takeoff pulley. The pulley and the power option it presented did not, however, interfere with operating the washer by hand. The hand lever used a push-pull action. It could be operated either from a standing or a sitting position and was "so perfectly balanced that it [was] mere child's play to keep it running." As with all wooden tub washers, the homemaker was advised to keep a little water in the tub at all times so that the wood wouldn't dry out and leak. Figure 4-5 gives a list of what was needed to do laundry back in the early 1900s.

First Maytag Contributions to Washer Technology

Such was the washing machine industry that L.B. (Bud) Maytag entered when he came to work for his father and brother in 1910. Although he had graduated from Iowa State College in Ames with a degree in mechanical engineering, Bud Maytag professed little interest in making farm equipment. Having sold both farm implements and washers, he observed that washers were a better pursuit than farm implements because they cost less and the market potential was far greater.

A Complete Laundry Cupboard

In a 1919 booklet Maytag told the homemaker that every laundry cupboard would be more complete if supplied with the following materials:

Beeswax or paraffin used to fill up and make smooth sad irons. It should be tied in a cloth for easier handling.

Common salt, a neutral compound, used as a scourer for soiled irons, or to set colors.

Ammonia, in diluted form (household ammonia), and Borax, a white powder. They are both mild alkalies, and of great advantage in softening water.

Sal Soda, or washing soda, also of help in breaking hard water—although an alkali should not be used too freely.

Vinegar, used to set colors.

Powdered Chalk or Fuller's Earth, used to absorb stains.

Figure 4-5. Elements necessary for doing a thorough laundry job, from a post–World War I Maytag pamphlet.

Fresh out of college, he was given the then insignificant washer portion of the business while his older brother Elmer ran the farm equipment operation and F.L. went on to other things. Bud found the arrangement ideal and turned out to be the guiding hand that led Maytag to world dominance in the washer business during his 16 years with the company.

Growing up in a small Iowa town, Bud had enjoyed the fruits of his father's success. He represented Newton High School at Teddy Roosevelt's 1905 inauguration and accompanied his mother and older sister Lulu on a European tour in 1909. Yet all was not gilded for the Maytag boys. Bud actually had begun his stint at his father's company at the age of 11, spending school vacations in the foundry, skimming molten metal for fifty cents a day.

F.L. had essentially left Elmer in charge of the company in 1909. Although he never relinquished the title of president, day-to-day operations were handled by Elmer. In 1910, Elmer married Ora Kennedy. Fred Maytag II was born to Elmer and Ora in 1911.

Howard Snyder: Keeping Maytag Ahead of the Pack

Breakthrough! The Swinging Reversible Wringer, 1911

The first of many Maytag industry firsts came in 1911, courtesy of Howard Snyder, whom you met briefly in Chapter 3. The company introduced a washer powered by an electric motor—not in itself unique, but it included a new swinging reversible wringer, a major improvement. Water-filled rinse tubs no longer had to be moved into position for the wringer. Instead, the wringer was easily swung into position over each of the two rinse tubs or the laundry basket. The wringer could be reversed to back the clothes out if the load was too bulky (see Figure 4-6).

The catalog copy read:

> The Maytag swinging reversible wringer is equipped with every possible safety device to protect clothes, fingers, and the rolls. In case a foreign substance gets into the rolls, the lever on top instantly releases the pressure. All that's necessary is to press the lever down. This pressure release lever and instant reversible features of the Maytag wringer absolutely do away with the possibility of injury to fingers or clothes.

Washer Tail Wags Farm Dog

Bud Maytag was named to the board of directors in 1911. It was the biggest year in the history of the young company. As F.L. Maytag commented:

> The year 1911 witnessed the beginning of phenomenal development in the company's business, when an electric-driven washing machine was added to the line of feeders and husker-shredders.

Maytag enjoyed record sales again in 1912. Washer production more than doubled. In 1913 and 1914 washer sales increased again, despite a three-month shutdown following a temporary dip in sales. As the importance of washing machines increased at Maytag, Elmer was named treasurer and manager, and Bud became sales manager.

Breakthrough! Multi-Motor Makes History, 1915

Operating out of his Chicago office, F.L. Maytag learned about a business-man seeking financing for a gasoline engine. F.L. saw the potential for powering a washer for the Farm Belt, where electricity was not available. He secured a six-month option on the stock of Elgin Wheel & Engine Works of Elgin, Illinois, and ordered 25 motors to experiment with.

Figure 4-6. *Good Housekeeping* ad featuring the swinging reversible wringer.

Back in Newton, Howard Snyder shared this optimism and equipped washers with the motors. They were taken to state fairs in an early form of market research, and F.L. went along to hear the comments. Favorable public reaction generated an order for an additional 100 motors, and in late fall another call went out to Elgin, this time for 1000 engines to be delivered early the following year.

In 1915, for the first time in the history of the Maytag Company, income from washing machine sales exceeded that of farm implements. Lured by the Multi-Motor magic, F.L. Maytag returned to active management of the company. During the nearly six years of his absence, the company, under the leadership of Elmer and Bud, had managed to earn almost as much money as F.L. had squandered during the same period on his various ventures.

By the end of 1915, washing machine production had increased 125 percent as a result of demand for the Multi-Motor. In an interview, F.L. said:

> I have been forced to quit trying to get business. The problem with us now is to take care of the business we have. We simply cannot do up our output in striking distance of our orders.

In 1916 Maytag purchased the Elgin company and moved the operation to Newton. Washer production doubled that year and nearly half were Multi-Motor equipped. But success was not automatic. The engine needed further refinements, which Howard Snyder provided. Next, the factory workers had to learn new metalworking skills. Then prejudice against a two-cycle engine had to be overcome. No one had yet made a successful two-cycle fractional horsepower engine (see Figure 4-7).

Design and Development: Two-Cycle Success

In the typical four-cycle internal combustion engine, intake, compression, ignition, and exhaust take place during two revolutions of the crankshaft, only one of which—the ignition cycle—is a power stroke. This was the type

Figure 4-7. This 1917 *Saturday Evening Post* ad extolled the virtues of the Maytag Multi-Motor.

of engine commonly used in automobiles and airplanes of the day. Oil used to lubricate the engine is contained in its own closed system.

In a two-cycle engine, the intake and compression cycles are combined as the piston moves upward and the ignition and exhaust cycles are combined in the down stroke. Each revolution of the crankshaft is a power stroke. Oil to lubricate the pistons is mixed with the gasoline. Outboard marine motors are a common application of the two-cycle engine, as are most lawnmowers.

The Maytag Multi-Motor had cooling fan blades built into the flywheel that blew air across the diagonal fins of the cylinder head to keep the engine cool. It was tested to operate 72 hours continuously under full load. The half-horsepower size used on washers weighed 35 pounds. It contained only 29 parts, including all bolts and screws, and only 5 *moving* parts. Maytag was a tireless advocate of simplicity.

One prominent dealer stopped his pen in midair when the Maytag salesperson mentioned the washer had a two-cycle engine. The dealer commented that he couldn't believe a small concern in Newton, Iowa, could make a successful two-cycle engine when a great many large companies, with unlimited capital and engineering talent, had tried and failed.

Then there was the rural homemaker, who had to operate the washer and was not familiar with operating a gasoline engine. She needed to be convinced that the Multi-Motor was easy to start and safe to operate, noisy as it was. Early versions had protrusions around the power takeoff pulley that could be stepped on to rotate the pulley and start the engine. Later models had a separate foot pedal.

The Biggest Producer of Small Gasoline Engines

Despite these obstacles, Maytag sold three times as many Multi-Motors in 1916 as it had thought possible at the beginning of the year and ultimately became the world's largest manufacturer of small gasoline engines. Maytag became the biggest and best producer of these gas engines for the same reason it ultimately became biggest and best in wringer washer production—by perfecting the product and manufacturing techniques to the same high quality and dependability standards. During a brief period of 1916, Multi-Motor inspector L.G. Weaver rejected all but 6 percent of the Multi-Motors because early production was not precise enough to provide adequate compression between a cast-iron piston and the cylinder wall. Snyder and his associates continued to whittle away at the problem until it was solved.

The world market quickly discovered the product that needed no external power source, and Multi-Motor washing machines were shipped to Australia, Holland, India, France, England, Canada, Peru, San Salvador, Cuba, Java, New Zealand, Philippines, Sweden, Norway, China, Denmark, and Hawaii. The Multi-Motor proved popular overseas throughout its production, particularly with missionaries around the world who seldom had access to utilities. Figure 4-8 describes how the wash was done at this point in time. It comes from the first of many definitive Maytag laundry guides.

Expanded Applications for the Multi-Motor

In addition to emancipating rural homemakers from the drudgery of the washboard and boiler, the Multi-Motor-equipped washer also provided a source of power for other jobs. The Hired Girl could be operated by an outside power source, but the Multi-Motor-equipped washer became the outside power source for a butter churn, food chopper, bone grinder, ice cream freezer, and other devices, even while doing the family wash (see Figure 4-9). The one-half horsepower engine was utilized by printers, jewelers, dentists, machinists, and others in addition to those doing the laundry. A one-horsepower version introduced later was used in other applications where additional power was needed. In 1919, Maytag sold 500 one-horsepower Multi-Motors to the Mower-Motor Company in Detroit, which produced the first power lawnmowers.

A list of other possible uses included an air compressor for milking machines, blacksmith shop blower, cream separator, small electric generator, feed mill, fruit sprayer, grindstone, fanning mill, pea huller, pump, rowboat, shearing machine, and "any other light machinery that comes within the power limits of this marvelous little motor."

All this cost just five cents' worth of gasoline for the average wash, plus a little oil to mix with the gas at a ratio of 25 to 1.[3] Although a 5-year-old could manually crank the Pastime, it took a 10-year-old to start the Multi-Motor with his or her foot. It was no doubt a mixed blessing for youngsters who were assigned the chore of doing the wash while dreaming of the day they could mount the compact motor on a go-cart or bike or find some other exciting application.

A company catalog described the Maytag Multi-Motor as the lightest yet most powerful and most convenient little engine ever built. The copy read a little like the Boy Scout Oath: "light, strong, durable, simple in construction, smooth running, quiet, clean and economical." (See Figure 4-10.)

---

[3] Maytag Multi-Motor oil containers and mixing cans still delight antiques hunters.

The Maytag Way to Wash

The same instruction booklet cited in Figure 4-5 gave these hints on successful laundering.*

> Wet the clothes, rub them lightly with soap and soak for a few minutes before placing in Maytag washer. Use water of a comfortable temperature and replenish whenever the water becomes dirty. Garments should be left wrong side out to protect the right side from dust while drying. Fifteen minutes' washing in the Maytag washer should be sufficient to clean any garment.
>
> Then put clothes through the wringer. Never attempt to wring clothes by hand. It is not only hard work, but it strains and weakens the fabric. For blankets, woolens, and all heavy materials, the wringer must be loosely adjusted.
>
> If white clothes are washed with Fels-Naphtha** and the Maytag washer, there is no necessity for boiling. The clothes will be clean and fresh.
>
> After the clothes come through the wringer, they should be thoroughly rinsed in comfortably warm water; at least two rinsings are desirable. Use the wringer for rinsing and bluing waters—in fact, whenever possible.
>
> Sunshine, moisture and fresh air are the greatest bleaches. Could we command a clean grass plot, pure air and sunshine, there would be no need of bluing. Clothes become yellow from careless washing and careless rinsing more often than from any other cause.
>
> To wash colored clothes, run them through heavy suds in lukewarm or cool water and rinse thoroughly in cool or lukewarm water, wring and hang out. If washed in this way, fast colors will not rub or fade. White and colored clothes should never be washed in the same water. In these days of uncertain dyes, the color in goods often runs and will spoil white clothes if they are placed in the same water.
>
> Muslins, prints, and ginghams should be ironed on the wrong side whenever possible as it makes the material look like new. To wash black taffeta, wash in three baths containing Venetian soap. Rinse and stiffen with gum arabic water and a little vinegar or rub the fabric with a sponge dipped in beer. Wring between cloths and iron on the wrong side.

*This washing instruction manual was distributed at the end of the first World War.

**A yellow, very caustic Naphtha bar of soap that was sold in groceries.

Figure 4-8. Tips from Maytag on getting cleaner, brighter clothes.

Figure 4-9. A drawing demonstrating some of the labor-saving applications of the Multi-Motor.

Letters to Maytag With Two-Cent Stamps

Maytag received "love letters" from satisfied users even in the days of wooden tubs and gasoline engines. These were reproduced in a company catalog of the era:

"The Maytag Multi-Motor Washer runs smoothly, operates easily and is O.K. in every way."

— G.L.C., Green, Iowa

"Every farmer's wife should own a Maytag Multi-Motor Washer. It relieves them of nearly all the drudgery of farm housework."

— A.E.P., Kenmare, N.D.

"I was skeptical about the Maytag Multi-Motor Washer and had little confidence in it before I tried it. But it gives excellent satisfaction and I have not a single complaint to make."

— R.E.B., Howell, Mich.

"I have seen a great many different kinds of washing machines, but the Maytag Multi-Motor Washer is the best washer I have ever come in contact with."

— C.V.H., Henry, S.D.

Figure 4-10. Proof of customer satisfaction—excerpts from letters sent in by users of the Multi-Motor washer.

An Industry Association for Washer Manufacturers

Although some 120 companies were making washers at the time, an appliance partnership of sorts emerged when an industry association for manufacturers of washing machines was formed in 1916 with 61 members. When this group, eventually called the American Home Laundry Manufacturers Association, was dissolved in 1966 as a prelude to formation of the larger Association of Home Appliance Manufacturers a year later, only 17 of the 120 manufacturers had survived.

Wartime Problems

Because Maytag, along with most washer companies, did not engage in war work, it suffered severe materials shortages in the period between 1917 and 1922. Newton had, by now, earned the title "Washing Machine Capital of the World." Over a third of all the washers manufactured in the U.S. at that time were built by the four companies in Newton.

In August 1918, the War Industry Board limited production in the washer industry. Maytag was forced to lay off 35 percent of its work force. Because of the government restrictions, production was flat during the war years. Foretelling the demise of the farm implement business, the marvelous Maytag corn shredder was discontinued in 1919.

Turning Away From Wood

Breakthrough! The Millrace Principle, 1917

In their search for a distinctive product advantage in the larger market served by electricity, Elmer and Bud Maytag had wanted to get away from wood, which eventually rotted and leaked. In 1917, an all-metal cabinet washer was introduced using the Maytag *millrace principle*.[4] A perforated cast-aluminum cylinder was mounted horizontally to rotate inside a metal tub. Clothes were loaded through a door in the top and tumbled as the cylinder turned, forcing hot, sudsy water through the soiled clothes. It was

---

[4] The millrace principle was so named because of its similarity to the pattern of water running over a millwheel in a stream. With the millrace principle, clothes tumble within a rotating drum. Indented baffles lift clothes and soapy water and let both tumble to the bottom again.

This effective washing principle is susceptible to overloading. So much as a handkerchief too much and the load rides around the drum like a donut.

a vast improvement over the old milk-stool agitator method of the mechanized washboard (see Figure 4-11).

It looked different too. A company catalog described it:

> Here is a washing machine which you have only to look upon and compare with any you have ever seen to decide that it has no rival in the matter of refinement. Every mechanical part is enclosed by the simple graceful cabinet which transforms the machine to a most attractive article. The swinging reversible wringer is especially designed for strength, efficiency and convenience as well as for harmony with the attractive design of the cabinet.

The washer incorporated two Maytag firsts—the millrace washing principle and the divided wringer. The latter featured instant tension release, with wide separation of the rolls and quick, easy movement to various working positions. The gasoline engine apparently couldn't be made to fit, because the washer came only with an electric motor or with a pulley to accommodate a belt from an external engine or some other source of power.

But the Multi-Motor was far from dead. In 1918 twice as many Multi-Motors were sold as were electric models. The wooden tub, however, lost its exclusivity as over 500 cabinet washers were built.

The cylinder washer, which was the first application of the principles later used in all front-loading automatic washers, was to be eclipsed at Maytag within five years by the even more remarkable Gyrafoam washing principle, which is still in use. However, the Bendix automatic washer, introduced in the late 1930s, still tumbled clothes in a cylinder, but loaded from the front rather than the top. The principle also was used in all attempts at manufacturing combination washer-dryers, a product that disappeared in the early 1960s (see page 182).

The Washer That Couldn't Be Built

Breakthrough! The Cast-Aluminum Tub, 1919

"When there is a real need, there can be found a means of supplying it," was a long-standing credo around Maytag that fit the search for a new and better tub. Maytag had studied the possibilities of aluminum and thought that this metal, properly cast, would provide a sturdy, rigid tub, light in weight—one that would not dent or rust and could be finished attractively. As early as 1915, an experimental aluminum tub had been cast, under Howard Snyder's supervision, but the problem was one of economical quantity production. Snyder had begun his aluminum study in 1912, the year he was placed in charge of the "experimental department."

Figure 4-11. This elegant Deco-era ad from a 1920 *Saturday Evening Post* featured Maytag's new cabinet washer design and breakthrough millrace principle.

Being told by the experts back in 1912 that a seamless aluminum tub was impossible to cast, Snyder and his people set out to do it themselves. It was one thing, they found, to cast various aluminum pieces for assembly into a cabinet washer and quite another to cast a 30-inch tub weighing nearly 40 pounds in one operation. Yet the outstanding advantages of a seamless tub molded to the desired shape kept them at it. Finally, in 1919 they solved the problem and put the tub into production in a new model.

The Model 70, Electric, and Model 72 With Multi-Motor

The trim new washer had a square cast-aluminum tub with rounded corners, a convenient and efficient wringer set low above water level so that heavy, wet clothing need not be lifted high out of the water to be fed into the rolls, and an arrangement to adjust the washer's height to the convenience of any homemaker. The new Model 70 electric, with its revolutionary seamless aluminum tub, was an instant hit (see Figure 4-12).

Inside the tub, a novel cast-aluminum dolly rotated back and forth, suspended under a flat aluminum lid. The tub was wide, and thanks to its

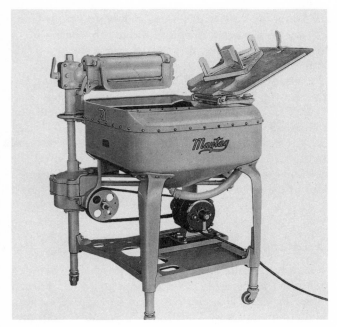

Figure 4-12. Maytag's Model 70—the "washer that couldn't be built."

cone-shaped bottom, particles of dirt washed from the clothes fell to the center and were not rewashed back through the clothing. A Multi-Motor version was also marketed as the Model 72.

Feast and Famine: The 1920–21 Recession

Despite the promise of the new gray aluminum washer, business stayed flat. The perceived need for a washer was yet to be established in consumers' minds. Only 2 percent of American families owned washing machines at the time. Even so, Maytag had the largest factory in Iowa following a half-million dollar expansion. From 1915 to 1920, Maytag grew from 2000 dealers to 11,000 and from 18 to 75 sales representatives. Maytag also had a funded debt of $615,000.

Bud Maytag's advertising (see Chapter 1) had convinced the "modern" woman to want a washer, and the Maytag plant had a 9000-washer backlog at the beginning of 1920. In an interview, Bud later said the problem with his sales force was no longer one of selling but rather of making satisfactory excuses for the company's inability to deliver. In June a new foundry went on line and production capacity was doubled. August sales exceeded any month on record.

Suddenly, though, things took a turn for the worst, and Maytag headed for a severe downturn. About the time that Newton's Iowa Mercantile Company, the "Big Store," was displaying a gray aluminum-tub Maytag in its Christmas window, Newton's washing machine factories were laying off 675 workers, including 350 of the 450 then employed by Maytag.

Maytag sales in 1920 had totaled a record $3.7 million. Then Newton was hit, like the rest of the country, by the unexpected—but thankfully brief—recession of 1920–21. In 1921 the company showed a loss of $280,387 on sales of $1.3 million. Nearly $90,000 of the loss came from a failed threshing machine company, the last one utilizing Maytag band cutters and self feeders. The payroll was cut by more than half. The nation survived the momentary turbulence and hitched its trousers before proceeding through the unmitigated growth of the 1920s.

Changing of the Guard

The slump may or may not have contributed to the power struggle between the generations that resulted in the withdrawal of 63-year-old F.L. Maytag from active management in 1921. He relinquished his post as president, and Bud took over as the company's leader. F.L.'s first withdrawal around 1910 had been voluntary, but his second withdrawal was not. His habit of coming and going, often jumping in and issuing orders on his sporadic returns, without regard for the plans of those he had left nominally in charge, proved a source of great frustration for both Elmer and Bud. F.L.'s unwise and unsound investments in railroads and automobiles, among other things, had earlier thrown the Maytag company heavily into debt.

Presumably, Elmer and Bud wanted to ensure that the old man would not be able to use the promising company's assets to bankroll any other questionable deals. In his memoirs, retired Maytag executive Robert E. Vance explained, "Due to these circumstances and given the forceful personalities of the three individuals involved, over a period of time a difficult struggle ensued. The end result was the practical withdrawal of F.L. from the active management of the company." F.L. became chairman of the board, Bud president, and Elmer secretary and treasurer. The three constituted the board's executive committee. The change was announced in the Newton *Daily News* as F.L.'s retirement.

Bud Maytag was at the reigns of the company during a time when Maytag needed to simultaneously hold off creditors and develop more business. Issues of design quality and prevention in the modern Baldrige context refer to shortening product and service introduction cycles. In the late teens and early 1920s, Maytag needed to do more than respond to changing markets. The company set out to be the very agent of change in the home appliance marketplace.

No one really knows just how much of a driving force Bud Maytag was in those days. However, in an attempt to position himself in company history, in 1960, then director Bud Maytag drafted a letter to company management.[5]
Referencing the years before he assumed the presidency in 1921, he wrote:

> F.L. about took the company with him and probably would have had it not been for E.H. (Elmer). We were considerably worse than broke. There was a long tough road ahead. I inherited the job of trying to stiff-arm five banks from St. Louis to New York, to each of which we owed $100,000 that we knew we couldn't pay unless something spectacular happened.
> My very first move was to go to Howard Snyder and say,
>
> > Howard, we're never going to get anywhere in the washing machine business with almost identically the same machine that 110 other manufacturers are making. So, I want you to design a machine that is brand new and unique in every way. Don't put a

---

[5]When Elmer died in 1940 and Fred Maytag II became president and CEO, Bud was invited back to serve on the Maytag Company board of directors, which he did until 1966. He was replaced on the board then by his son, L.B. (Bud) Maytag Jr., president of National Airlines at the time. When Fred Maytag II died in 1962, Bud, and later Bud Jr., were the only Maytags connected with the company. Bud died in 1967 and his son in 1990. Other than stock holdings, there have been no Maytags connected with the Maytag Company since.

stick of wood in it if you can help it, change the shape or anything else you want to do, but make it completely different in
appearance because my job for the indefinite future is to be
promising these banks that we really have something sensational
coming out and that if they'll just give me some time, we'll get
the job done.

I also told him I didn't want to lay eyes on it until he was ready to wash.
From there on I spent what seemed like hundreds of sleepless nights on
the Pullmans going to and from banks and finally one day Howard
phoned me to come up and watch him wash.

What I saw was the square aluminum tub machine all polished up
within an inch of its life and I knew at first glance that this was *it*.

Bud was a total personality contrast to his older brother, although they
shared a family resemblance. Even there Bud had the best of it. Where Bud
was outgoing and flamboyant, Elmer was reserved and less volatile under
stress. While Bud eventually rebelled and quit, Elmer, who was five years
older and infinitely more practical, quietly stuck it out and dutifully made
the best of the situation.[6]

Bud grew up a tall, handsome man with an urbane sophistication belying
the fact that his education took place at Iowa State College of Agriculture
and Engineering in Ames, a land-grant institution that excelled in its chosen specialties but would not be thought of as worldly. However, Bud managed to get around. A charmer, he fit the image of his self-styled role as a
marketer. He was a great believer in the power of advertising and attributed
his efforts in that area to the significant growth of the washer end of the
business between 1910 and 1920.

The Move to National Advertising

A feature article in the *Des Moines Register* in 1920 told Bud's story.

When Bud arrived on the scene, mechanical engineering degree in
hand, the company was making, as a sideline, a hand-operated washing
machine. His father gave him the washing machine end of the business
to "cut his teeth on." For five years the washer business grew but there

---

[6] An anecdote about Bud and his brother clearly illustrates the basic difference between the
two. It seems that Bud, a champion amateur golfer, constantly pestered Elmer to try the game,
but his brother had no time for it. One day Elmer finally gave in to Bud's pressure and agreed
to play a round. Suitably equipped with clubs, a ball, and perhaps even plus-fours, Elmer stood
at the first tee while Bud hit his drive. After some rudimentary instruction from his brother,
Elmer then addressed his ball and struck it a blow. He turned to Bud and asked, "What hap-
pens now?" "We walk down the fairway and hit the ball again," replied Bud. Without another
word, Elmer turned, got in his car, and drove away.

was nothing spectacular about it. Then came the gasoline engine washer. The opportunity for developing such a machine and selling it broadcast over the great farming territory of the Middle West appealed strongly to the imagination and business sense of young Bud Maytag.

With boyish enthusiasm, Bud Maytag's mind leapt on to the future. How to make the business greater? How to make it nationwide in scope? At this critical moment, Bud Maytag was bitten by the advertising bug.

> Something had to be done to make us step out from the pack and forge ahead. That something was national advertising. I knew from that moment on that advertising was the thing to do. I don't know how I came to realize it, for I had no experience with advertising, but I somehow felt it was the very thing we needed.
>
> After selling the idea of national advertising to my father, I had to sell it to the sales force, because I knew they had to believe in it before they could profit by it. It was simply unheard of. Some of the company officials thought I was crazy, and that Dad was rapidly losing his mind for letting us scatter 22,000 hard-earned dollars to the four winds.

As a matter of fact, $22,000 barely bought enough advertising to do any good. A full page in *The Saturday Evening Post* cost around $5000 then for one insertion. The *Register* article continued with Bud's own story:

> Right then was the crucial point in the company's career, and I have always felt proud of my father, who had built up this immense business, nursed it through innumerable setbacks, and established it on a firm and paying basis by the most conservative of methods, because he was progressive enough to take a chance on a new venture like this—which to him at the time must have seemed like throwing money away.
>
> He gave me $22,000 of rope with which to hang myself, and I knew we must get back $22,000 worth of profit from it. I kept a careful track of where that $22,000 went and what came of it. The first six months after we started advertising in national magazines, we received 5500 inquiries.
>
> Out of this number 95 percent were new people—that is, people living in sections of the country where we had no dealers. This showed me that we were covering the washing machine field only to the extent of 5 percent, and that we were overlooking just 95 percent of possible business. I figured that of these 5500 inquiries, surely at a conservative estimate we could sell one out of four. That would bring us in practically the amount we had expended for advertising.
>
> But it didn't work that way at first. The washing machine business was so new they first had to sell the washing machine idea before they could begin to sell the Maytag washing machine idea.

That is, we had first to talk just plain washing machine to a woman, because up to that time, she never had such a thing, and the whole idea was strange to her. Nowadays you can see that the sales operation is entirely different. The modern woman is educated to the washing machine idea. All that remains for a salesman to do is convince her that his washing machine is the best.

In three years, we were spending five or six times as much on advertising as we did the first year. In five years, we increased our business 1200 percent.

F.L. never publicly disclosed why he chose Bud over Elmer to head the company. Perhaps it was because Bud was the more dynamic and was a college graduate. Maybe it was because Bud's end of the business became dominant. In any event, Elmer was hurt by the slight, although he never complained publicly. While Bud was not quite a prodigal, Elmer's role was somewhat akin to that of the prodigal's brother.

5
Growing Pains

The Twenties—A High-Times, Hard-Times Decade

Maytag's Overnight Transformation to a Corporate Culture

If anything is constant at Maytag, it's change. Taking the long view liberates the organization from needing to be the first or the fanciest. Instead, the focus is on becoming, and *staying,* the best. An enduring commitment to continual product improvement doesn't grab many headlines. Trains that run on time don't make news the way trains that crash do. Quietly and patiently sticking to the knitting is how Maytag makes its own luck. Yet, every once in a while, ongoing innovation has produced a truly revolutionary advance that has had a catapult effect on the business.

Maytag was catapulted into the national spotlight over a period of two short years when the solid small company, emerging despite the struggle to escape a heavy debt burden, blossomed into a wildly successful enterprise, growing like Topsy and pushing wheelbarrows full of money to the bank. Sales volume in 1924 was six times that of 1922, and earnings grew even faster. Employment tripled during the period, and then doubled again in 1925. The company paid off all its debt—not to owe money again for more than 50 years.

F.L. Maytag and his children became millionaires virtually overnight. The final 15 years of F.L.'s life were spent aboard the gravy train. Maytag's success, based on continued pursuit of innovation, eventually allowed the privately held company to go public.

Gyrafoam and the Phenomenal Model 80— The Innovations That Revolutionized Washing

Breakthrough! The Agitator Principle, 1922

The foundation for the stock offerings and the cause of the Maytag Company's blossoming prosperity in the mid-1920s was the invention of the Maytag "Gyrafoam" washer. As with so many world-shaping innovations, the invention of the "Gyratator" could be called a "planned accident."

One day in 1920, a group of Maytaggers was monkeying with a washer in an attempt to reconcile the inherently inefficient transfer of power from the motor below the tub to the agitator on top. As the story goes, the metal "milk stool" agitator (look back at Figure 4-12) hanging under the lid fell off, flipped over, and landed upside down in the bottom of the aluminum tub. Looks were exchanged, the genius of fate was instantly recognized, and the challenge was accepted on the spot. If the dolly could be made to work at the bottom of the tub instead of hanging from the lid, the mechanical gear/driveshaft assembly that transferred power to the top of the lid from the motor underneath could be eliminated.

Howard Snyder is given credit for the innovation because he headed Maytag's experimental department at the time and had already contributed countless other innovations over the years. By plugging away at continuous improvement, Snyder and his people were ripe for the lucky moment, and were smart enough to pay attention to such accidents. Snyder and Bud Maytag were both part of the planning group.[1] The fortunate accident was not overlooked, because the Maytag research group was actively striving for improvement as part of Bud's effort to get a leg up on the competition.

Innovation Begets More Innovation

The solution to the problem of putting the dolly at the bottom of the tub was not easy, though, and a great deal of time was spent trying out various configurations. The most important breakthrough came as the dolly's pegs were replaced with fins that set up interesting new currents in the washtub (see Figure 5-1). The original function of the dolly and pegs was to pull the clothes through the soapy water to generate the washing action. Instead of dragging the clothes through the water, the new fins forced the water through the clothes, creating a much more powerful washing action that was, at the same time, much gentler on the clothes. The result was cleaner

---

[1] Years later, in a letter to Maytag management, Bud took credit for planting the bug in Snyder's ear that led to the technical breakthrough.

Maytag invents the modern agitator.

In 1922 Maytag came up with what many regard as its most important "first" — a new washing method that rocked the entire washer industry.

Up to then washers cleaned by means of a device under the lid that dragged clothes through the water. Maytag replaced this with a finned agitator at the *bottom* of the tub. Named the Gyratator™, it cleaned by water action alone.

Maytag's revolutionary bottom-of-the-tub agitator cleaned clothes by forcing powerful currents of hot, soapy water through them. This cleaned more thoroughly yet more gently than previous methods.

This new washing technique which Maytag called the Gyrafoam™ principle was unlike anything else on the market.

Maytag coupled the Gyrafoam™ principle with its aluminum tub in Model 80, a new washer that took the country by storm. It proved so popular that Maytag discontinued making all other models in order to meet the unprecedented demand.

Figure 5-1. The finned Gyratator was the secret to Maytag's innovative Gyrafoam washing technique.

clothes with less wear and tear. To this day, Maytag engineers believe that simplicity is the ultimate sophistication. Years later, the so-called gutless wonder, named because of the absence of complicated mechanisms inside the washer housing, would bear the legacy of Maytag simplifications that improved performance as well as quality and dependability.

Breakthrough! Solving the Low-Post Problem, 1925

Maytag's designers were not through yet. The Maytag Gyrafoam washer had an Achilles heel. The driveshaft post to which the agitator was affixed was under water during the wash cycle. This permitted corrosion to occur around the underwater seal, so that the washer could develop a leak after a period of time. The solution Maytag engineers found was to replace the low post with a tall agitator post to keep the shaft driving the agitator out of the wash water, as shown in Figure 5-2. Maytag made the switch on January 1, 1925, and produced a repair kit with the new agitator to replace any having problems in the field.

Marketing the Model 80

The Model 80 washer, which featured the new Gyrafoam principle, was introduced early in 1922, but it took a little while for the world to beat a path to Maytag's door, although that happened soon enough. The new washer was radically different from anything else on the market, and it cost more money. Even though it was vastly superior in performance, people

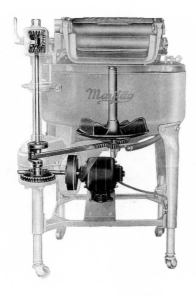

Figure 5-2. The Model 80, which underwrote Maytag's phenomenal growth during the 1920s.

had to be shown its virtues (see Figure 5-3). F.L. himself was the first to demonstrate and perhaps unwittingly set the precedent for the most effective way to sell the Gyrafoam washer—by demonstration.

Four prototypes were built for demonstration purposes. F.L. had one crated and boarded a westbound train with the washer, advising the office folks that he wouldn't be back until he had a carload order.[2] It isn't certain whether F.L. assumed this role because of his superior salesmanship or because he could best be spared from the day-to-day operations of the company.

The Great Sales Trip of 1922

After crossing the vast prairies of Iowa and Nebraska, F.L. made a first stop in Denver. Taking the machine to his hotel room, he set it up and called in dealers. For two days they came, saw, and marveled, but disappeared when he asked for the order. Across the Rocky Mountains, Salt Lake City was F.L.'s next stop, but an entire week there produced only polite interest and

---

[2] A carload is 50 units, even though a boxcar actually holds 75 units. The highest discount a dealer could get was for a carload order of 50 units. Any quantity above that was the same price.

Figure 5-3. The Model 82 was the same as the Model 80—except that it featured the Multi-Motor.

still no orders. Across the desert, a week in Los Angeles followed with identical results.

Maytag must have been frustrated if not desperate by the time he set up the Model 80 Gyratator in his Oakland hotel room, but he hit the street and cold-called the dealer nearest his hotel. Though the two men had never met, F.L. had been told that A.C. "Ted" Schleuter was a "go-getter" in the washer business.

Schleuter was not interested. He had 200 washers in stock from another manufacturer and had just come from Detroit, where he had placed an order for an additional carload. F.L. persisted and Schleuter finally agreed to call at the hotel and see the Model 80 at work, agreeing to bring some greasy overalls for demonstration purposes.

He showed up about 5:30 p.m. and watched the washer wash. Intrigued, he came back after supper. Leaving late, he told F.L., "If you can sell my salesmen tomorrow, I will see you again tomorrow night." The following day the salesmen came and witnessed the swish-swashing action of the marvelous machine. They were sufficiently interested to spend most of the day around the washer. Later that evening the dealer returned and, convinced, signed up for the precious carload F.L. had promised his staff back in Iowa. It turned out to be the shrewdest thing that Schleuter ever did. He went on to become the Maytag distributor for the entire state of California and a multimillionaire in the bargain.

The Start of Something Big

After three weeks on the train and in hotel rooms, F.L. returned across the desert, the mountains, and the great plains, arriving back at the Maytag offices in Newton on March 20, 1922. Production of the new washer began in April. Trickles of orders became floods. Work on all other products was halted, and all facilities focused on the Model 80. A night shift was added and employment doubled. The production rate was increased to 100 washers a day in June, but the factory was running a month behind in fulfilling orders.

Public demand for the new washer made the Maytag dealer franchise a valuable commercial asset, and Maytag made the most of it. Eleven thousand dealers sold Maytag products in 1921, some with mainly farm implement ties. By 1925, the Maytag Company had aligned itself with only the 3000 biggest and best appliance dealers in the country. The product was on allocation for most of that time. In November of 1922, the Maytag Company gave a banquet in Oakland for the A.C. Schleuter Company in recognition of having sold its seventeenth carload of Maytag washers in less than

Figure 5-4. By 1926, Maytag was setting industry records for the size of product shipments to its branches.

eight months. And in 1923, Ted Schleuter, both a distributor and a dealer for Maytag, sold 92 carloads of Maytags.

Selling by the Trainload

Early in 1923 the first solid trainload of washers was shipped to the Philadelphia branch for eastern dealers. The 31-car trainload was valued at over $400,000 and set a freight speed record of 16 hours between Newton and Chicago. A second trainload was shipped to the Philadelphia branch in July, a third in September, and a fourth in November, totaling 133 carloads.

More trainload shipments followed, to both coasts. On October 12, 1926, five trainloads of Maytag washers were shipped to the Philadelphia branch (see Figure 5-4). Up until that time, it was the world's largest single shipment of merchandise, but was eclipsed in May of 1927 by an eight-trainload shipment, valued at $2.75 million, also to Philadelphia.

The Trouble With Success

With the almost immediate acceptance of the Gyrafoam washer, the company's limited manufacturing facilities were quickly overtaxed. Sources for manufacturing materials had to be found and convinced that they would be paid. Managers and workers had to be hired in numbers greater than ever before. Space had to be built quickly, and perhaps most important, all had to be organized, coordinated, and controlled in order to take profitable advantage of the opportunity.

By the end of 1923, the company was financially sound and was the acknowledged leader in the washing machine industry. Meanwhile Bud, as president, focused on marketing and did not become involved with employee or community relations. His contribution was the creation of an effective marketing organization that is still reputedly the finest in the appliance industry. One of the ads for the Model 80 is shown in Figure 5-5.

The dramatic market acceptance of the Gyrafoam washer opened vast opportunities to the small manufacturing organization and enormous challenges as well. The cylinder-type washer was sufficiently different from anything else on the market at the time, and the skeleton of a national sales organization had started to take shape. Now, with a product so much in demand and with the competition far behind, there was a window of opportunity to hand-pick sales representatives and expand territorial distribution at the same time. Bud handled this responsibility, and many of his marketing policies and some of the distribution structure are still in place. Elmer was to build the product and develop the corporation.

Enlarging the Factory

It was at this time and under these circumstances that Elmer Maytag made perhaps his greatest contribution to the company. If the company was to franchise superior sales outlets, it felt an obligation to supply them promptly and adequately. A modern aluminum foundry was in hand, but the gray iron foundry lacked capacity. There was a small machine shop and, fortunately, large areas of floor space left over from the farm machinery business. Elmer used what he had to the fullest, but it was obvious that Maytag would be primarily an assembly plant for the time being. He hired a young purchasing agent, Walter Clauser, who proved to be a genius in locating suppliers, negotiating prices, and getting deliveries to keep the assembly line humming.

Assembling parts purchased almost entirely from subcontractors proved to be an expensive way to manufacture, and only the lack of competition permitted Maytag prices to support it. With some resistance from

Figure 5-5. The sales strategy for the Model 80 was bold and simple: the product sells itself. This ad from the mid-1920s predates similarly premised Honda automobile ads by about 65 years.

Bud and a great deal from F.L., who didn't want to turn his cash into brick and mortar, Elmer initiated a building program that by 1926 provided total factory space of 600,000 square feet, including a six-story building alive with conveyors and other materials-handling equipment.[3] It was a long time before the sophisticated mechanization of the factory was complete, but as it progressed, cost savings were produced that permitted the reduction of wholesale prices just when serious competition began to catch up.

[3] That 1926 six-story factory building was recycled 60 years later into swank, carpeted, air-conditioned office space, a few years after wringer washer production was halted there in 1983. It became Maytag's technical center with a handsome modern facade at a cost much lower than building a new facility. Even though the white-collar types have moved in, there is still a machine shop on the first floor. New employees joining the corporate staff in Newton probably have no idea of the origin of the modern-looking technical center in which they work.

In a sort of chicken-and-egg scenario, Maytag's tendency to take the long view has led to a cycle of investing capital resources in areas of the company that, in turn, generate more capital resources to invest. Of course, Maytag always had access to cash following the Gyrafoam infusion.

Innovating in the Sales Process

Breakthrough! Demonstration Selling, 1923

With all due respect to the creators of Honda's "Danny," whose dilemma bears an uncanny resemblence to that of Old Lonely, the Model 80, when demonstrated, literally sold itself—about sixty years before the Honda. In fact, this phenomenon soon gave rise to a slogan Maytag used with both wholesale and retail customers, "If it doesn't sell itself, don't keep it." (see Figure 5-5 again). When they saw it at work, dealers bought it. But both dealers and the company soon recognized that it had to be demonstrated.

The company's answer was to hire commission salespeople and send them out to dealers who had purchased a quantity of washers. The sales rep would assist the dealer for 30 days, offering instruction on how to sell by demonstration. The new sales technique had three steps. The first step was to schedule a demonstration, the second step was to do the demonstration, and the third step was to close the sale. The sales pitch was saved for the third step. No sales pressure was applied during the first two steps.

For many dealer sales people, the first step was the hardest. It meant door-to-door cold canvassing, ringing doorbells, and asking to do a demonstration. The following description of how one dealer salesman started his career appeared in a 1928 issue of *The Profit News,* Maytag's field publication.

I started selling Maytags in March 1927, with only $2.70 in my jeans. Strolling down the street, I saw a Maytag in the window, walked in and asked if they needed any salesmen. The answer was "yes" and I was told the good things about the wonderful Maytag Company and what a wonderful organization it was to be connected with. I asked if they were selling any Maytags and the answer again was "yes." I laughed, for after two years in the real estate business I thought it almost impossible to sell anything in Florida. Finally, I said I would try it.

Next morning I started to work. I drove out with one of the boys to make a demonstration; then I was convinced that the Maytag was really as good if not better than they had said. I was really enthused next morning when they gave me a truck and I started out to book demonstrations.

I drove up one street and down the other wishing that someone would stop me and say that they wanted to buy a washer. Finally I collected enough courage to go up to the door. After I rapped several times, a lady came to the door with a long face to know what I wanted. I asked if she would be interested in buying a washer and she said, "No, my husband has been out of work for several months and we have no money." I tried the next house and heard the same story.

I walked down the street for several blocks and tried another house. I told this lady that I wanted to show her how to save some money. She was interested and agreed to a demonstration.

The salesman finally changed his tack and decided to ask customers if they were interested, not in washers, but in saving money. It worked.

From then on I averaged about two demonstrations a day for three weeks but not a sale. I had ten Maytags out on demonstration and at the end of the fourth week I closed nine sales.

After that I never let anyone tell me they hadn't any money for I knew that was only an easy way to get rid of me. I found that the days were too short because so many hours means so many calls and so many calls means so many demonstrations and so many demonstrations means so many sales. The law of averages will take care of you.

Two Selling Secrets: Call After Supper, and Make It a Numbers Game

Maytag salespeople soon learned that the best time to try to close the sale is immediately following the demonstration, when the customer's interest is always greatest. They also learned that 90 percent of major appliance sales need the consent of both husband and wife. However, the demonstrations frequently took place during the day when the husband wasn't home.

Many women told the salesperson that their husbands wouldn't let them buy a Maytag washer when in fact they were simply afraid to ask. The sales reps soon learned that the wives were often grateful if they did the asking. That's why many successful Maytag salespeople spent their evenings calling back after daytime demonstrations in order to catch *both* husband and wife at home: after supper, dishes done, kids in bed, evening paper and ashtray at the ready. Male sales resistance seemed at its weakest when the house was full of after-dinner cigar smoke. The husband was often surprised to learn how shabbily he had been treating his wife and how much he himself would benefit from sparing her the drudgery of hand laundering.

If the woman won't commit to a purchase after a successful demonstration, the wise salesperson knows its the husband who must say yes. The good salesperson always found an excuse to come back when both husband and wife were together. No sale was considered lost until both said no.

The formula that emerged from the Maytag demonstrations worked out that for every six demonstrations, three washers would be left in the home for further consideration and one sale would result. Those not sold would be picked up and cleaned up for another try. A Maytag sales rep quickly became an expert in washing clothes.

A War Story From the Field

A 1927 issue of *The Profit News* recorded one salesperson's story of a particularly difficult sale. It was 10 p.m. and the demonstration was over. Mom was sold but felt the price was a bit high. Dad wanted to "wait and pay cash." The salesperson gently persisted, and the man was finally sold on the deferred payment plan. Then two married daughters arrived. Not wanting to lose $160 from their inheritances, they lobbied against the purchase. Then the high school flapper daughter showed up and added to the salesperson's woes. "Oh, no," she wailed, "If you buy that, I won't get the fur coat you promised." That got the attention of the two older sisters. "I didn't get a fur coat in high school, and furthermore I had to wear cotton stockings," one of them said. In an abrupt about-face, they urged their parents to buy the washer, reasoning that a washer was much more practical than a fur coat.

Buying on Installment: The Maytag Acceptance Corporation

In those days before the Great Depression, about 25 percent of Maytag washers were sold for cash, the rest on the installment plan. The down payment averaged about a third of the sales price. The company established the Maytag Acceptance Corporation in 1927 to finance Maytag dealers and handle other installment paper. Located in F.L.'s beloved Chicago, the finance firm purchased time contracts from dealers for the price of the contract less 10 percent. When the contract was paid off, the dealer got the remaining 10 percent. In 1928, Maytag Acceptance raised the minimum down payment to $15 from the previous $10. In response, both the Kansas City branch and Maytag-Chicago, a city distributor, formed their own contract purchase companies.

Exclusive Franchises: Fighting for the Right to Sell a Maytag

One of Bud Maytag's marketing policies, initiated in 1924, was a franchise program giving dealers protected territories.[4] During the first year the company canceled the franchises of seven dealers in a two-week period, declaring war on "bootlegging" (selling washers outside of the assigned territory). The practice led to open warfare between dealers in Indianapolis. One dealer stopped indiscriminate selling only after a neighboring dealer and his salesmen came over en masse and threatened to clean house. Three years later the company announced it would not honor product guarantees on bootleg washing machines.

Marketing the Maytag Way: The Wet-Spaghetti School

One of the most significant differences between Maytag's approach to marketing and marketing practices of other appliance manufacturers is the concept of pulling product through the dealer organization by creating retail demand rather than concentrating on pushing product through the wholesale channels. Compare the policy to a strand of wet spaghetti: it's easier to pull it than to push.

In a nutshell, the difference between pulling product through a dealer network versus loading up dealers with product (as auto manufacturers are still doing) is the difference between taking the short view and the long view. If the patience and resources are available to take the long view, there will be no logjam of product to congest the corridor that runs from the factory to the consumer. Furthermore, the company's cash or credit won't be held hostage in inventory.

Pressuring dealers to sell product by loading them up tends to create adversarial relationships between dealers and manufacturers. At the very least, the dealers feel as if the manufacturers don't understand and/or care about their problems. From the days of F.L., Maytag has valued its dealer relationships highly, and it shows in the descriptions of the relationship that you hear from both dealers and company personnel.

Beginning with the product demonstration emphasis of the 1920s, Maytag salespeople have always helped their dealers move the product at retail.

---

[4] The practice was later rendered illegal by federal regulatory legislation. Licensing agreements remain a part of Maytag marketing policy, although without exclusive territories.

As a result of the close working relationship over the years, many synergistic sales promotions were developed. The "72-Hour Maytag Mad Marathon" originated at the wholesale level to honor F.L. Maytag's seventy-second birthday in 1929, and is still practiced today. The marathon dealer remains open for 72 straight hours, offering extra bargains in the wee hours. "Catch me asleep," the dealer challenges, "and you get your washer free."

Another promotion is the "Back Door" or private sale. The dealer sends invitations to customers, inviting them to visit the store after hours, coming through the back door or being admitted only by special invitation, for special bargains. The secret of this and all Maytag promotions is that they all mean what they say. The marathon store is really open for 72 hours straight. Nobody gets into a private sale without an invitation. Whatever the promise, it is kept. This policy of going the extra mile and of being totally honest with the public has endured throughout the years and has become proverbial with Maytag. It's also one of the things that makes Maytag promotions successful. Over the long haul, the public learns to believe not only in the product but also in the company.

Dealers must adhere to the same standards of straight dealing in order to receive support from their company representative, including the financial incentives supporting the promotion. In 1928, to encourage retail sales, the company went so far as to pay its salespeople commissions on *retail* rather than *wholesale* orders. A major marketing policy initiated in 1926, requiring cash on delivery to dealers, was retained for 50 years until market conditions required a return to dusted-off 30-day terms. The 50-year success of such an unheard-of requirement further demonstrates the value of a Maytag franchise.

Door-to-door selling and demonstrations by Maytag dealers were valuable so long as consumers were new to washing machines and so long as the Gyrafoam principle was unique to Maytag. As other washing machine makers adopted the agitator principle, paying Maytag a royalty to use the technology,[5] much of the distinction diminished and so did the emphasis on demonstration selling.

"If You Build It, They Will Come"—Building Commitment Through Factory Visits

As the Maytag plant in Newton was expanded and modernized to accommodate the popularity of the Model 80 Gyrafoam washer, plant visits by dealers and their salespeople became popular. Seeing firsthand how the

---

[5] At one time, over 80 manufacturers paid Maytag to use its agitator patent, until a 1939 court ruling invalidated the patent. A similar situation existed with the Maytag wringer patent.

washers were made gave a salesperson greater confidence and product loyalty when selling. Dealers still visit Newton, but now it is Plant 2, home of the automatic washer and dryer, that is the magnet.

More than witnessing the assembly of Maytag products, Maytag sales personnel experience the esprit de corps of the factory. This experience shapes attitudes about Maytag products and sticks with salespeople who would otherwise only know one another by business card or a sales meeting group photo. The tradition of an annual year-end convention for the entire marketing group was begun at the turn of the century when the company still made farm equipment. The last annual sales convention in Newton was in 1926. Since then, meetings have been held regionally. Maytag field personnel still visit Newton on a regular basis, but rarely at the same time.

Family Feud: Conflict Between the Generations

During the early 1920s, Elmer and Bud Maytag had a growing problem with their old man. While nominally turning over the reins in 1921, F.L. retained his ownership interest, along with the top title of CEO, and continued as patriarch of his old-fashioned German family. He undoubtedly regarded this relationship as his due and his sons initially yielded, though grudgingly. But as the company increased its wealth, F.L. spent more and more time in Newton. As CEO, but without benefit of the overall planning, he became the proverbial loose cannon, rolling into town and into the plant and office, taking potshots at will.

The explosion came in 1926 when Bud apparently decided he had put up with enough and suddenly resigned. Little mention and no credit came to him during the lifetimes of his father and brother. It was almost as if he had never been part of the team. The golf course Bud donated to the country club left more of a mark on Newton than did his executive career.

The Hotel Had a Back Door

Some hold to the view that Bud was as exasperated with his father's peccadillos as with his blustering management style. Marital estrangement was fully evident by 1926 when F.L. built a million-dollar, five-story hotel in downtown Newton so he would have a place to live. His top-floor apartment had a back entrance that led directly to the street below. Rumor had it that the stairs were used by mysterious female guests.

F.L.'s daughters, Freda and Lulu, sided strongly with their mother, Dena. When she died in 1934, they made certain her portrait was given to the First Presbyterian church in Newton and not left in the big home built about the same time as the hotel. Young Fred Maytag II and his new bride lived in the house briefly before it was torn down as an unsalable white elephant to avoid paying property taxes. Apparently there's a reason that Dena Bergman Maytag and daughter Freda lie together on the opposite side of Newton Union cemetery from F.L.'s marvelous mausoleum.

The Third Maytag President and CEO

After Bud's departure in 1926, Elmer assumed the presidency *and* chief executive's office with the understanding that F.L. would concentrate his still significant abilities on sales, public relations, advertising, and the other aspects of marketing that Bud had left behind. However, F.L.'s growing ego-centricity went considerably against Elmer's grain, even though he seemed better able to cope than Bud had been. To the credit of both men, they had their showdown in private. Without any fanfare, Elmer emerged as the unquestioned chief executive officer. While F.L. didn't appear changed, he never again openly challenged Elmer. From there on out, F.L.'s chairman-ship seemed increasingly honorary.

Finally alone at the helm of the company, Elmer began his reign at a time when the country was experiencing its greatest business boom in history. The Roaring Twenties brought a seemingly insatiable demand for goods and services. Prices, debt, interest rates, and the stock market all skyrock-eted. While all this made it relatively easy to finance expansion and price his product at a highly profitable level, Elmer became uneasy. To him, it all looked too good to be true. He decided to consolidate gains and prepare for stormy weather that might lie ahead.

Maytag Goes Public

In the mid-1920s, company financing still depended on bank loans, as it had from the beginning. Even during periods when banks were eager to lend, Elmer Maytag remembered the times when they had nervously called in their loans. His goal was to become independent of bank credit, and in 1927, the year Maytag made its one-millionth washer, he began to make plans for a public stock offering. Virtually all the common stock was in the hands of family members who were reluctant to part with their proprietary position. With the help of the New York investment banking firm of J. & W. Seligman & Company, an arrangement was worked out to issue three classes of stock in 1928.

When Maytag was incorporated in Iowa in 1909, F.L. owned the company pretty much lock, stock, and barrel. That's how it stayed when the company was recapitalized as a Maine corporation because of a change in Iowa law. Prior to Maytag's first recapitalization, Iowa corporations did not need approval of the secretary of state to sell their stock. The new law also restricted indebtedness or liability of an Iowa corporation to less than two-thirds of capital.

In 1919 Maytag had secured $600,000 in 6 percent serial gold notes from a Chicago bank. They were retired in 1924. That December, in another recapitalization, the company established 15,000 shares of 7 percent preferred stock and an equal number of shares of prior-preferred stock, both at $100 par value. Authorized common stock was increased to 100,000 shares, although only about 40,000 shares were issued, almost entirely to the family.[6]

Less than a year later yet another capital reorganization plan was adopted, this one a proposal from Hornblower & Weeks, investment bankers. Under this plan Maytag reincorporated under the laws of Delaware, becoming a publicly held company with 2.4 million shares of common stock with no par value. A quarter-million shares were sold to Hornblower & Weeks at $15 a share. The proceeds were used to pay off the preferred stock issued the previous year. The stock was listed on both the New York and Chicago stock exchanges.

Selling the Company and Keeping It, Too

Generous dividends were paid on the common stock and it sold for a new high of $30.50 on April 22, 1927. Then came 1928. While neither a sales nor earnings record, results that year produced an incredible 24.18 percent earnings ratio. Seligman, with assistance from Blyth, Witter & Company, developed the recapitalization plan adopted by shareowners in May 1928.

Three types of securities were issued. First, 100,000 shares of $6 first-preferred stock was made available to the public at $100 a share. Owners of this stock had priority in liquidation and for payment of dividends, plus the right to name a majority of the board of directors if preference terms were defaulted. Proceeds were earmarked to retire outstanding bank loans and pay other debts. It was callable at $110 a share.

Next was an issue of 320,000 shares of $3 cumulative preference stock to be put on the market at $50 a share at such times and in such quantities as seemed advisable to provide working capital. It was subordinate only to the first preferred as to liquidation and dividend priority and carried the right

---

[6] It would seem reasonable to assume that Howard Snyder and other key executives held stock in Maytag during F.L.'s tenure.

to name one member to the board of directors in case of default. It was callable at $55 a share.

The third issue consisted of 1.6 million shares of new common stock, the same amount outstanding of the previous common issue. Since most of the previous common was held by the Maytag family, so was most of the new common, the only stock with voting rights. It was listed on the New York Stock Exchange and large quantities were offered for sale by the family in order to establish a market and to diversify their investments. But they kept control of the company at the same time.

Over the next several months there was such a demand for the preferred that the entire issue of $3 cumulative preference stock was sold, and for the first time in history, the company had a bulging treasury. The common also sold well. The first 12,000 shares of first-preferred stock were retired before the end of 1928. Common stock dividends totaling $1.52½ cents a share were declared in 1928, in addition to paying the preferred dividends.

Never Again

When the recapitalization was completed and the company was independent of bank debt, Elmer vowed never to use bank credit again. During the Depression, Maytag fell behind in dividend payments on the $3 cumulative-preference stock, and in 1933 those owners elected a member to the board as provided. He was Cyril J. C. Quinn of J. & W. Seligman & Company. After dividend arrears were made up, Quinn was retained on the Maytag board of directors until his death in 1975.

At one point director Quinn suggested that Maytag borrow funds at between 2 and 3 percent interest to redeem preference stock that was paying 6 percent, but Elmer remembered his vow. Despite the obvious economic advantages, Maytag didn't borrow the money. The sense of a long view, the dedication to principle over profit, had apparently been successfully handed down from F.L. to his sons.

The last of the first-preferred stock was redeemed in 1950, and the $3 cumulative preference stock was retired in three transactions between 1955 and 1959. Thus Maytag again became the exclusive property of the common shareowners, now over 8000 strong, just three years before the death of Fred Maytag II, the last of the family to hold the company reins.[7]

---

[7] Although it was rumored through the 1950s that the Maytag family controlled the majority of the company's stock, the fact is that the family held only about 5 percent. With the Maytag family being scattered and, in some cases, estranged, it's unlikely the Maytag holdings would have been voted as a block.

6

The Dawn of Social Responsibility in Manufacturing

Evolving Attitudes on Company Stakeholders—The Turbulent Thirties

The Early Roots of Labor Unrest

The labor movement that swept across the United States during the Great Depression reached Newton, Iowa, and the Maytag Company in 1937. Labor organizers found fertile ground. While F.L. had planted the seeds for much of the paternalism that union organizers would turn into unrest, he probably could have successfully resisted that tide, but he was no longer there to handle "his boys."

Just four months before his eightieth birthday, F.L. Maytag died in far-off California. He became ill at his new Beverly Hills home and died in a Los Angeles hospital on March 26, 1937. Death was attributed to a heart ailment. Newspaper headlines that March screamed of strikes and lockouts across the country.

Unions and labor unrest did not appear suddenly on the Newton scene. What must have been the first Maytag strike occurred on Tuesday April 14, 1897, when 8 of the 28 workers at the Parsons Band Cutter and Self-Feeder company walked off the job after a fellow employee was fired for "impertinence." The newspaper account identified the strikers as the "best" workers. Their strike demand was for a new shop superintendent to replace George Parsons. The next day the molders at Skow Brothers Foundry joined the strike as a sympathy gesture. The foundry was making castings for Parsons. The strike was settled on Saturday and everyone returned to work on Monday. Parsons, one of the original four partners, hung around for about a year.

While a number of strikes took place in Newton over the early years in both industry and retail, none of the striking employees were represented by unions at the time. Some of the earliest union-led strikes to affect Iowa were in the coal mines. Nationwide coal strikes in 1919 and 1922 impacted severely on Newton, since city utilities, homeowners, and industry depended on the fossil fuel. In 1931, 200 Polk County coal miners enrolled Newton Coal Company miners in the union by force. Four years later, 350 Jasper County coal miners joined 400,000 union members in a nationwide strike.

A former southern Iowa coal miner who went to work for Maytag in the early 1920s recalled that the miners always went on strike in the summer, rather than be laid off.

Wages and Hours

Wages have never been the major issue in a Maytag strike. In 1910, following a 6 percent wage increase, 28 cents was the Maytag factory average hourly wage. There was no wage increase in the office. Younger workers at the time were pushing for a 9-hour day and a half-day Saturday, but older workers didn't like the idea of a reduction in hours. In 1914, Maytag was the first Newton employer to go to half-day Saturdays. Employees worked 10-hour days rather than 9 to accumulate the same 54 hours a week. This plan was started by George Westinghouse, who died that year. It wasn't until 1933 that Roosevelt's National Recovery Act reduced the workweek to 40 hours.

All Newton factories closed Christmas Day beginning in 1912, and Labor Day was made a holiday beginning in 1914. There was a long-standing tradition of Christmas gifts. In 1903, all employees received a turkey and cranberries. The men got a box of cigars and the women an equivalent gift. The office staff, in turn, gave F.L. a Morris chair—the early version of a recliner. In 1907, F.L. obtained a list of needy folks and sent groceries in addition to the turkey. Some also got a check for $10. In 1914, Parsons company employees got turkeys, and One Minute workers got the day off with pay plus a $2 gift certificate for their wives. At Maytag, everyone got a $2 gift certificate, including the third of the work force that was laid off. The war in Europe and uncertain business conditions caused production to fall off and only the washer work force remained at full strength. A 1918 Christmas gift to Maytag employees was a $500 Prudential life insurance policy for those on the payroll six months to one year, a $1000 policy after one year, and an additional $100 for each year of service up to a maximum of $2000 in coverage.

F.L. always paid his employees well and that policy has continued to the present. Historically, Maytaggers have been the highest paid workers in the appliance industry. According to a company publication in 1930, Maytag was paying the highest wages of any company west of the Mississippi.

The Evolution of Employee Benefits

During his stewardship, Elmer sponsored a number of other innovative employee benefits, including the Employees' Relief & Benefit Association, financed by member dues and company contributions. Benefits were paid when employees missed work because of illness, long before sick leave was invented. A doctor hired by the association served employees at no additional cost, their families at modest extra cost, and the company on a fee basis for first-aid and hiring physicals. Company-sponsored programs have long since replaced these pioneering attempts at employee benefits.

The Incentive System: Heavy on the Carrot, Light on the Stick

Unquestionably the most valuable employee benefit was the 1908 piece-work pay plan that permitted employees to set their own pace and earn in relation to productivity. Other piecework plans were in disrepute because employers abused them and cut rates as efficiency improved. Seeing the production numbers and costs come across his desk, Elmer believed that if the rate was set correctly, both the company and worker would benefit. It was his policy not to change an established rate unless an outside supplier could underbid the work, the rate was clearly out of line with other similar jobs, or the job itself was substantially changed. The system produced extraordinary earnings for competent workers and tended to weed out incompetents and malingerers.

Is It Paternalism? Or Is It Corporate Social Responsibility?

The Maytag boom of the 1920s coincided with a slump in Iowa coal mining. Iowa coal, while plentiful, is generally of poor quality with a high sulfer content. In the early twentieth century, coal was mined across southern Iowa both in shaft mines and strip mines. John L. Lewis, later the irascible head of the United Mine Workers, got his start in Colfax, Iowa, 10 miles west of

Newton. As the most accessible coal disappeared, so did many miners' jobs. Out-of-work coal miners lined up for good-paying Maytag jobs.

However, there was no place for the workers and their families to live. During much of 1922 and 1923 Newton had a tent city. Men lived in boxcars on rail sidings and in tarpaper shacks. Every rentable sleeping room was occupied during the week by workers who went home to their families only on weekends.

Housing, Food, and Fuel for Hard Times

Elmer Maytag recognized the problem and did something about it. His actions were typical of the many times he pragmatically came to the rescue of employees. But Elmer was such a quiet and unassuming personality, his altruism stayed a well-kept secret. Meanwhile, his more publicity-conscious father was worshipped by "his boys." While F.L. had often toured the plant and knew many on the work force by name, that was not Elmer's style. He seldom saw the inside of the factory. In addition, the size of the work force had grown fourfold and many of the workers were new to the area. Nevertheless, Elmer seemed always to have the employees' best interests at heart. His concern for Maytag employees, when viewed from a historical perspective, appears genuine.

In the face of all the problems related to such rapid growth and the change to arm's-length employee relations, Elmer managed to keep faith with the policies that had driven Maytag over the years and maintained the level of excellence that F.L. had established. By hindsight, it can be seen as an incredible achievement, particularly by a man lacking much charisma. Such great change in a such a brief period has occurred only twice since in Maytag history, once during Fred Maytag II's stewardship in the post–World War II years and again in the 1980s when Dan Krumm was CEO.

Elmer attacked the housing shortage by going into partnership with a Newton building contractor, W.W. Smith. Together they bought and subdivided tracts of land, bought up vacant lots, and built hundreds of modest homes, which were sold to employees. The mortgages were held by Elmer's Jasper County Savings Bank and paid off by payroll deduction.

Later, during the hard times of the Depression, when there were layoffs, payments were waived and the owners had the option of catching up or extending the terms. On the other hand, when the payment came out of a short-workweek paycheck, the employee might be left with only $3 to make do for two weeks.

Other employee needs were not always readily met by the community and at least some local merchants were inclined to gouge. Elmer, impatient with the retail community, had carloads of coal brought in, set on a siding, and sold to employees, who hauled it away themselves. On another occasion, he had carloads of potatoes shipped to Newton for employees.

The Infamous Gasoline Station: Taking Exception to Company "Philanthropy"

One of Elmer's paternalistic moves later backfired. A company gasoline station was built in 1923, and employees from the president on down could buy gasoline with coupons charged to their paychecks. These moves got the attention of local merchants and moderated their greed.

At first, employees applauded Elmer's attempts to stabilize retail prices in Newton. However, in the years that followed, outside agitators for organized labor found such behavior fertile ground for raising employee suspicions. Appreciation later turned to resentment as management was painted as an exploiter of the workers. Eventually, anything that smacked of paternalism was phased out. While only a modest example of the benevolent paternalism exercised by the Maytag family over the years, the gasoline station became a symbol used effectively by union organizers a dozen years later.

Paternalism: A Subtle Problem

While F.L. had always treated his boys well, he also decided what was best for them as a proper German patriarch always did. The net effect was a sort of noblesse oblige that carried over to his son Elmer, who responded more from compassion than from rightful reign. While this situation was far more prevalent when an entrepreneur owned the business, paternalism is not unknown among modern managers who don't actually own the company but merely act as if they do. It is equally resented wherever present.

Typically, the employee receives a nice present and is expected to show proper appreciation by attending an event or whatever. This pattern goes back to the turn of the century. In 1901, for example, F.L. declared a half-holiday and gave everyone tickets to Buffalo Bill's Wild West Show, which had stopped in Newton.[1]

There are numerous other examples. The office force once got free tickets for an organ recital at the local Methodist Church, but the ultimate was probably Maytag Night at a tabernacle revival series. The center section of the tent was reserved for company officers and employees, led by F.L. Another time, he gave everyone the afternoon off and tickets to the Jasper County Fair.

Elmer started a twilight factory baseball league. The Maytag team was accused of being semipro, although they came in second to the One Minute team in 1924. The fact is that more than one factory supervisor was hired because of his baseball ability. Once hired, Maytag "ringers" generally turned out to be good supervisors.

---

[1] During the performance, a horse landed on one of the managers and his wife, but they escaped serious injury.

The Maytag employees' family picnic was begun in 1927 to celebrate F.L.'s seventieth birthday. Over 7000 people participated in the parade to the fairgrounds and the games, treats, speeches, and picnic dinner. The picnic always was held on a Saturday, and everyone wore a white outfit and a Maytag overseas cap in the parade from the plant to the fairgrounds. Showing up for the parade was not optional. For his seventieth birthday, F.L. announced, without previous fanfare, a collective $130,000 bonus to employees with more than three years of service. A band and chorus of 80 performed a tribute to F.L. The evening of round and square dancing was cut short by rain.

It all seems quite innocent, even charming, but union organizers and strike leaders would see it in a different light.

Meanwhile, Maytag Bends But Isn't Broken by the Great Depression

Despite the stock market crash that brought on the Great Depression, 1929 was the year of Maytag's prewar record sales and earnings, which were an astounding 27.15 percent of sales. While employment was not a record, the payroll was.

The Depression began to hit Maytag and Newton seriously in 1931. As an economy measure, the board of directors voted a two-week vacation without pay for all factory employees, including salaried foremen. They also voted a 20 percent cut in factory, branch, and main office expenses by reducing personnel, salaries, or both. Also lost in the cutbacks were the annual employees' picnic, county fair tickets for employees, and similar benefits. That year, production was cut in half. The payroll also was half that of the previous year and was cut by half again in 1932, the low point for Maytag. Its two-millionth washer produced that year was one of fewer than 75,000 made by fewer than 1000 employees—the first time since 1924 the work force had dipped below a thousand. The average worker took home less than $700 that year. The company eked out earnings of $100,000, a miniscule 2 percent of less than $5 million in sales. But Maytag never lost money during the Depression.

Marketing and Product Development Strategies for Hard Times

Price-Driven Marketing: Maytag Models 10 and 11

Two daring marketing programs helped save the day during the depths of the Depression. Both can be credited to Elmer, essentially as financial decisions. Both suggested that he knew something about the ratio of price to demand, and maybe a little about psychology as well.

The first was the introduction of a low-priced washer with a porcelain-coated steel tub, the Model 10, in April 1933 (see Figure 6-1). It wasn't the first Maytag with a round tub or a steel tub but it was the first to sell well, because its retail price was $59.50, compared with more than $100 for aluminum tub washers. The earlier models hadn't sold well because sales commissions were meager and because sales reps had been indoctrinated to believe that square tub aluminum washers were the best. But in the face of almost no sales in 1932, the low-ball model was a godsend. A similar Model 11 featured the Multi-Motor.

One dimension of the Maytag washer story is told in annual production statistics. For example, wood tubs predominated until 1922, when aluminum tub washers took over. Production of aluminum tubs peaked in 1926, but that type prevailed every year except 1932 and 1933, when cheaper steel tubs were more popular. As a result of the introduction of the Model 10 steel tub in 1933, more than four times as many steel tubs as aluminum tubs were sold that year.

The following year, 1934, saw a dramatic turnaround in the popularity of aluminum tub washers because of a second and most spectacular marketing ploy. A dramatic jump in employment and doubling of the payroll between

Figure 6-1. The steel tub Model 10—priced to sell during the Depression.

1933 and 1934 resulted from the switch to selling Model 30 deluxe aluminum tub washers over the porcelain steel tub Model 10. The vitreous enamel porcelain steel tubs were purchased from an Ohio company and the aluminum tubs were made in Newton by Maytag employees.

Model 30: Repositioning the High End

When a new Model 30 washer was introduced in late 1933, little changed from the Model 90 aluminum washer it replaced (see Figure 6-2). The flagship of the Maytag fleet sold at retail for $139.95.

Elmer Maytag had been wintering in Florida since 1928 and took up almost permanent residence in 1934. The climate there had proved beneficial for both his and his son Robert's health. He was there in January 1934, when Maytag's field marketing organization held a meeting in Newton. The marketing people were in the dumps. Despite the improvement in sales volume generated by the Model 10, sales commissions had not kept pace. Business was tough. They all clamored for a price reduction on the top of the line.

Claire Ely, retired marketing vice president, was working for the Minneapolis branch at the time and was in the room when F.L. opened the meeting. As Claire tells it, F.L. first asked them how they'd like a $59 aluminum washer. Yes, they sure would. If anyone can make an inexpensive washer, F.L. told them, Maytag can do it. More cheers. Of course, he went on, freight would cost the same as for the more expensive model. Service cost would probably be more because it couldn't be as well made and dependable. The final straw was that of course commissions would be very small. Despair returned.

Long Distance Hoakum

"I'm just not sure what we should do," he concluded. "Maybe we should ask Elmer what he thinks." F.L. picked up a phone and made the call to Florida. After some preliminary politeness, he told Elmer that the boys wanted a lower price on the Model 30 and went through some of the earlier discussion. Elmer's response was, "If we do anything, we should go all the way." He then announced that effective immediately, retail price of the washer would be $89.95, carload dealer cost $45 and sales commission $6. At first the men were too stunned to respond, then they brought the house down.

Demand was so great, some of the dealer orders placed that January were not delivered until June. The marketplace virtually exploded, and Maytag was in the driver's seat. While the price was protected on earlier orders, pricing edged up almost monthly until it stopped at $114.95. Sales that had increased by $3.5 million in 1933 went up by another $6 million in 1934, and earnings both years ran about 14 percent of sales. Sales didn't continue at that brisk pace during the remainder of the decade, but neither did they decline from year to year.

Figure 6-2. The Model 30—The Old Gray Ghost: One of Maytag's all-time best-sellers.

Shouldering the Responsibility Locally

In 1931 Elmer had been tapped by President Hoover to serve in his Unemployment Relief Organization, headed by Walter Gifford, president of AT&T. The organization included a real cross section of businessmen, politicians, labor leaders, planners, educators, and the like. Elmer came away from that experience with the conviction that government, listening to all those voices, simply could not deal directly and effectively with the ailing economy. If Maytag employees were to be helped, it would have to be locally, and it was probably up to the company.

One significant local program was the great woodpile scheme, instigated by Elmer with the aid of the Newton Jaycees, headed by Bob Vance, who worked for Elmer at Jasper County Savings Bank. The two got together to carry out Elmer's plan. He owned some river bottomland that contained substantial stands of timber. It would make good firewood for Newton homes, most of which were heated by hand-fired furnaces that could burn either coal or wood.

Elmer donated the timber and Maytag furnished tools and trucks for cutting and hauling the cord wood. Maytag employees were offered work cutting the wood at $5 per cord. The Jaycees' role was to coordinate the sales of the wood. Elmer paid the Jaycees a 50-cents-a-cord commission out of his own pocket and the company handled the bookkeeping.

The Jaycees, long on manpower and short on money, jumped at the chance. The project was a success from the start and continued through two winters. Many thousands of cords of wood were sold, nearly every worker took wood for some of his wages and extra money flowed in the community. Some of the wood could still be seen stacked behind Newton houses years later after most had switched to oil furnaces.

Elmer the Man: A Not-So-Subtle Problem

Nevertheless, a primary cause for the union organizing and the 1938 strike at Maytag was the deepening belief in the minds of many employees that management was no longer as sympathetic to workers or their needs as it had once been. Elmer Maytag's introverted personality contrasted with that of his father and was misinterpreted by some as condescending. The attitude and behavior of outlander labor negotiator Art Taylor contributed even more to a feeling among workers that they must look out for themselves. A union official at the time was quoted as saying, "The main thing we wanted was an end to the absolute domination of the management." In Elmer's era, management meant "the family."

Elmer did not have the dominant, magnetic personality of his father, nor was he as polished and extroverted as his brother Bud. He sometimes suffered unfavorable comparison with others in the family because his talents were less obvious. He had the ability to quickly reach the bottom line, but he lacked the facility of speech and persuasion to carry others along with him. He fell back on authority, brevity, and bluntness.[2] His orders seldom included the reason why and never invited discussion. He left the impression that he was hard boiled, unapproachable, and rigid. Yet he went out of his way to solicit input before reaching a decision. Some felt his bruskness covered a shyness he didn't want exposed.

Elmer could hold his own with high-powered executives, politicians, and professionals but for companionship he preferred the common people. He liked to spend his time at his dairy farm talking bloodlines and production records or in a farmer's barnyard talking crops and weather.

As a youth he had enjoyed holidays on a farm and the interest stayed with him all his life. His entry into the dairy cattle business was typically amateurish and the culmination was typically top drawer. He owned over 4000 acres of Iowa farmland and the most magnificent herd of Holstein-Frisian cattle anywhere. Maytag is part of the lengthy name of many a pedigreed cow or bull even yet.[3]

---

[2] Once Elmer responded to a lengthy letter from a General Motors officer expressing an interest in merger:

> Dear Mr. (So and So):
> No.
> Yours Truly,
> E.H. Maytag

[3] Maytag Blue Cheese: Dairy farming ultimately grew into a major Maytag family endeavor. Elmer had built an impressive herd. After Elmer's death, Fred, after some searching, found a way to make his father's dairy herd pay off. He learned of a method developed at Iowa State College for making blue cheese, using a penicillin mold for the veining. By the end of 1941, the dairy farm had produced its first batch of Maytag blue cheese. Sold almost entirely by mail order, it developed a reputation as one of the finest blue cheeses in the world.

Fred was proud of the cheese business, but not of the cows. The prize bloodline started by his father in 1922 was sold off in 1949, leaving a working herd to supply the basic cheese ingredient. The dairy farm sold all its cattle in 1992 and now purchases all its milk needs. That announcement prompted an editorial in the *Des Moines Register*.

Milkers for Maytag

Maytag has sold the cows on its Newton farm to an Oelwein dairy operation, and in the future will buy all the milk it uses in the blue cheese it markets. Maytag farm manager James Stevens said it is getting too tough to find workers willing to take on the twice-daily, seven-days-a-week chore of milking.

C'mon, Maytag. What about all those lonely appliance repairmen who are bored to tears? They could even do the work sitting down.

The Maytag dairy was inherited by Fred's sons, Fritz and Kenneth, and continues as a successful mail-order business. Fritz (Fred Maytag III) also runs a microbrewery in San Francisco that makes Anchor Steam beer and he owns a vineyard in the wine country north of the Golden Gate bridge. Neither son has ever been involved with the parent company.

His enthusiasm for Florida led to his investment in a partially submerged island near Miami Beach that became one of the most exclusive residential areas along the coast. Failing health kept Elmer in Florida most of the time from 1934 until his death in 1940.

Events Go From Rosy to Slightly Red

The introduction of Models 10, 11 and 30 gave Maytag the boost it needed to get back on track. Labor benefited as well. Employment jumped from an average of 983 in 1932 to 1116 in 1933, and a whopping 1995 in 1934. A 5 percent wage increase went into effect August 1, 1933, the year Iowa voted to repeal Prohibition. Jasper County voted dry. Elmer declared a moratorium on interest payments for employees purchasing houses from Maytag-Smith, the company itself, or Elmer personally. No interest would be charged from July 1, 1934, until July 1, 1935, when it would be 3.5 percent.

Despite all he had done for employees before and after he became president and throughout the Depression, Elmer's name would soon turn to mud in his hometown. In March 1936, the United Electrical, Radio, and Machine Workers of America was formed and it affiliated with the Congress of Industrial Organizations.[4]

The Infamous Jobs-for-Pontiacs Affair

Of all the incidents and events used by William Sentner to stir up unrest among Maytaggers, probably the most effective was the situation that tied buying a Pontiac to steady employment at Maytag. Enter F.L.'s cronies Joe Longwell and John Herbst.

F.L. was estranged from his family. He was well past 70, and most of his friends of earlier years were dead. Those left were awed by his immense wealth. He was in the paradoxical position of being worshipped by many but liked by few. A man of F.L.'s temperament found this situation intolerable. The void was filled by a small group of what George Umbreit later called "unprincipled individuals," headed by Herbst and Longwell.

Herbst was made plant superintendent despite upper management's objections. Longwell, owner of the Pontiac dealership, was an intimate at F.L.'s hotel suite. Naturally, the community came to believe that Joe was a

---

[4] In 1949, the union was tossed out of the CIO at the national convention in Milwaukee because it was believed to be communist-dominated. One known communist was William Sentner, a vice president of the 700,000 member national union and also a district organizer for the CIO. He played a major role in the great strike at Maytag.

good one to have as a friend. For example, when the school superintendent hoped to interest F.L. in buying uniforms for the high school band, he thought it wise to mention this first to Longwell. Shortly afterward, the school got its uniforms, and it was hinted to the superintendent that his car was getting old and perhaps he should be thinking about a new one—a Pontiac.

Hiring practices were arbitrary in those days. The personnel manager would go to the gate, look over the lineup, and select a worker on a whim. This "shape-up" led to injustices. Once a person was hired, the foreman had absolute authority in assigning jobs, pay, and working hours, a major consideration in times of short workweeks. There was only one sure way to beat the system.

Anyone who bought a Pontiac on credit would find a job waiting at the plant and could be assured of work for at least so long as the car payments stretched. Nothing was ever stated openly, but trial and error soon proved the method to be infallible. Joe Longwell sold the Pontiac—for about $700—and John Herbst provided the employment security. This practice generated considerable resentment, especially among employees who did not need or could not afford a new car.

This, along with company houses, birthday parades, and the continuing annoyance of mandatory YMCA dues, provided Sentner with all the ammunition he needed to foster a strike. One reluctant YMCA dues payer thought he had found a solution. When faced with the forced question, he asked instead to have a junior membership deducted and given to some poor youngster in his name. His next paycheck excluded deductions for both a youth membership and an adult membership.

The Last Will : The Last Straw

F.L.'s will was a last straw to workers who had been confident that he would not neglect them. A rumor around town had it that an eightieth birthday giveaway would dwarf what F.L. had done on his seventieth. Plans already were under way for a pageant to be staged by the Newton Chamber of Commerce that would have been bigger than anything Newton had ever seen. But all of that went by the board with F.L.'s death a few months before the anniversary.

Then came the will. F.L. left nearly $2 million to a total of 194 beneficiaries, including distant relatives, management associates, office help, servants, Hotel Maytag employees, and even employees of Longwell Motor Company, but nothing to the production employees. Maytag main office and branch office employees who had not shared in the 1927 birthday gift would receive $1000 each, along with employees of Jasper County Savings Bank, Hotel Maytag, Ceylon Court,[5] and Longwell Motor Company, the last suggesting F.L. may have had an ownership position.

Longwell inherited all personal effects located in F.L.'s apartment in Hotel Maytag with the power to "distribute them to any of his relations or close friends who may care to have any of them." The Pontiac dealer also was one of five who got $25,000 each. Two of the others were company executive George Umbreit and banker Ray Bailey.

Hotel manager Ernie Zeug was given an undivided half interest in the hotel. John Herbst was one of several receiving $10,000 gifts. Another was Father T.J. McCann, rector of Sacred Heart Church and close friend of F.L., and a third was the widow of F.L.'s former partner, W.C. Bergman. Her inheritance was to be paid in $900 annual installments.

The balance of the estate after specific bequests was left to his son Bud. The will specified that Elmer and his two sisters had previously been provided for. The will was drawn up in February 1936 with the two sons as executors, along with attorney Tim Campbell. A codicil that November replaced the sons with Ray Bailey, suggesting further estrangement.

The estate totaled some $10 million, the largest ever probated in Iowa, and taxes totaled over $500,000, that figure having the same distinction. F.L. also carried the largest insurance policy in the state, for $1.5 millon.

---

[5] A keystone of F.L.'s increasingly extravagant lifestyle was Ceylon Court on Lake Geneva, Wisconsin. He bought the 400-acre estate in 1928. The building had originally been the country of Ceylon's exhibit at the Chicago Columbian exposition of 1893. It had been disassembled, moved to Lake Geneva, and reassembled as part of the huge estate.

It was large and ornate with much use of exotic woods. The main building featured ornate and symbolic carvings of the many kinds of native woods fastened together with wooden pegs to form the structure. The carvings carried into the house, which was furnished and decorated with jades, porcelains, ivories, paintings, tapestries, carpets, and furniture, all of oriental design and in keeping with the architecture.

Also on the grounds was a boathouse with living quarters above, a large greenhouse, swimming pool and bathhouse, and a seven-room gatehouse just inside massive iron gates, which normally remained closed. There was a large formal garden of intricate design as well as other gardens, lawns, and landscaping, all maintained with utmost care. Throughout the estate were huge porcelain vases and statuary from Ceylon (now Sri Lanka).

F.L. spent his summers in Ceylon Court and entertained royally, including family, friends, and employees. His hostess there was the wife of a field employee, who presumably remained married all the time she was presiding as gracious hostess for F.L. The hostess' marital status as well as F.L.'s estrangement from Dena were no secret to the family members, employees, and other guests at Ceylon Court.

After F.L. died in 1937, Elmer began using Ceylon Court as a summer home but did little entertaining outside of the family. The place required a large staff of servants and gardeners and was sold after Elmer's death in 1940 because it was difficult to staff during World War II.

Getting Organized

Herbst was $10,000 richer but out of a job. A Newton native, he had worked at Maytag for some time before being named production manager in 1936. In March 1936, the new electrical workers union had been formed. It affiliated with the CIO. The following year that union had a contract with Maytag and Herbst was replaced by Art Taylor, a hard-driving executive from the East with a reputation as a union-buster. Taylor had worked for Westinghouse and the New York Central railroad, among others. He was paid the same salary as George Umbreit, vice president and treasurer, which put him high in the pecking order.

Fred Maytag II later described the situation:

> The relationship between employer and employee was close, friendly, and sympathetic. The managers and owners adopted a paternalistic attitude towards their employees and bestowed personal philanthropies upon the community. It was assumed that our employees, whose wages were well above the average for the area, were completely happy and it was a source of great pride that no serious attempt had ever been made to organize a labor union.
>
> Then, in 1937 it happened. A group of disgruntled employees called in a CIO organizer, held a meeting in a rented hall, and a few days later we were confronted by representatives of the United Electrical, Radio, and Machine Workers and the accomplished fact that all but a handful of our employees had joined their union.
>
> Apparently, our employees weren't quite so happy as we thought!

Local 1116 of the Electricial Workers Union was organized April 20, 1937. When union officials met with Umbreit and Roy Bradt, marketing vice president, nine days later to discuss negotiations, they claimed a membership of 1400. F.L. Maytag's body had not been in his mausoleum 30 days. The American Federation of Labor belatedly sent an organizer to Newton on May 3. He found little encouragement and left a week later.

Hammering Out the First Union Contract

The day he departed, a delegation from Local 1116 headed by Wilbert (Web) Allison, first local president, met with company officials to present their contract proposals. A national officer of the United Mine Workers, CIO, spoke at a Maytag union meeting that evening.

The company's response was to request proof that the union did in fact represent the Maytag workers. In reply, the local produced evidence of 1700 dues-paying members. Negotiations started June 1, and the union accepted the company offer June 9 by a vote of 1339 to 234. Provisions of the first contract included a 5 percent wage increase, a 40-hour week, weekly pay instead of biweekly and a grievance procedure making use of shop stewards. The first wildcat walkout occurred June 17 when assembly workers objected to the presence of an alleged antiunion worker. The dispute was settled five days later when the man joined the union.

1937—The Year of Unionism and Strikes

The all-pervasive atmosphere of trade unionism rocking the country in 1937 encompassed Newton as well. The UE not only had organized Maytag but also had set up locals at the One Minute and Automatic Washer companies. Another local included employees of Parsons Company and Newton Foundry. All negotiated contracts in 1937.

Other local unions also flourished, such as the United Garage and Oil Station Workers, which had a week-long strike in August 1937. The CIO Retail Clerks union struck for three days in July, and the Montgomery Ward store was the scene of picketing during a two-month strike by the same union in August and September. Shopping habits were upset and some women refused to venture out on the courthouse square without their husbands.

A union organizer orchestrated a walkout of employees at the White Way Cafe after an employee was fired. They returned to work when she was rehired. The AFL Typographers Union struck the *Newton Daily News,* and Maytag workers picketed the newspaper office in violation of an injunction that limited pickets to employees.

The UE held its first state convention in Newton. Over 5000 people attended a Labor Day celebration organized by the CIO. In September, the CIO organizer, L.J. Martin, was given a job at Detroit headquarters and was replaced by William Sentner, who presided over the CIO District 8 convention in Newton the following month.

Just as Art Taylor was the chief protagonist for the company, William Sentner played that role for the union. A native of St. Louis, he had been a construction worker before becoming a full-time union organizer in 1935. He had joined the Communist party in 1934 following a police beating during a picket line dispute. He had attended Washington University in St. Louis and had been arrested many times. A front-page editorial in the *Newton Daily News* accused Sentner of defying law and order, inciting mob spirit, using vile language, threatening to blow up the town, and bragging about being in jail 28 times.

The CIO claimed credit for breaking up Longwell's "employment agency" when five Maytag employees sued him after they were laid off and couldn't keep up their car payments. They claimed Joe had guaranteed work so long as the payments continued. Before the suit came to trial the following spring, Longwell requested a change of venue, claiming he couldn't get a fair trial in Jasper County. But he saw the handwriting on the wall and bailed out before the first of the year. He leased his building to the Ford dealer as of January 1, 1938, and went out of business. He had arrived in Newton in 1926 from Des Moines and established his car dealership at the age of 35 and departed 11 years later. He had just purchased his building for $15,000 a few weeks before—from the F.L. Maytag estate. Longwell died suddenly during a visit to Missouri in 1942.

The CIO ran a candidate for school board in the 1938 election. The candidate lost amidst the largest turnout in school election history. With labor agitation in the factories and also in the stores where they shopped, interfering with their local newspaper and even attempting to influence the education of their children, Newton's conservative citizens were upset and ready to take sides.

The Great Strike of 1938

Local 1116 was feeling its oats as the original Maytag contract neared expiration. The company requested a National Labor Relations Board election, wishfully thinking that union support might be waning. An antiunion headquarters was established in the Hotel Maytag. The NLRB-supervised election showed overwhelming support for the union. The vote was 1188 for and 269 against.

It must have been difficult for Elmer and his associates at the company to accept the cold reality of their unpopularity. In their disbelief it was natural to blame the outsiders for their problems, for coming between the company and its employees. The community by and large took the same view.

Flush with success, the union demanded a closed shop, dues checkoff, 25 percent raise, 10 percent night pay differential, paid vacation, and a guaranteed annual wage. The company rejected the concept of a guaranteed annual wage, closed shop, checkoff, and paid vacation, but suggested a 40-hour week. Business was in a slump, and the company regarded a paid vacation as the equivalent of a pay raise, which wasn't in the cards. The contract expired as the union rejected the company proposal, but union members voted not to strike. They contested the company's claim that Maytag paid 5 percent above industry average wages.

The company recessed talks and requested a conciliator, but then Maytag made the move that made a strike inevitable. Perhaps it was thought that a forceful action might intimidate the workers. Management was wrong. On a Saturday, the company posted notices in the plant that, because of poor business, a 10 percent wage cut would be effective immediately. On Monday, employees reported to work, even though the union was aware of the notice, and then refused to work under the wage cut, walked out, and set up a picket line.

Art Taylor became a symbol of the company's intransigence. He was perceived as an arrogant outsider with no feeling for local conditions and no inclination to learn, and he quickly earned the animosity of the workers. He was joined on the company negotiating team by a young lawyer from a Chicago firm that specialized in labor relations, interpreted by the union as union-busting. Umbreit and young Fred Maytag II, grandson of F.L. and Elmer's son, completed the team. Fred found the episode a significant learning experience. Notably absent from the company team was Elmer, who had departed for Ceylon Court and took no direct part in the proceedings.

The Friday before the walkout, the union held a mass meeting on the downtown square. Over 1000 people heard Sentner deliver a long, involved, highly emotional speech. He sneered at the manner in which the Maytag family lived, indicating they could well afford a pay raise for the workers. The wild oratory, slurs against the Maytag family, huge crowd, tumultuous applause, and the resulting electric atmosphere all set the tone for the confrontation that followed.

Showdown at the Factory Gate

The first few weeks of the strike passed peacefully enough. Then talk of a back-to-work movement began. Eventually, more than a third of the factory workers were ready to return to work. About 350 strikers occupied the plant for a week in late June to forestall a return by the others. A conference led by Iowa Governor Nelson Kraschel ended the sit-down when the company agreed to keep the plant closed.

Because local law enforcement proved to be woefully inadequate, the community started to organize a civilian posse to keep order as the tension mounted. On July 18, about 500 workers returned to work, and eight carloads of washers had been shipped out by late afternoon. In contrast to the quiet at the plant, a large crowd gathered at the junior high auditorium for the opening of the NLRB hearings on the charge that the company was out to break the union. Production at the plant quietly continued the next day with no attempt to halt returning workers.

Sensing that they were losing their grip, union leaders made plans that night for an all-out effort to keep the plant from opening the next day. The strikers expected to be met by armed deputies. Suddenly, the meeting was galvanized by the news that the Democratic governor had called out the National Guard. A detachment of 250 guardsmen moved in during the night to establish martial law and close the plant "until the future peace in Newton is definitely guaranteed." General Matthew Tinley was notified that evening at his Council Bluffs home. He arrived in Newton late that night and set up headquarters in the Hotel Maytag. He got to bed about 6 a.m. but was awakened 20 minutes later with the news that a riot was in progress at the plant.

Milling around company gates since dawn was a large mob of strikers, back-to-workers, wives, spectators, peace officers, and armed vigilantes. Scuffles erupted. One man was hospitalized. But General Tinley's appearance was sufficient to quiet tempers, and the trouble was over by the time troops arrived. The tension was broken. The town was titillated with the spectacle of armed men patrolling the streets and machine guns set up overlooking plant entrances. The National Guard camp in southwest Newton became a magnet for young boys.

Aftershocks

With pressure to open the plant mounting, Governor Kraschel made a serious blunder. The NLRB proceedings were a continuing aggravation in the community and the governor closed the hearings, prohibiting them anywhere in the state. In Washington, the governor's action was branded illegal, and the hearings were moved to Des Moines and ordered to resume August 4.

Semisecret conferences with Elmer Maytag and his son Fred, attorneys for both sides, the general, and the governor continued. Finally, on August 3, the governor announced he was ordering the National Guard to reopen the plant the next day. The terms agreed to were that all legal action against the union members would be dropped, 12 troublemakers would not be rehired, and the original 10 percent wage cut would stand. Any additional cuts would be limited to 5 percent. If 1938 earnings covered the required preference dividends, a 5 percent pay increase would be granted for all of 1939.

In his statement, the governor glumly added, "This proposal in no sense of the word represents my personal views, nor do I desire to comment except to say that I am convinced that it is the best offer available at this time...."

Next morning the union held a mass meeting and members were urged to return to work. While some wanted to hold out, the majority were tired of futile gestures. They marched directly from the meeting to the plant and went to work. The strike was over, but the bitterness lasted for a long time. Families in Newton remained divided for a generation. The NLRB hearings in Des Moines went on the rest of the summer.

Fred Maytag's father-in-law, Kenneth Pray, was an academician in social studies from Philadelphia and was characterized by his own daughter as a "bleeding liberal." That is until, while vacationing, he attended the NLRB trial in Des Moines one day. Ellen Pray Maytag reported that her father turned overnight into a redneck reactionary after hearing the testimony. He was particularly affected by the vicious outpouring from some of the strikers' wives. He said it reminded him of Madame Lefarge and the women of the French Revolution.

Learn Your Lessons and Move Forward

It must have been very unpleasant and even frightening to be a Maytag family member in the middle of all the controversy. Young Fred, at 27, could easily have reacted like his father-in-law. Instead, he observed and learned a great deal about human nature and labor relations. While Sentner was the same satanic figure to him as to his fellow Newton citizens, Fred did not see the rank-and-file strikers in the same light. He could accept the fact that grievances existed. He kept the same concern for employees that his father and grandfather had shared. It proved to be another case of enlightened self-interest.

The strike came about because of fear, misunderstanding, mistrust, and a breakdown in communications. As the summer weeks wore on and tensions mounted, weariness as much as anything contributed to a conclusion. The Maytag Company was not destroyed. The union was not destroyed. The community was not destroyed. Each had learned some lessons on how to live with one another.

Maytag could have destroyed Local 1116 at the end of the strike. Three months without income had placed union members in dire economic straits. Antiunion sentiment was strong in the community and throughout the state. Yet after production was resumed, the management, down through the foreman level, bent over backward to refrain from encouraging antiunion activity.

Once labor was organized, Maytag never attempted to reverse the process. Management felt that a strong union was desirable to enforce contract provisions and avoid wildcat work stoppages. Over the years the company and labor bargaining unit have worked well together, and that cooperation has always been most apparent when it came to the subject of quality and dependability.

Postscript

When Maytag built its automatic washer plant in Newton in 1949, both parties made a serious mistake in establishing a separate bargaining unit for the new plant, with its own seniority provisions. The move seriously hampered mobility between the plants. It took years to eliminate the problem.

In 1949, the CIO expelled the UE because of alleged unAmerican activities on the part of some top officers. However, the CIO, then dominated by Walter Reuther's United Auto Workers, waited before pushing a replacement union, and in the interim, the UAW was given a free hand to attempt to organize the former UE locals.

Many new employees had joined Maytag after World War II with the opening of Plant 2, where the automatic washer was built. They did not share the loyalty to the UE held by Plant 1 workers, who still remembered the strike. All the union officers were from Plant 1, where three-fifths of the bargaining unit worked. A new slate of officers from both plants was proposed and narrowly won election in 1951. The real objective was to find a new international union to affiliate with. In the interim, if the UE found out, it had the power to take over the local and seize the treasury.

The financial problem was handled by opening individual accounts for all union officers and stewards who would need to be paid and depositing enough money in each account to cover six months. Then came the question of which union to join. The board met with representatives of the Machinists, IUE, UAW, Teamsters, and others. The objective was to link up with a union that was clean and free, and offered democracy to its locals.

It was also during this period that Walter Reuther became the most progressive and articulate labor leader in the country. He had just successfully struck the auto industry for the first fully funded, actuarially sound pension program for industrial workers in America, with the slogan "Too young to die and too old to work." The UAW was also the only union that offered strike benefits to members. An enthusiastic endorsement from the UAW local at the John Deere plant in nearby Ankeny, Iowa, completed the persuasion for the board to recommend the UAW to its members. An NLRB election was arranged, and the UAW received about 97 percent of the vote. Six members voted for no union.

Negotiating a New Contract

With the help of UAW officials, the new Local 997 prepared to negotiate a common contract for all plants. According to a union account, the company team included "a high-class negotiating lawyer from Chicago, and for the first time in history, Fred Maytag was on the company's committee."

It took close to six weeks to negotiate the first UAW agreement. "We made more gains in that first contract," the account went on, "than we had made in the past six years." Gains included three new holidays, additional vacation, a skilled trades training program, improved language in the incentive program, a wage increase, and an agreement to negotiate a pension plan. Edris (Soapy) Owens, elected president of the local in 1952, achieved a combined seniority system.

Local 997 has been involved with two major strikes at Maytag. In 1955, the strike was over the company's refusal to grant a supplemental unemployment benefit (SUB) plan. The strike was settled without SUB, but it became part of the 1956 contract. Another strike occurred in 1971, principally over ineptitude by both parties.

Achieving Full Participation

Quality comes from everyone pulling together. Everyone on the payroll must be focused on the same objective. Maytag has always stressed the importance of its people, more than institutions or methodology. Maytag's pattern of behavior through the years indicates a genuine regard for the

Figure 6-3. Maytag legendary quality is possible only because of a quality work force. The aluminum foundry is pictured here, pre-World War II.

value of people at all levels, from bargaining unit through management ranks to the executive level. Figures 6-3 and 6-4 illustrate the changing face of Maytag's work force.

Fred Maytag II put it this way:

> I happen to believe that a [person] makes [the] most effective contribution and achieves the greatest personal satisfaction when [there is] a sense of really being a part of the organization—when [the person] believes honestly that the decisions [made] and the actions [taken] have a direct effect on the success of the total operation.

Emphasis on Training

Under the leadership of Fred Maytag II, Maytag management showed a willingness to change, and many new programs were introduced in the postwar

Figure 6-4. The Dependability People.

era. With progressive and prudent people at the top, the company showed leadership in recruitment, training, compensation, and communications. In the late 1940s Maytaggers were being told, "You are already doing things that the rest of the world only talks about."

Maytag's preference for promoting from within has led to a strong supervisory training program. In other words, Maytag cultivates its leaders from those in the ranks. The company recognizes that its culture of quality won't come along with a manager hired away from another company. Instead, Maytag actively seeks out tomorrow's leaders whenever possible from among its own. The emphasis on internal promotion began in earnest with development of the automatic washer following World War II.

Manufacturing the automatic washer required building and staffing a whole new plant. New skills had to be learned and mastered. The cadre was picked and worked as a team from the outset. The success of that initial effort led to a continuing supervisory training program and then to a pre-supervisory program in which likely candidates are selected from employee ranks for a year's training before being given supervisory jobs.

Another program trains marketing and administrative candidates recruited from college campuses. It takes up to two years and rotates trainees through numerous departments, using on-the-job rather than strictly a classroom approach to avoid elitism. Begun in the 1950s, this program was the starting point for past and present CEOs Dan Krumm and Leonard Hadley.

Communicating With Lead People

One of the most effective means of communicating with supervisors is the Maytag Management Club. Every employee supervising others or possessing special status because of the professional or technical nature of his or her work is considered a member of management and eligible to participate. Participation in the Maytag Management Club runs at approximately 90 percent of those eligible to belong. The club is affiliated with the National Management Association. Executives participate, but club leadership is in the hands of rank-and-file members.

Fred Maytag described the Maytag Management Club's success:

> It has been one of the most important factors in building esprit de corps, uniting [people] into a smooth working team and developing a sense of being members of the whole organization rather than just employees of the company.

The club is nearly 50 years old, and a regular annual feature almost from the beginning has been a report from the CEO and financial division on results of the previous year as published in the annual report. Other management incentives included a generous bonus plan and restricted stock options. All employees benefit from educational assistance grants. A weekly salaried job-bidding process promotes fairness in advancement.

Ensuring Common Ground With Labor

Over the years, Maytag has achieved good understanding of its corporate objectives, particularly the total quality and dependability emphasis, with plant workers, despite dealing with two sometimes militant unions. One reason may be Fred Maytag's outlook: "It is fundamental in our policy that labor and management have so much in common, and so few differences, that neither can afford the luxury of fighting."[6]

---

[6] As a state senator, Fred Maytag spearheaded passage of Iowa's right-to-work law, prohibiting a closed shop because "it is fundamental in Maytag policy that every employee is free to belong to any union of his [or her] choice or to no union at all." On the other hand, he led the fight to increase unemployment benefits and workman's compensation in Iowa.

7
Enlightened Self-Interest

From Philanthropy to a Formal Policy of Community Service

"It's so good to have a nice industry like Maytag. We might have had a brewery."
A RARE NON-MAYTAG RESIDENT OF NEWTON, IOWA

Public Responsibility—Creating the Environment for Quality

Public responsibility in the private sector has many names and many facets, but all relate to the interplay between a company and the general public. It is one of the four groups identified by Fred Maytag II in his credo hanging in the lobby of Maytag's headquarters building. Each of the groups— customers, employees, shareowners, and the public—respond to a quality company. Each has a need the company must fulfill in order to be successful and remain in business. Public responsibility also is among the core values and concepts of the Malcolm Baldrige Award.

Other names for public responsibility might include corporate good citizenship, philanthropy, community relations, social responsibility, and envi-

149

ronmental concern. Several mutual funds provide investors with the opportunity to own the stock of companies that are regarded as socially responsible.

Interested parties include government at all levels, plant communities, educational institutions, charitable organizations, environmental activists, and do-gooders of every stripe. Public activities include paying taxes; supporting public projects from building a library to fighting a war; giving to charitable causes; properly handling air, land, and water wastes; recycling; providing equal opportunity for all; and generally being a pillar in the community.

Quality Can't Exist in a Vacuum

Advocates of the short-term, bottom-line approach to management may have trouble justifying expenditures of time and money in the name of public responsibility. The argument goes that a company is in business to make money to provide for everyone who has invested in the enterprise. These advocates concede that customers must be kept happy, and that it may save money to keep employee turnover down, but, they wonder, where's the payoff for all the rest of that stuff?

Short-termers don't understand the value of investing in quality either. Being a short-termer in business becomes a self-fulfilling prophecy of mediocrity. To stay in business requires long-term public acceptance. A resentful plant community or disapproving general public ultimately will have a negative impact on the enterprise. More to the point, an appreciative community and approving public will have a positive effect on all aspects of the company's affairs, including good feelings on the part of employees, shareowners and the all-important external customers. Those good feelings translate into longevity and money in the bank.

Hey, Big Spender—The Philanthropic Beginnings of Social Responsibility

When in 1926 F.L. Maytag found himself reined in on the management front, he discovered new ways to express himself. The Maytag ship had arrived so he now had plenty of money at his disposal to (1) give away, (2) bankroll the high life, and (3) purchase the center of attention. He raised personal philanthropy to a fine art, lived off the fat of the land, and presided regally over company functions at home and abroad, often staged to serve his growing need for gratification through adulation.

F.L.'s contributions, while exceedingly generous, carried his unique trademark. He had the audacity to assess family members for a proportionate share of all his major monuments, most of which carried only *his* name. His reasoning must have been that all the family members' wealth initially came from his personal industry. To his credit, F.L.'s philanthropy reflected his concern for the community, the same concern that had earlier caused him to become involved in local politics and chamber-of-commerce-type activities.

Hospitals

Both his first and final contributions benefited Newton in a significant way. The first, while he was mayor and before he became truly wealthy, was to host a fund-raising dinner that collected $24,000 of the $70,000 needed to complete the building of Mary Frances Skiff Hospital. The major gift of $100,000 had come from Vernon Skiff, Jewel Tea magnate, to honor his wife shortly after her death. Skiff had grown up in Newton and both he and his wife are buried there. Skiff was persuaded to make the 1919 contribution by a committee that F.L. Maytag chaired. The community got behind the fund drive with F.L.'s encouragement, and the needed funds were raised. F.L. was on the building committee and one of the first trustees when the hospital was dedicated in 1921.

Another of F.L.'s medical contributions, in 1931, was to donate $150,000 for the Maytag Research Laboratory for tuberculosis at the Southeast Presbyterian Sanitarium in Albuquerque, New Mexico, where his daughter Freda had been a patient. She had lived in Colorado and New Mexico since contracting an illness in 1914. Her mother's frequent and protracted visits to Freda, beginning with a year's stay at Silver City, New Mexico, may have contributed to the Maytags' marital estrangement. Freda, married and divorced, spent the rest of her life in the Colorado Springs area. It's possible that her presence there influenced her brother Bud's decision to settle nearby when he left Newton in 1935.

Higher Education

F.L. was generous to several midwestern colleges, including Coe in Cedar Rapids, Iowa; Monmouth in Illinois; and Parsons in Fairfield, Iowa, which gave him an honorary degree in 1926. His major educational philanthropy was the establishment of a $50,000 student loan endowment at neighboring Grinnell College in 1927. He became a trustee, beginning a chain of Maytags on that college board that continues to this day.

The Community

In 1927 F.L. (and his silent-partner family members) contributed a $250,000 YMCA building to the community. His generosity was tarnished, however, when he required each and every Maytag employee to become a member. (See Chapter 6, the section on paternalism.) Even though the company subsidized the dues, membership was not optional.

T.R. Smith, a Newton native and retired R&D vice president, recalls working in the machine shop to earn money for college. He had grown up best buddies with Fred Maytag II and more than once had sat at a dinner table presided over by the domineering F.L. Feeling that he needed his money for college tuition and seeing no benefit in YMCA membership, T.R. declined his foreman's invitation to join. Summoned to the factory superintendent's office, he had the offer explained more thoroughly, ending with a clear choice—join or be fired. He joined.

Building of the Maytag Hotel in downtown Newton in 1926 was regarded by the community as a contribution, although F.L.'s real motivation doesn't seem to have been lost on anyone. The hotel was leased and later sold. It was a grand edifice and later became the first air-conditioned hotel west of the Mississippi. F.L. was the first guest and maintained a suite on the fifth floor the rest of his life.

F.L.'s final gift to the community was in fact a living memorial lacking only his statue to be complete. In 1935 the community, state, and whole Midwest, including Chicago, were involved in the dedication of the swimming pool and bathhouse at Fred (F.L.) Maytag Park, presided over by Ronald "Dutch" Reagan. The formal dedication of the park was held on what would have been F.L.'s eightieth birthday, July 14, 1937, four months after he died. F.L. had acquired the former county fairgrounds and created a magnificent 40-acre park at a cost of $325,000.

It included the Fred Maytag swimming pool and a Fred Maytag bowl for band concerts and such. Tennis courts were added soon after. His generosity (once again supplemented by the family anonymously) included a $200,000 endowment for perpetual maintenance, to be looked after by a board of trustees, empowered to serve for life, that included his cronies. The park manager was a brother-in-law of Pontiac Dealer Joe Longwell, one of the trustees. That endowment served the park for a generation before inflation pushed the property into city hands.

Churches

Although F.L.'s brother Ted is better remembered for his church involvement, F.L. built a $75,000 citadel for the Salvation Army. In his dedication speech he recognized that organization's work with the indigent. Most of the other Newton churches benefited from his largesse at one time or another. He contributed organs to several churches, including a $15,000 Austin pipe organ to the First Presbyterian church, the Maytags' home church.

F.L. was generous to Sacred Heart Catholic church and had a close relationship with the rector. Father T.J. McCann, ordained in 1908, came to Sacred Heart two years later and served that parish until his retirement. He was fast friends not only with F.L. but also with Elmer and later with Fred Maytag II. He bent church rules to officiate at F.L.'s funeral, held in brother Ted's Methodist church, because it was the largest in town.

In 1929 F.L. built a $5000 parsonage for the Evangelical Association of America in Laurel, where his father had been a pillar of the German Evangelical church. The elder Maytag had been born a Lutheran in Germany but converted to the Evangelical church and helped organize a congregation in the Laurel area. He was a devout member and undoubtedly F.L. had ample exposure to that church while growing up. As is not unusual with the child of a fervent churchgoer, F.L. seemed less than devoted to the church.[1]

The Principle of Enlightened Self-Interest

The Maytag philosophy given the name "enlightened self-interest" by Fred Maytag II was his justification for everything Maytag has done for the public good, as well as what it does for its customers and employees. He described it as taking the long view. It could be called a quality attitude, a class act, prerequisite to a quality result. He said:

> We must operate in an atmosphere of approval, not only from our customers, but from our employees and the general public as well.

Enlightened self-interest is not altruism. It is self-interest in the sense that it is done for the purpose of furthering the corporate cause. It is just good business. Company time and money can be spent to benefit others, because in the long run the company will benefit in kind. Bread cast upon the waters does seem to return.

---

[1] F.L.'s brother Ted was a dedicated, tee-totalling Methodist. He was a delegate to the national conference of the Methodist Episcopal church in 1927 and two years later contributed $50,000 to Taylor University for the Maytag Memorial gymnasium. He also served on the board of Iowa Methodist Hospital in Des Moines.

Ted's handsome house stood at the end of the block containing the homes of Elmer and F.L. Maytag. Legend has it that one day during prohibition Ted answered a knock at his door and found a bootlegger looking to deliver his contraband to the F.L. Maytag home. Without acknowledging the man's error, Ted Maytag accepted the order and proceeded to pour it all down the drain after the man departed. Ted was fatally injured in a 1931 auto accident while en route to a Methodist church meeting in Muscatine, Iowa, on the Mississippi River.

True altruism, where the left hand doesn't know what the right hand is doing (that is, free of the knowledge of potential gain), is just not possible. There is always a payoff in giving, if only inside oneself. Fred Maytag II, who formalized Maytag's corporate giving, put serving the need first but felt the company deserved credit for doing good with the shareowners' money.

Fred Maytag's Early Years

Although the Maytag family practiced public responsibility from the first, it was Fred II who formalized the company approach to public concerns that grew and changed from the beginning until his era. Although Frederick Louis Maytag II was named after his illustrious grandfather, he was always known as Fred by everyone in the company and the community. The expression "From shirtsleeves to shirtsleeves in three generations," which seems to apply in so many wealthy families, didn't fit the Maytag situation—at least not in this case. The reason may be that Fred wasn't *born* to priviledge. He was already in his teens by the time wealth came to the Maytag family.

Nor was he spoiled or coddled at home. Like his father and uncle before him, he spent summer vacations in the shop during high school. One summer, when Fred announced to his father that he had decided to take up golf, Elmer sternly informed him that he had better learn to work before he learned to play.

An Entrepreneurial Child Prodigy

Fred and boyhood chum Tom Smith (whom you'll meet again later) went through dozens of schemes intended to make money, including mowing yards, building birdhouses, and giving pony rides. A memorable attempt was Sunny Boy Hair Oil, concocted by Fred and Tom and bottled by Tom's younger brother Bob at "Midwest Lab" (the Smiths' basement). Although the stuff was actually sold to local barbershops, the enterprise went broke. Tom and Bob were sons of W.W. Smith, Elmer's partner in the employee housing business.

As an Eagle Scout, Fred went to the Boy Scout World Jamboree in 1927 at the age of 16. He finished high school at Culver Military Academy and then graduated from the University of Wisconsin in 1933 with a degree in political science. While at Wisconsin, he met his future wife, Ellen Pray of Philadelphia.

Although he was engaged, Fred set off on a year-long trip around the world, a graduation present from his father. He returned in August 1934, and immediately spent two weeks on active duty with the National Guard at

Camp Dodge, Iowa, as a second lieutenant. Apparently he had earned ROTC credentials at either Culver or Wisconsin, or both.

Fred Begins His Maytag Career

Fred's first assignment at Maytag was to learn about marketing. He went to work October 1, 1934, in the Indianapolis office under branch manager Les Green. He and Ellen were married that November. They traveled extensively for the company, and Ellen also became familiar with Maytag people in the field. The couple spent extended periods of time in Texas, California, and Portland, Oregon.

In the fall of 1935, they returned to Newton, where Fred worked as a regular employee in the sales department. He made a film of the manufacturing process for use in the field. *The Story of Maytag* was named one of the 10 best nontheatrical films of 1936, the year Maytag made its three-millionth washer. The couple's first child, Ellen Louise, was born that year.

During this period Fred became more and more disillusioned with his grandfather's proclivity to stir things up in the absence of Elmer, whose increasingly debilitating illness was keeping him in Florida. He made up his mind to leave the company. Several executives tried to talk him out of it but got nowhere until Will Sparks, company secretary and a long-time employee, had a heart-to-heart with him. Sparks pointed out that F.L. was nearing 80 and wouldn't be around too much longer and that Elmer's illness would prevent him from resuming control, so it was going to be up to Fred to keep the company going. Fred decided to accept the challenge and stayed on at Maytag.

A Quick On-the-Job Education in Leadership

Sparks was right. When F.L. died early in 1937, Fred found himself a sort of de facto executive without portfolio, working with George Umbreit, and a 25-year partnership between the two men was forged. Fred had become a vice president and director the previous year, at a salary of $5000. Now at the tender age of 26, he became immediately embroiled in a patent infringement lawsuit, was a negotiator in the 1938 strike, and suffered through the trauma of having to fire people, including production manager John Herbst, who had been involved with the notorious Joe Longwell in the jobs-for-Pontiacs affair.

The year 1937 also saw Fred's first personal philanthropic endeavor. He had been the speaker at the previous year's Newton High School commencement. He decided to share his travel experience and offered a European trip to a graduating senior. The first winner was announced in 1937, but world events precluded any further awards.

Elmer died in July 1940. At the age of 29, Fred was named president. Umbreit became executive vice president and the partnership was official.

The Ultimate Challenge in Social Responsibility—War

Participation in a war effort represents the ultimate public responsibility, not only for government but also for other groups, including employees, shareowners, and the community. During World War I, Maytag and the rest of the washing machine industry were uninvolved in the war effort, presumably uninvited, and suffered greatly from lack of materials during the period from 1914 to 1918. To an amazing extent, business and the public were left to function as best they could while America fought the war in Europe.

With the coming of World War II, things were far better organized and mobilization was total. As early as October 1940, Maytag was cooperating with the national preparedness program. It received its first defense contract, for $150,000, in March 1941. A $1.5 million contract for Martin bomber parts was announced in September. At yearend, after the attack on Pearl Harbor, it was announced that further contracts had been awarded, but there would be no more announcements for security reasons. The Newton National Guard unit had been called up early in 1941. The four-millionth washer was produced in May 1941, but because of the rush to complete civilian production, there was no celebration.

Total Conversion to War Work

The last wartime washer was built April 14, 1942, and only repair parts were manufactured for the duration. The plant operated on three shifts, and workers were constantly being recruited.[2] Maytag was a subcontractor for Martin, Goodyear, and Allison, among others. Chief products were heat-treated aluminum castings for airplanes and engines, tank track pins, and hydraulic actuating cylinders for bombers. Guards were hired and the plant was fenced in. Families of employees could no longer enter. Maytag collected a half-million tons of metal for a scrap drive. Other Newton indus-

---

[2] Because of the shortage of men, women were called on to detassel hybrid seed corn that fall, a hot and dirty task essential in the production of hybrid seed corn that had traditionally been done by men. Also, a dozen women completed 300 hours of machine shop training. In 1943 the first women were hired to work in the Maytag factory.

tries also converted to war work. There were no Christmas lights downtown for the duration, and daylight saving time was begun.

Maytag spent more than $2 million on new facilities for war work, including a new aluminum foundry. Aluminum castings were made for Rolls Royce and Allison airplane engines and machine gun turrets. Twelve kinds of electrical actuators were produced to operate landing gear, wing flaps, and bomb-bay doors on flying boats and heavy bombers like B-17s. There were 26 models of hydraulic cylinders made to do similar jobs on medium bombers and fighters, such as the B-26, P-38, P-39, P-47, and P-51, and for Britain, parts for the Spitfire, Lancaster, and Mosquito planes.[3]

The Continuous Improvement Ethic Doesn't Stop in Wartime

Probably the most significant contribution to the war effort came with Maytag's redesign of hydraulic actuating cylinders. Fred had reorganized the experimental department into a new research and development department in 1941, headed by his childhood chum, Tom Smith, now an MIT graduate in electrical engineering. Tom reduced the number of parts in one hydraulic cylinder from 136 to 69 and another from 145 to 28, with large savings in weight (see Figure 7-1). The redesigns saved the government over $1 million in 1944 alone. Maytag also doubled the strength of Allison engine castings without any increase in weight, extending engine lifespan from 180 hours to 500 hours.

The quality and dependability of Maytag hydraulic cylinders brought offers of enough new business to hire an additional 2000 workers, but Maytag had neither the facilities nor the human resources to handle the work.

Wartime Developments in Employee Relations

War bond rallies were major events during the war. At Maytag, a committee was formed for employees to buy a bomber, and the *Bomber Drive Bulletin* was initiated. The drive went over the top in two weeks. However, the weekly publication, now called the *Maytag Bulletin* survives to this day, nearly 50 years later. Its popularity during the war came from publishing columns of news and pictures of relatives and employees in the service. Popularity continued after the war because the weekly publication covered its employee audience as though it were a small community. It also quickly

[3] Maytag's name was associated with another World War II aircraft. The low-powered, single-engine plane used by artillery spotters earned the nickname "Maytag Messerschmitt" because it sounded like a Multi-Motor to farm boys turned soldiers.

Figure 7-1. Engineer Tom Smith, who was heir to the innovation mantle of Howard Snyder, demonstrating one of his parts reduction designs for hydraulic cylinders to Fred Maytag and military procurement brass.

developed a reputation for factuality—if you read it in the *Bulletin,* it was true. The *Maytag Bulletin* remains an effective employee communications tool, passing a new readership test every week as it is distributed at plant gates. Few copies are left after employees leave and none end up on the floor. Figures 7-2 and 7-3 show the first *Bulletin* and one of the most recent editions.

The war bond committee later became the workers' activities committee, organizing athletic teams and a bowling league. A family picnic was held with a contest to select a Maytag Slacks Queen among women working in the plant. Mary Ellen Johnson was picked from 30 candidates. Speaking at the coronation, Fred Maytag suggested that the program become an annual event, and it did for a number of years until it became difficult to recruit volunteers to help stage it. Besides, television was tough competition for the program's audience.

The committee soon changed again to a labor-management council composed of an equal number of members elected by workers and appointed by the Maytag president. The group administers all employee activities not tied to the bargaining unit, operating with funds from vending machines located throughout the plants and offices.

New Postwar Horizons

As early as 1943, Fred Maytag was named chairman of an appliance indus-try committee on postwar conversion. Maytag's directors authorized R&D to proceed with development of an automatic washer as rapidly as possible. In a 1943 talk to members of the newly formed Maytag Twenty-Five-Year Club, just prior to observance of the company's fiftieth anniversary, Fred said that after the war, the company would not be satisfied just making wash-ers. Although he couldn't predict what the company would be making 50 or 25 or even 10 years into the future, he said:

> We'll continue to grow and make a contribution to society commensu-rate with that of the past 50 years. We won't even try to go back to the making of washing machines until we've done our part to win the war. But I know that from the experience of the past two years, we will not be satisfied with just making washing machines.

Asked later to elaborate on this idea, 32-year-old Fred Maytag admitted that he was looking pretty far into the future: "There will be a tremendous demand for washers and ironers, and reconversion of our factory will take longer than most people realize. Other products will have to wait."

Speaking at a radio forum, Fred urged gradual reconversion of war plants. "Military demands will decrease as the war progresses and the grad-ual reconversion will prevent mass unemployment from developing as the cutback is made." He did not see the immediate development of miracle products. "Much production will be a resumption of prewar goods for a year or so. New models and merchandise must be developed before release, and the public must be educated to new products."

Conversion to Peacetime

Meanwhile, the war went on and civilians faced meat, butter, and cheese rationing. But factory war work was declining. Fred told an employee group why Maytag had refused cost-plus contracts.

> We made a decision in 1941 when we went out for war contracts that we wanted this work on a competitive basis, at a fixed price, and that we would stand or fall on our ability to produce for that. The results have been outstanding. As a result of redesigning work by our engineers and of production efficiency in our factory we have been able to cut the cost of these items to save taxpayers $1 million this year.

Maytag's union sponsored a conference in 1944 in Newton on the subject "Community Leadership for Reconversion and Postwar Employment." Fred

Maytag *bomber drive* Bulletin

NEWTON, IOWA JULY 1, 1943 BULLETIN NO. 1

"BUY-A-BOMBER" DRIVE BEGINS

A Free Bond Given Each Week During Bomber Campaign

Extra Awards for All "Ten Percenters"

Here's a chance to win up to three War Bonds free!

In order to further the Buy-a-Bomber drive, the company has agreed to award War Bonds in a weekly drawing to be held on Friday afternoons under the auspices of the Workers' Committee, for the duration of the bond drive.

All names of those who have pledged themselves to buy bonds through the payroll allotment plan will be placed in a container and thoroughly shuffled. Then one name will be drawn by a service man home on leave who will be invited to the plant to make the drawing.

YOU MAY WIN $75

If the person whose name is drawn is participating in the payroll allotment plan, he or she will receive a $25 Bond. If it so happens that the person has pledged 10%, but less than 15% of earnings, the prize will be doubled and the lucky worker will receive $50 in bonds. If, however, the person has pledged above 15% a total of $75 in War Bonds will be awarded. Following each drawing, the award will be made by a different member of the Workers' Committee.

The Committee urges that you make your maximum pledge today so that you can get in on the chance to win one or more bonds in tomorrow's drawing. Your Bomber Captain will see that your pledge reaches the auditing department without delay.

PICTURES WANTED

If any member of your family is in the armed forces, the editors would like to receive a photograph. Please include name, rank, branch of service, and name and address of parents, together any other information which may be of interest to relatives or friends. Either hand the picture to Dorothy Evans, Armed Service Editor, in the engineering department, or deposit in the Maytag Bulletin NEWS BOX in the plant entrance at the southeast clock house. All pictures will be returned.

"Let's Get Going," Says Bond Drive Committee

Caught by the candid camera while making plans for the "Buy-a-Bomber" War Bond drive, the Maytag Workers' Committee is seen examining bond drive posters in their meeting room at the plant. Left to right (standing): Bryan Barrett, Al Fisher, Joe Hyld, chairman, A. B. Conwell (seated) Mrs. Letha Martinson, S. J. Hardaway and Mrs. Stella Harpole.

Dept. "Bomber Captains" Are Named

So that every Maytag worker may conveniently learn at first hand the details of the "Buy-a-Bomber" bond drive, and make his pledge without delay, "Bomber Captains" have been named in every department, and for every group of twenty workers. They have full information on the payroll allotment plan and can supply you with the forms required to authorize payroll deductions.

Look in the following list of names for the Bomber Captains in your department. Contact the person you know the best, and talk over with him your plans to PLEDGE AS MUCH AS YOU CAN AFFORD TO SAVE out of your pay check each week for the bonds that mean "money in the bank "when you need it more than you do today.

BOMBER CAPTAINS

Office—T. J. Thorson, A. K. Rollins, Eva Meng, Thelma Palmer, Elmer Boot, W. D. Wilding, Robert Vance, Iva Schultz.

Department D-26: Electrical Department—Everett Nible.

Department D-27, Laboratory —Wayne Farland.

Department 29, Research and Development—Howard McBride.

Department D-37, Police Guard —George Raridon.

Department D-23, Employment —Mrs. Dorothy Murphy.

Department D-24, Engineering —Shirley Irwin, Mable Raridon.

Department D-25, Watchmen— Bob Reynolds.

Department 32—Beulah Johnson.

Department 32A—Mrs. Cora B. Shadle.

Department 33 — Mrs. Letha Martinson.

Department D-16, Pattern Shop —Harry Eke.

Department D-17, Tool Room —Magnus Neilsen.

Department D-18, Receiving and Storage—Drew Walker, Don Eaton, Doris Watson.

Department D-5, Heat Treating and Plating—First Shift, Harley Knox; Second Shift: Frank Hollister; Third Shift: Glenn Hotger.

Department D-7, Wood Shop— Ora Provin.

Department D-10, Eclipse Assembly—Cyrus Faber.

Department 4, Casting Finishing—First Shift: W. C. Farrow, C. Fish, H. Snook, B. McAfee; Second Shift: D. K. White, H. Masters, H. Miller, T. Lester; Third Shift: E. K. Goodhue, H. Thomas, R. E. McKeag, W. C. Pieper.

Department D-11, Martin Assembly — Glenn Pickering, Fred Wheeler, Paul Gillaspie.

Department D-13, Inspection Department — First Shift: Dean Elder; Second Shift: Bruce Il-

(Continued on Page 2)

Gets Going With A Big Bang As Air Raid Bomb Bursts

Workers' Committee Announces Plans

With scores of Maytag workers in shop and office increasing the amount they have already pledged for War Bonds, and with many more signing up for the first time, the Maytag "Buy-a-Bomber" War Bond drive literally got underway with a "bang" today when an air raid bomb was exploded as a "starting gun" as the four o'clock shift took over.

The bomb was exploded by Mayor A. M. Miller, commander of the OCD.

Following a meeting of more than 150 workers who have been named "Bomber Captains" to solicit pledges, the plan to pledge enough for bonds to buy a bomber and win the famous Treasury "T" Award Flag moved into high speed in every department.

A "MARAUDER" THE GOAL

Through arrangements with the United States Treasury department and the Glenn H. Martin Company, every cent now pledged, or to be pledged, by Maytag workers to purchase war bonds will be credited toward the purchase of a famous Martin B-26. The great fighting ship will be christened the "Maytag Marauder" and flown to the front from the Omaha plant of the Martin company as a contribution of the men and women at Maytag.

Actually, the bomber does not cost the bond subscriber a cent, since he receives all the bonds he buys, it was pointed out. In fact, you get back $4 for every $3 you invest, as that is your return under the rate of interest paid by the government to holders of War Savings Bonds.

"Just as soon as everyone pledges his full share, the bomber will be purchased, so the quicker you sign up for all you can afford to SAVE, the sooner we'll get the great ship on its way to smash the Axis," a spokesman for the Workers' Committee declared.

The Bomber Captains, whose names appear in another column of this paper, are prepared to accept your order for bonds today. They have supplies of the Treasury Department bond purchase pledges and copies of the payroll authorization for deduction of the amount you feel is

(Continued on Page 5)

Figure 7-2. First issue of the *Bomber Drive Bulletin*.

W E E K L Y

Bulletin

OF PUBLICATION

MAYTAG
100
Years of Dependability

FOR AND ABOUT MAYTAG COMPANY EMPLOYEES   FEBRUARY 18, 1993, VOL. 51, NO. 7

Cole named to head company's Herrin laundry operations

Gary L. Cole has been named vice president, operations at Maytag Company's Herrin, Ill., laundry manufacturing facility, as announced by Richard J. Haines, Maytag Company president.

In his new assignment, Cole replaces Frederick P. "Rick" Foltz, who recently was named vice president and general manager at Admiral Company, Galesburg, Ill.

Cole, 49, began his career with Jenn-Air Corporation, Indianapolis, Ind., in 1969 as manager of market services and later became an applications engineer. Cole later was named national sales manager for Jenn Industries, a former subsidiary of Jenn-Air Company, which manufactured commercial and industrial ventilation equipment. He was named executive vice president and general manager for Jenn Industries in 1983.

In 1989 Cole was named to his current position of vice president, operations at Jenn-Air Company.

A native of Indianapolis, Cole attended the General Motors Institute, Flint, Mich., and served in the U.S. Air Force. He and his wife, Patricia, have two children.

Services to be held for retired division sales manager Joe J. Shackelford

Joe J. Shackelford of Littleton, Colo., retired Western division sales manager for Maytag Company, died early this week at his home. He was 65. Services will be held tomorrow in Littleton.

Shackelford joined Maytag in 1956 after selling his retail operation, a propane gas and appliance business in Bentonville, Ark. He first served as a regional manager in the Kansas City branch, covering northwestern Oklahoma and southern Kansas. In 1958 he moved to the Omaha, Neb., area, and in 1961 was promoted to branch manager of the former Jacksonville branch. Shackelford was named Western division sales manager in 1967 when Maytag Company organized its distribution centers into three divisions.

Born in Dalhart, Texas, Shackelford grew up in Fayetteville, Ark., where he attended the University of Arkansas. Prior to joining Maytag, he served in the Pacific with the U.S. Navy.

Survivors include two sons.

Competitive appliance industry issues challenges for the '90s

Meeting the challenges of the '90s in the fiercely competitive appliance industry, where the fight for market share continues to intensify, was the focus of Richard J. Haines', Maytag Company president, annual address to the Maytag Management Club on Monday evening.

Explaining that the firm initiated several programs during 1992 designed to meet these challenges, Haines stated, "We put into place a number of programs that were designed to support our strategic business plan, that have already begun to make a difference in our profit margins and will continue to keep us competitive in a market that is intensely so."

The need to maintain the quality and dependability of Maytag products remains a top priority for the company, Haines noted, and has resulted in the formation of a washer quality improvement team.

"The automatic washer is the cornerstone of the Maytag Dependability Store," he stressed. "And for us to continue our dependability claim of 'lasts longer and requires fewer repairs,' we must ensure we work to protect this 'reliability' edge."

The team functions with the knowledge that service call rate (SCR) is not only the number of repairs per washers produced, but also a measurement of how well the appliance meets the expectations of consumers. This team is responsible for significantly reducing the SCR on washers during 1992 and, in fact, surpassed its goal.

Continuing his review of 1992, Haines noted the successful negotiation of the labor contract, "The contract is one that we believe will yield long-term benefits for all involved particularly, in the area of health care."

In today's atmosphere of teamwork and continual improvement, Haines pointed out that perhaps an even more promising result of negotiations was the signing of a letter of understanding. This is an agreement with the union to explore further employee involvement in seeking higher levels of quality, teamwork and productivity.

"I find this agreement particularly significant — because mutual trust and cooperation don't happen overnight — they require the right attitude on everyone's part. This agreement indicates that a cooperative attitude is developing ...," he said.

"I believe that our employees, at all levels, have a vested interest in the success of our company, and given the opportunity — they want to be involved, participate and contribute to its success. We need to let that happen."

Another high point for the year was the upswing into full production at the Jackson Appliance Company.

(See 'Challenges' on Page 2)

Figure 7-3. The *Bomber Drive Bulletin* survives today as the *Maytag Bulletin*—a reputation for factuality remains.

was on the panel, along with William Sentner, now a UE vice president. The women in the audience applauded when Fred said, "The vast majority of women working in Newton will want to return home and let men overseas take over their places." They did return home, but they didn't stay. Women returned to the Maytag labor force almost immediately. By May 1946, 486 veterans were on the Maytag payroll, including 5 women.

Whistle Blowing—The Old-Fashioned Way

Fred had been planning the stunt for some time, so he was ready when the announcement came of Japanese surrender on August 12, 1945. He rushed from home and blew the factory whistle at an unusually early hour. Two days later, he blew it again when VJ day was officially recognized.

Maytag had done its duty and was appropriately rewarded with E flags, T flags, and assorted other recognitions, including one for victory gardens. The next couple of years, however, were an unrelenting hassle with a government that didn't want to surrender the reins of power. The main offender was the federal Office of Price Administration.

America has never repeated the all-out industrial effort of World War II. A limited involvement accompanied the action in Korea when Maytag built tank track parts.[4] Neither Maytag nor most of America got involved with Vietnam. Almost all defense work is now performed by full-time players doing government work with little room for volunteers.

Public Service: The Ultimate in Government Relations

A good corporate citizen has a responsibility in politics and government not unlike a private citizen. Business does not operate in a vacuum. So enlightened self-interest helps to bring business and government together.

Fred Maytag II grew up in the Republican party and became a major player in the Iowa GOP. It was his nature, moreover, to give himself fully to an endeavor. So in 1946, when an aging and ineffective state senator from Jasper County needed replacing, Fred announced his candidacy, defeated the incumbent in the primary, and went on to be elected to a four-year term in the Iowa Senate.

---

[4] The building constructed for that project, although subsequently used for many operations, including manufacturing automatic washer transmissions for years, was still called the Tank Track building by old-timers, before it became the home of Newton Polytechnic Campus of Des Moines Area Community College.

He provided leadership at a level not often found in an elected body, but having served his purpose, he did not run for reelection. He remained active in the Republican party for the rest of his life. He chaired the Republican state convention in 1952, the year of the great battle between General Dwight Eisenhower and Ohio Senator Robert Taft. Fred was a supporter of Taft, and the conflict was bloody at the Jasper County convention, where a group of young turks took control from the precinct caucuses on and sent an Eisenhower delegation to the state convention. Fred was also a gentleman and closed ranks. He chaired the Republican state convention again in 1960, and was a delegate to the national convention that same year that nominated Richard Nixon.

Following in the Founder's Footsteps

As a state senator, Fred was following in the footsteps of his grandfather, who also made a name for himself in state government, serving 8 years as state senator at the turn of the century. F. L. had been a progressive Republican follower of Teddy Roosevelt and a strong supporter of Iowa governor and later U.S. senator Albert B. Cummins.

F.L. also had served on Newton's city council earlier and spent a term as the city's mayor. He was appointed to various boards and commissions. Both Maytags received strong encouragement to be a candidate for governor and U.S. senator, but neither ran for higher office.

In the case of Fred, his political ambitions came into conflict with his company role and became the proximate cause of his creating a professional management team for Maytag. (See Chapters 8 and 9.) Had he not been stricken with cancer, he might well have become a national political figure.

PAC Money and Participation

Fred died before the formation of Maytag's political action committee (PAC), but he was well aware of the effectiveness of the United Auto Workers PAC in Jasper County politics. The Maytag good government committee raised its funds by soliciting voluntary contributions from a broad range of management. Unlike some, it did not obtain money from a handful of top executives whose salaries had been padded to reimburse them for their contributions. The company had no say in how the funds were distributed. Candidates from both parties received support. Unlike many business PACs, funds were never given to candidates for the same office. The criterion was simple—which candidate would be most supportive of business and most effective in that support. Both state and federal candidates continue to receive funds.

The company had been represented in the political arena by a Washington representative since the World War II days of procurement. The move from a reactive posture to a proactive political stance came gradually. Today, following corporate expansion, Maytag seeks support from the congressional delegations of Iowa, Tennessee, Illinois, and Ohio, where plants are located. The company is also active in the government relations of its industry group, the Association of Home Appliance Manufacturers.

Growth of Environmental Concerns

A quality company that maintains state-of-the-art production facilities must also have a strong safety program and long-range concern for the environment—for the sake of employees, the community, and planet earth. Perhaps nowhere will short-term thinking come back to bite more quickly than failure to adequately deal with potentially damaging by-products and waste.

Standards of acceptable conduct have changed drastically over the years as the frontier mindset in which there's always plenty of everything has given way to recognition of the environment as a closed ecosystem. To keep the focus on quality, the workplace must be clean and safe. Visitors to Maytag plants frequently remark on the cleanliness of work stations and aisles and on how busy everybody seems to be.

Busy But Not Careless

Safety is part of the religion preached daily in Maytag facilities. An unsafe workplace cannot be efficient over the long haul. At Maytag, safety standards are right alongside quality standards in every job description.

When Maytag Killed the Cows

An example of changing environmental standards is the handling of a toxic by-product of the electroplating process. Maytag uses plating to provide superior wear on load-bearing parts or to build in corrosion resistance. Chrome and zinc are the most common coatings. The effluent from the chrome plating process is highly toxic.

In the early 1950s, some of that same waste found its way into a plant sanitary drain and flowed into a nearby creek. The water level was low and the waste wasn't sufficiently diluted when some grazing cows drank from the stream, with fatal results. Fred Maytag took immediate steps to prevent a reccurrence and then constructed a state-of-the-art chemical waste treatment facility at Plant 2, where the plating operations were moved. At Plant 2 it was not possible for any toxic wastes to enter the city sewer system. Separate catch tanks and drains funneled any spill to the treatment plant, along with all wastes needing treatment.

An Award-Winning Improvement

The new facility resembled a city sewage treatment plant except that it also supplied tertiary treatment to neutralize any solution. The end result was water purer than that coming out of the city water supply (see Figure 7-4). With typical focus on constant improvement, Maytag proceeded to reuse the treated water, of better quality, and saved many dollars on its city water bill.

Fred was an avid hunter and fisherman, a trustee of Ducks Unlimited and member of the Izaak Walton League, which may explain his going the extra mile to ensure that Maytag could never pollute again. In any event, the company waste treatment facility became a source of pride and was the basis for a number of state and national awards.

Meeting Other Concerns

Earlier, the company had installed equipment for eliminating aluminum and porcelain dust from the air. Before it was torn down, the Plant 1

Figure 7-4. The chemical waste treatment facility at Maytag's Plant 2.

boiler room smokestack received smoke abatement equipment back when coal was still used as fuel. An installation was made to safely burn discarded oil. Today, filters capture solvent from the painting operation. Cardboard cartons are recycled, along with scrap of all kinds. In short, Maytag is an environmentally conscious operation. Few members of the community are fully aware of the great lengths that have been taken to prevent Maytag from becoming a poor neighbor, but they have nothing to complain about either.

The Maytag Company Foundation: Formalizing Charitable Giving

A major public responsibility for any business is contributing financially to worthwhile causes—whether home community drives, state or national charities, or programs tailored to the individual company's desires. Maytag does some of each. A business is fair game for all sorts of requests, from tickets to the firefighter's ball to a major institution's capital fund drive.

Maytag's generosity over the years has taken various forms. Founder F.L. first led community fund drives for projects like Skiff Hspital and finally used his own immense wealth to give the community highly desirable major gifts that served as monuments to the man. He was also generous to institutions of higher education.

Bud's single major contribution to his home community reflected his personal interest when, in 1926, he gave the Newton Country Club a new golf course, probably still the finest nine-hole links in Iowa. He moved to Colorado Springs following his mother's death, and among his contributions to his adopted community was the design of a golf course at the Air Force Academy.

Elmer was strongly motivated to help young people get an education. He saw the need to replenish the community's supply of professionals as well as engineers and managers for his business. But it was not Elmer's way to give gifts. Rather, he was involved in an elaborate network of low-cost loans to get the job done. Besides, F.L. did an impressive job of giving Elmer's money away, along with that of other members of the family, to support his pet causes.

In Fred's case, he shared an interest in higher education and felt the same obligation to his home community but, typical of him, saw the need for an organized approach. In 1953, he formalized the company's charitable giving under the Maytag Company Foundation, Inc., and also formed the Maytag Family Foundation, which became a formidable force from his estate.

The bulk of giving from the company foundation went to education in one of several ways. The first and largest program, now 40 years old, is the college scholarship fund, which aids both students and the schools they attend. Until 1992, the program was open to all Newton High School seniors and also to children of employees, wherever they attended high school. About a third of Newton factory employees live in surrounding communities, and the children of Maytag field employees were also included.

Awarding of a scholarship is based on academic achievement, leadership, and extracurricular accomplishments, but the amount given is based on need. The grant may include full tuition plus fees and books, half that amount, or an honorary stipend. It is normally renewable during the undergraduate career.

In 1990, the company foundation became the Maytag Corporation Foundation with infusions from Magic Chef and Hoover foundations. The company foundation had supported the Iowa College Foundation since the beginning, along with several other grants to higher education. An educational gift-matching program is in place for all employees.

Today, the college scholarship program is open nationally to up to 25 children of corporate employees. Reflecting an emerging national trend to promote precollege education, Newton schools will benefit from a $125,000 contribution to their model technology plan for all grades in lieu of future scholarship eligibility. It is Maytag's belief that helping local schools acquire the latest in high-tech equipment and programs improves the quality of education for many students who never attend college.

The primary purpose of the Maytag Corporation Foundation is to demonstrate good citizenship in those communities where Maytag operating divisions are located. The foundation concentrates its giving locally and in three primary areas—aid to education, community betterment, and cultural activities. The budget in 1992 was $2.6 million.

Fred's Philosophy

In a talk given in the 1940s, Fred Maytag expressed his philosophy on corporate giving, particularly to higher education. "We must accept a measure of social responsibility," he said. "My personal opinion is that the overwhelming majority of stockholders will favor the development of a program of judicious giving to education." He pointed out that the corporation had emerged in the prior half-century as the major form of business enterprise. Formerly, corporate profits were passed on to shareowners to spend as they saw fit.

Speaking of a time when most stockholders were individuals, not pension trusts, and government was not yet expected to care for everyone's every need, Fred said:

Today, with the corporations being used as the greatest tax collection agency of all time, most of the profits are siphoned off by government before they reach individual shareowners. Therefore, giving at the corporate level is vastly more effective than at the stockholder level.

The corporation becomes the instrument in our time through which we can continue to do for a free society what, historically, the individual has always done. Even though the returns are not direct or measurable, they are nevertheless very real and over the long term will bring benefits both to the corporation and to its individual owners.

Fred Maytag sensed a diminishing appreciation among young people for the profit motive that formed the backbone of the American way of life he cherished. In the late 1950s, Maytag commissioned an educational film called *Eddie Incorporated,* which featured a young boy operating a lemonade stand. The issues that Eddie had to deal with in the film paralleled good corporate business practices and a well-balanced business ethic.

The film was another example of Fred Maytag's enlightened self-interest, yet it doesn't seem to have had much impact on the tide of public tolerance for increasingly larger and more invasive government or on the public's languishing appreciation for the vital role of business in American life.

8
Postwar Maytag

The Dependability Ethic Meets Competitive Pressure

Taking the Long View

Maytag's enlightened self-interest philosophy of taking the long view was applied to products as well as policies and people. Both Fred Maytag II and Tom Smith, head of research and development, were full of ideas for new and different products following World War II, but the focus first had to be on resuming washer production and then bringing out an *automatic* washer.

The company did expand its appliance line right after the war by entering the gas range and freezer business, using products manufactured by other companies to Maytag specifications. Globe American Corporation of Kokomo, Indiana, which made metal lifeboats during the war, was a producer of quality gas ranges. Globe's total postwar production was taken by Maytag, following purchase of a 40 percent interest in the company. A small chest-type food freezer was manufactured to Maytag's design by Artkraft company of Lima, Ohio. Both products reached the market in 1946.

Tom Smith: Heir to the Inventive Genius Mantle of Howard Snyder[1]

Breakthrough! The Famous Model E, 1939

Wringer washer production was resumed in 1945 with the Model E, first introduced in 1939 (see Figure 8-1). It was the first major contribution of Tom Smith, who spent three years on the project. The Model E remained the top of Maytag's wringer washer line for 44 years, an incredible design achievement.

Smith, who had worked in the machine shop to earn college money, graduated from MIT with an electrical engineering degree in the Depression year of 1932 with no job prospects. A year later he was offered his old job back at Maytag but at less money. He took it. In 1934, Elmer Maytag offered Tom a job in the experimental department, where he started by performing clerical and drafting duties. He was one of two engineers and five machinists in the department. Smith's first project was to design a two-cylinder modification to the gasoline engine, which went into production in 1937.

As that job phased out of the experimental department in 1936, he began work on the Model E. His design objectives, some of them self-imposed, included appearance, lower cost, quietness, and ease of operation. He made use of sheet metal, die-castings, and plastics. The gray aluminum tub wringer model of the day had a wringer lever that was difficult to operate and an automobile type gear shift. Smith began by designing a new power drive, which he showed to F.L. in 1936.

When MIT offered Smith a scholarship in its department of business management in 1937, the disorganization and lack of direction he felt at Maytag, perhaps owing to F.L.'s interference, made the MIT offer attractive. He decided to take the scholarship and told Fred Maytag, his boyhood friend. A few weeks later Fred called him and asked him to stay. F.L. was dying and there were going to be lots of changes. Fred told him, "We will need you."

---

[1] Howard Snyder was more than the mechanical genius F.L. had discovered in Minnesota back in 1896. Over the years, the two men became close friends. Snyder accompanied F.L. on many of his Maytag junkets and amused Maytag sales people across the land with his wry humor and fascinating stories of invention after invention.

Snyder was born in 1869 and died in his Newton home in 1927 at the age of 58. He had been weakened by a 2-year bout with pernicious anemia. Trips to the Mayo Clinic, Johns Hopkins University Hospital, and Battle Creek, Michigan, had failed to slow his physical deterioration. An attack of pneumonia finished him off.

F.L. visited Snyder's bedside the day before the mechanical marvel passed away. Accounts of the scene describe F.L. holding Snyder's hand as Snyder, near death, reportedly said, "I wish we could take just one more trip together." F.L. later described Snyder as, "...the best friend I ever had."

Figure 8-1. The first postwar Maytag was the Model E, first introduced in 1939. This *Woman's Home Companion* ad announces Maytag's return to normal production.

Breakthrough! The Low-Post Agitator, 1939

Smith stayed and rapidly became a legitimate heir of Howard Snyder—resident genius. He next developed a fingertip control for the Model E wringer and a low-post agitator, using a shaft seal made of stainless steel, synthetic rubber, and nylon. The low post had presented serious problems for the original Gyrafoam washer.

A New Look—Putting the "White" in White Goods

Smith had given the washer a streamlined look, making a slotted sheet-metal skirt for the aluminum washtub. However, management wasn't satisfied with the appearance and retained industrial stylist Harold Van Doren to brighten the look. Van Doren and Smith collaborated, and Van Doren came up with a new look, using a deep, slotted skirt. Smith thought he could improve on it and smoothed out the skirt, hiding all mechanisms. Given the choice of presenting both designs, Van Doren went along with Smith's look, which they sold to the executives. The Model E was painted white—a daring departure from the dappled green, tan, or gray common to appliances at the time.

If It Ain't Broke...

The Maytag field organization was less than enthusiastic about the new washer that Smith's continuous improvement had produced. First of all, it again had a low-post agitator, which had caused them well-remembered problems. Second, the agitator in the new model was made of plastic at a time when the word plastic was synonymous with cheap. Finally, they were having no problem selling the Model 30, the "old gray ghost." Why change?

A Sales Conspiracy Foiled

As Claire Ely, then a Maytag salesman in St. Paul, tells it, his dealers had gotten together and decided to boycott the new Model E. They had decided that each dealer would order 5 of the new washers and 45 of the old. (A carload was 50 washers.) Ely called on his largest dealer first. He made out an order for the dealer consisting of 45 Model Es and 5 of the old model. The dealer objected and Ely used his best sales technique. He told the dealer that the company, world leader in the washer business, had come out with an improved washer that customers would soon be demanding because of features and styling. (It was the industry's first white appliance.) He couldn't let the dealer make the mistake of a lifetime by not getting on the bandwagon. Ely prevailed and was able to show the signed order to his next unbelieving dealer. So it went, and the Model E was launched in the Twin Cities. Ely was right: the Model E sold well. Figure 8-2 shows a Model E as it was typically displayed on the dealer floor just prior to and just after World War II.

The Model E was the top of the line for Maytag from 1939 until World War II ended production in 1942. During that time, some design deficiencies showed up. The washer needed to be beefed up for use in "Helpy-Selfy" laundries, which were gaining popularity in Oklahoma and neighboring states. These small businesses were the forerunners of the coin-operated commercial laundries to appear a decade later. Instead of washing a few loads a week, the washers in these laundries ran almost constantly. The die-cast gears driving the wringer did not prove adequate and were replaced with steel gears. Other improvements were made during the war, and a more desirable and dependable Model E had evolved by the time production resumed in 1945.

Answering Resistance From the Field

As plans were being made for resumption of washer production, Fred Maytag called Smith in and told him the field organization preferred to go back to the Model 32 gray aluminum tub washer. Smith was convinced that the Model E was a superior product and Fred agreed. The postwar line of wringer washers consisted of three models. The Model E had a full skirt surrounding its aluminum tub with the highly polished crown. The combination of the aluminum tub and the dead air space surrounding it kept wash water hot longer. While design changes were made over the years using improved materials, the Model E retained its appearance for over four decades, except when Maytag changed its logo from time to time.

Maytag Models J and N

The other two washer models had porcelain-enameled tubs. The middle Model J had a square tub, and the lowest-priced Model N had a round tub. All three used the same transmission and the same wringer (see Figures 8-3, 8-4, and 8-5). While there were three price points in the Maytag line, there was no difference in fundamental quality among them, just a difference in features. Maytag had learned the advantages of manufacturing on only one quality level. Workers can't be expected to change their standards from one model to another and still feel they are building a quality product—another example of enlightened self-interest. To this day, the Maytag Corporation

Figure 8-2. Your friendly Maytag dealer. This is Mr. Spaulding, standing next to his top-of-the-line model.

Figure 8-3. The improved Model E.

Figure 8-4. The mid-priced Model J also had a square tub.

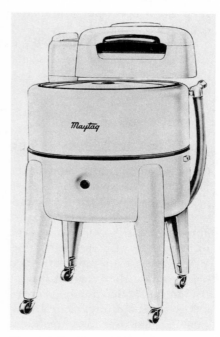

Figure 8-5. The round tub Model N, lowest in price.

stresses the same concept of a single level of quality and dependability in all
Maytag products. A 1948 ad in *Better Homes & Gardens,* touting all three
Maytag models is shown in Figure 8-6.

A Rube Goldberg Device Only a Bureaucrat Could Love

The wringer washer, dependable as it was, almost came off the market a
decade earlier than its final demise. As consumer advocacy became
increasingly fashionable, Underwriters Laboratories mandated a safety
device that would stop the wringer if something got caught in it. Maytag's
solution was a foot pedal that acted like a dead man's throttle. When the
operator removed a foot from the pedal, the wringer stopped. But the
device had to be fail-safe and foolproof. Someone could simply place a
brick on the foot pedal and circumvent the safety feature. So Tom Smith
made a small leak in the foot pedal that gradually let air out until it
stopped functioning. The operator had to lift a foot from time to time to
keep the wringer operating (See fig. 8-2). It was a feature only a bureaucrat
could love.

When Maytag finally ceased making wringer washers on November 22,
1983, it had manufactured nearly 12 million washers, of which well over
half were still in regular use. Figure 8-7 shows Dan Krumm retiring the
wringer washer in 1983.

The Big Changeover: The Automatic Washer

Of all Maytag products, appliance or farm equipment, the longest in gesta-
tion was the automatic washer. The assignment was given to R&D in 1944 to
proceed posthaste with the design of an automatic washer, but when plans
were being made late that year for resumption of washer production, the
automatic wasn't going to be ready. Therefore, production resumed with
three prewar wringer models. Before it was approved for production in
1948, Maytag's first automatic model had gone through 12 tub designs and
6 different washer ideas. A dual agitator almost made the final design but
couldn't meet dependability criteria.

Then it came time to decide where to build the automatic. Invitations
came from all over Iowa, the Midwest, and eastern industrial states. Newton
met the challenge by upgrading utilities and providing more housing, and
Maytag reciprocated by having its plant site, a cornfield on the northern
edge of town, brought inside the city limits to be included in the tax base.

Figure 8-6. A 1948 ad in *Better Homes & Gardens* shows the E, J, and N models, now called the Master, the Commander, and the Chieftain.

Figure 8-7. It was the end of an era when the last wringer washer rolled off the line in 1983. CEO Dan Krumm presided over the emotional farewell ceremony.

The plant was designed on one level with continuous flow of raw materials in one side and finished products out the other. The initial layout would produce 500 units a day. It was opened in February 1949. Now, over 40 years later, Plant 2 has swallowed its original outline in almost constant growth and encompasses highly sophisticated automation (see Figure 8-8).

The original $7 million investment has been enlarged some 20 times. In the economics of manufacturing, the ability to pay ever higher wages is directly proportional to the capital investment required to make each worker more productive. Both the initial investment in Plant 2 and the additional funds spent to keep it state of the art came from retained earnings.

Figure 8-8. Plant 2, built to house the automatic washer division: Maytag began production of automatics in 1949.

For Maytag, A Postwar Proliferation of Competitors

By the time Maytag introduced its automatic washer, the marketplace had changed drastically from the one hauled up short by World War II. Before the war, Maytag literally owned the market for wringer washers, supplying over half of all washers sold. Its competitors largely were independent producers, smaller in size. (General Electric did become a major competitor, but it dropped out of the wringer washer field in 1954.) Maytag continued to dominate a greater share of an ever-shrinking wringer washer market (called "conventional" washers by the industry to differentiate them from the new automatic washers). Industry sales of automatic washers finally exceeded those of wringer washers in the early 1950s. An ad for Maytag's first automatic washer is shown in Figure 8-9.

By then, the competitive lineup had changed dramatically. Prewar washer brands included Apex, ABC, Easy, Speed Queen, Thor, and Nineteen Hundred corporation (soon to become Whirlpool, following a merger with refrigerator maker Seeger). Bendix had introduced the first automatic washer in the late 1930s. After the war the competition included General Electric, Westinghouse, Philco division of Ford, Kelvinator division of American Motors, Frigidaire division of General Motors, Whirlpool, Crosley-Bendix, White Consolidated, and Amana.

In the early 1950s half the washers were sold by appliance stores, mainly small independent retailers. Soon the marketplace came to be dominated

Figure 8-9. A *Ladies Home Journal* ad showing Maytag's first automatic. Note the Dutch Oven gas range, one of Maytag's first attempts to move beyond laundry equipment.

by large chains of discount stores and the merchandising might of Sears, Montgomery Ward, and others.

Maintaining Leadership Through Constant Customer Focus

Breakthrough! Breakthrough! Breakthrough!

Maytag held its own in the highly competitive postwar environment because it succeeded in transferring the quality of its wringer washers to the new arena of automatic washers. Maytaggers did it because their fundamental design criteria had been to produce an automatic washer that could wash clothes as clean as the Maytag wringer washer. It would have been tempting to change when and because everyone else was changing, but instead Maytag stuck to what it knew how to do. Despite the fact that it held off introducing an automatic until the company's quality standards were met, Maytag has never ceased to dominate the high end of the washer business, in the historic 1950s price range of $290 and above.

Continuing innovation brought Maytag automatic washers such features as automatic water level control, suds saver, cold-water wash (see Figure 8-10), two-speed wash and spin, front servicing, timed bleach injection, fabric softener dispenser, the simpler Highlander design with Helical Drive transmission, and a washer and dryer stacked pair utilizing a single electronic control for both units.

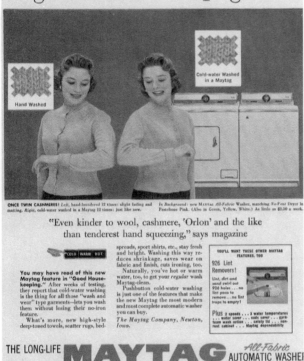

Figure 8-10. 195 Maytag invents cold-water washing.

Many innovations in the home laundry appliance field follow developments in detergents or fabrics. A slower spin speed to avoid setting wrinkles in synthetic fabrics is one example. Another involves Maytag's introduction of timed bleach injection. Independent research from Lever Brothers produced evidence that bleach added with detergent to the wash water nullified the effect of optical bleaches contained in detergents. If addition of the bleach is delayed for only a few minutes, the dye has time to attach itself to the fabric and then become impervious to the bleach action.

Within months, Maytag had introduced its timed bleach injection feature. Bleach is poured into an aperture and held in a reservoir that automatically dilutes it to proper strength and delays its introduction into the wash water until the detergent dyes are safely deposited.

Doing Away With Line Drying

The logical companion of an automatic washer is, of course, a gas or electric clothes dryer. Just as the automatic washer greatly simplifies washing, a clothes dryer automates drying clothes and eliminates the concern for favorable weather.

The clothes dryer is strictly a postwar development. Maytag introduced its dryers in 1953 and made improvements over the years paralleling washer changes.

Typical of the Maytag way was introduction of an electronic control (black box) that directly measured the level of moisture in drying clothes and turned off the dryer when the desired moisture content had been reached. Also typical, Maytag chose to design and manufacture its own control, while other companies purchased the device from a manufacturer of appliance controls. As with so many of Maytag's I'd-rather-do-it-myself components, the company achieved greater dependability, higher production quality, and manufacturing cost savings.

An early Maytag dryer model used a water film principle to eliminate the need for venting. Dryers produce hot, lint-laden air that usually is exhausted by venting to the outside. The water film dryer exhausted the air through the water film, cooling it and leaving the lint to go down the drain. While demand for an unvented dryer did not justify continued production, the principle was used later when Maytag designed its combination washer-dryer.

The Un-Breakthrough: A Good Idea Whose Time May Come Again

The washer-dryer combo is by far the most complex laundry product, combining two very dissimilar processes in a single cabinet. The history of this development illustrates well how continuous improvement waits for nothing. By the time a recovery could be made from a poor quality startup, both the market and the manufacturers had moved on. Demand for this product was promptly squelched by an industry quicker to market than to perfect its designs. Maytag and a few other manufacturers perfected their combination washer-dryers, but customers and dealers were too disillusioned by the service problems of earlier entries to pay attention. Some Maytag combination washer-dryers were still in use 20 years after their production was discontinued. With growing concern over water conservation, a market may someday return for the combination washer-dryer, which utilizes front-loading tumble washing action. The tumble washer uses less water than an upright agitator model. The original Bendix automatic washer used a front-loading tumble action, but had to be bolted to the floor to keep it from walking across the laundry room during spin cycles. It also was highly susceptible to overloading.

The Birth of the Coin-Op Laundry: Meeting a Specialized Market Need

With the advent of automatic washers, the early Helpy-Selfy laundries were transformed into Laundromats, a Westinghouse trademark concept offering the use of coin-operated washers and dryers. In the beginning, the coin laundries featured Westinghouse, Norge, and Speed Queen washers. For a time, coin-operated dry cleaning also was offered.

Maytag entered the field of commercial laundry sales in 1958 through a group of independent distributors, who supplied their customers with other products and location planning as well as the washers that provided the chief attraction. Distributors sold many turnkey operations to investors such as doctors and dentists. Other stores were small Mom-and-Pop businesses. Many of the stores were left unattended and often were open 24 hours a day. Some used attendants to handle drop-off laundry for patrons and to provide dry-cleaning pick-up service.

The Maytag name for dependability lent appeal, and the company soon became a dominant player in the commercial laundry business. The special commercial laundry washers had few differences. A brass water valve handled the much hotter water used in coin laundries, but essentially the coin laundry customer used an identical washer to the one found in the home.

Maytag quality and reliability made it an easy sell to re-equip laundries with Maytags instead of competing washers. That dependability left the owners little to do but collect and bank the coins. Maytag now dominates the coin laundry business like it once dominated the wringer washer market.

Innovation Eliminates Vandalism

Breakthrough! Electronic Funny Money, 1962

A major problem for coin laundries came from petty thieves who broke into the washers and dryers for the coins, often to support drug habits. The major losses came not so much from the money taken as from the damage done to the machines. So Maytag engineers brought creative thinking to the problem and solved it by removing temptation. They designed a receiver that accepted a plastic ticket instead of money. The ticket was damaged on insertion so it couldn't be reused. Nothing of value remained in the machine.

Tickets were sold by attendants, if the laundry had them, or by neighboring merchants, or from a dispenser built like a bank vault to discourage would-be thieves. Tickets were available with different printed circuits for competing laundries, and the circuits were disguised to discourage counterfeiting.

For those owners preferring to stay with coins, Maytag developed and made its own coin slide, seeing a need for improvement over those available on the open market. One advantage of the device was the ability to change the amount of money needed so prices could be changed, sometimes temporarily, without having to replace the coin slide.

Computer-Age Tools Aid the Laundry Business

Breakthrough! Computer-Trac, 1988

As with any system handling money—and quarters can add up to a great deal of money—security is a never-ending concern. Elimination of manual operations can improve both security and accuracy. In the 1980s Maytag introduced Computer-Trak to its commercial washers and dryers. A simple coin drop box replaces the coin or ticket slide. Electronics inside keep track of laundry cycles and can even tell the user, on an LED screen, the time remaining in the cycle. The owner can change prices quickly and easily enough to offer reduced prices at slow times of the day. The feature has become Maytag's most popular model.

Breakthrough! ACCU TRAC, 1992

ACCU TRAC was introduced to route operators in 1992. Using a hand-held reader not unlike those used to take inventory in grocery stores, a supervisor or collector takes a reading on each machine, perhaps as money is collected. When decoded back at the office, the ACCU TRAC reader tells the number of cycles run (and the amount of money that should be present), service problems, and other information. The system was developed by Maytag's R&D department.

Saturation and Growth in the Commercial Market

Once replacement of washers in existing stores had taken place, growth opportunity in the store field flattened. New stores cannot find new customers indefinitely and market saturation sets in. As neighborhoods change, old stores may close and new ones open, but the net demand for machines no longer grows appreciably.

The major growth area for commercial laundry appliances is in the so-called route operation. It started as commercial operators put washers and dryers in apartments and other multiple-housing areas. In some cases, landlords owned the units, but increasingly the route operator has hundreds or thousands of units out and pays the landlord a commission. A single organization can handle collections and repairs for a large number of units. Maytag dependability pays dividends for the route operators as well. Emerging lifestyles would seem to dictate continued growth in this market. College dormitories are a major market.

Homestyle Laundries for Everyone

Originally coin laundries used large double-load dryers that were not kind to clothes, overdrying and wrinkling most items. Then Maytag introduced its homestyle modules. Two home dryers were stacked and coupled with two washers to make the module. In laundries, banks of modules were lined up, each with a sorting table, to offer some privacy to the normally communal atmosphere of a coin laundry. The laundering results also were more homelike. These homestyle modules fit into many apartment installations, a plus for route operators.

As with the domestic laundry business, Maytag was a late starter in the commercial coin-operated laundry field, but by focusing on customer needs and applying customer-driven design improvements to meet those needs, it has become the acknowledged leader. Underlying both businesses is Maytag product dependability.

Name Alone Doesn't Sell a Product: Early Setbacks in Broadening the Product Base

The Maytag Dutch Oven gas range produced by Globe American from 1946 to 1955 was in every sense a Maytag quality product. It had features that were exclusive in the range business. It also had limitations. It was available only as a gas range and only in a 40-inch width. It also carried a quality price tag (look again at Figure 8-9, bottom).

Exclusive features included a deep cooker well in place of one surface burner and a Dutch Oven, with 40 pounds of insulation, that cooked on with the gas turned off. Of course, the customer had to learn how to use both.

Sales of the range line and the Maytag freezer sales (discussed below) were disappointing. High price was a limiting factor, along with limited model availability. Maytag was learning that there were not two profits to be made from a single appliance sale—one for the manufacturer and one for the marketer.

This lesson was driven home with the Amana experiment. Maytag had dropped the Artkraft freezer from its line in 1950, when it entered into an arrangement with the Amana Company, also located in Iowa, for Maytag to market chest and upright freezers and a combination refrigerator-freezer made by Amana with Maytag styling. In addition to disappointing sales and lack of a double profit, Amana experienced a service problem that Maytag couldn't live with, and the arrangement was terminated in 1960. Maytag also purchased ironers, first from Conlin and later Ironrite, but demand for that product practically disappeared in the 1950s, helped along by the arrival of no-iron synthetic fabrics.

While experimenting with outside product suppliers to supplement the Maytag line, the company had not for many years produced any of its own products for private-label use. It was axiomatic that "a washer by any other name" was not a Maytag. The truism was used as a sales argument against Whirlpool, whose biggest customer was Sears, for whom Whirlpool made products with the Kenmore label.

Head-to-Head With Whirlpool: The Case for the Shortline Manufacturer

One of Fred Maytag's postwar philosophies was in direct opposition to that of Whirlpool, which was emerging as Maytag's primary competitor. Following the 1954 merger that created the Whirlpool Corporation from Nineteen Hundred Corporation and Seeger, that company actively pursued the policy of becoming a full-line producer offering dealers and private-label customers all of the so-called white goods appliances—washers and dryers, gas and electric ranges, refrigerators and freezers, dishwashers, and trash compactors. The Whirlpool CEO and leading architect of the full-line philosophy was Elisha (Bud) Grey. In contrast, Maytag identified itself as a short-line manufacturer of home laundry appliances, with 95 percent of 1959 sales volume in that area.

During the postwar decade, the prevailing philosophy was that the retail consumer demanded a full-line supplier to whom that retailer would be tied exclusively—a common practice in the auto business. There would be no room for a specialty producer. Fred Maytag pointed out that the actual trend had gone the opposite direction, with retailers taking on additional brands as they grew in size.

Fred's position, the basis for his remarks before the New York Society of Security Analysts in 1957, was that there were certain criteria essential to success in the appliance business and that the short-line question was not one of them. His criteria:

FIRST, it is essential to develop and efficiently produce a well-engineered product.

SECOND, it is essential to secure efficient distribution, advertising, and servicing for that product.

THIRD, it is essential to develop and maintain a good relationship with the retail dealer who sells the product to the public.

He went on to show how Maytag, as one short-line producer, was able to meet those criteria and thus was not at a disadvantage in competing with full-line companies. Fred explained that cost starts with design:

We have a closely knit, highly specialized product development division. They operate on the basic Maytag idea that model changes should represent significant improvements, rather than simply an annual face-lifting. They are conscious of the continuing need to design for improved function, as well as simplified manufacturing. In the constant battle against rising labor and material costs, I believe that any manufacturer who wishes to stay competitive must find ways to produce more efficiently. This starts with design.

We are constantly striving to improve our product. Sometimes improvements are introduced unheralded and sometimes they result in a change of model. But one thing is certain: we never introduce a new model that is not an improvement over the one it replaces.

In our R&D division, three kinds of developments are constantly in progress. We are always striving for the ultimate perfection of present designs in order to eliminate all causes of product failure, to improve our manufacturing techniques, and to reduce costs. Secondly, we are continually concerned with the development of new models and new features to meet the changing needs of the customer. Finally, we have our long-range development program for the creation of completely new products.

The Highlander—Designing for Mid-Market

Studies indicated that while Maytag was a strong contender in the high-end automatic washer market, representing 47 percent of the total, it had no entry in the field of lower-priced automatics, consisting of 43 percent of the market. Fred realized that if Maytag could compete in the lower price class, the company could nearly double its market potential:

> One way to get a lower-priced product is to strip down an existing model—take off features until the desired price level is possible. That isn't the way our people work. A totally new washer was designed, one with a new drive mechanism, Helical Drive. The end result was a fully automatic washer with many extra features, a quality product that can be sold by dealers with confidence and at a normal profit. It is not a stripped-down promotional model. It is easier and less costly to produce and it can be sold at a lower price.

The Helical Drive transmission introduced on the Highlander washer was soon adopted on all Maytag automatic washers.

In the decade of the 1950s, 204 patents were issued to members of Maytag's R&D division and 111 applications were pending. Several large manufacturers had licensing agreements with Maytag under which they used inventions patented by Maytag.

Production Facilities—Vertical Integration

Continuing his argument, Fred said:

> In our manufacturing plants, we have what is perhaps the highest degree of integration of anyone in the home laundry field. We now produce just about everything that goes into our products except electrical motors, timer controls, molded plastic parts, and some few die castings. Thus, we are in a position to exercise a high degree of control over components and in many cases achieve manufacturing economies by producing components ourselves.
>
> In the past 10 years, we have invested $33.4 million in new facilities, more than doubling our manufacturing space. We have financed this expansion ourselves. We are in a strong financial condition with no debt. And may I state to you quite sincerely that in no instance has any modernization or improvement been rejected on the grounds that we couldn't afford it. We have been able to do all we needed to do. In light of all this, the ability to produce efficiently is not the exclusive prerogative of the full-line companies.

Maytag Addresses Distribution

Maytag has a rather unique method of distribution, selling directly to dealers rather than through the additional step of distributors or jobbers. For

Figure 8-11. Ad for the Highlander, another of Maytag's best-selling models.

many years the company also sold only for cash in advance or sight draft bill of lading. Fred Maytag:

> We believe that people are the heart of any marketing organization. Our careful selection procedures and our continuing training program are, I think, unusual in the appliance industry. I may state to you quite frankly

that Maytag has never found itself in a position where it could not do those things that need to be done in order to recruit, train, develop and put into the field an effective and efficient marketing organization.

Speaking to his third point regarding dealer relationships, Fred said:

The most important factor to consider is that the independent dealer—and some of them can be pretty independent—is primarily concerned with the manufacturer's policies and procedures that affect him. Just so long as a manufacturer can provide the dealer with a set of conditions that permit the dealer to sell competitively priced merchandise under a sound policy that gives the dealer self-respect in the job he is doing and that gives him an opportunity to earn a fair return on his labor and investment—just so long will there be independent dealers in adequate numbers to handle the products of that manu-facturer.

Maytag, with 15,000 dealers at the time, was not limited in that category.

Eschewing Artificial Obsolescence

Another 1950s trend in the home appliance business was the emergence of annual models, long a tradition in the auto business. It was started by General Electric in an effort to build volume for its extensive facilities at Appliance Park in Louisville, Kentucky, in a time of slack sales. Soon most other companies had followed suit.

Not Maytag. Fred Maytag's words ring with his conviction against a practice that for him marked perhaps the low point in American manufacturing:

We reject the concept of planned psychological obsolescence. The general practice is to produce a completely new line of models every year, come what may, most frequently embodying only a superficial face-lifting. This is supposed to stimulate the housewife to replace appliances that are still perfectly useful but that have gone out of style.

I happen to believe that it has hurt manufacturers, dealers and consumers alike. When a potential customer is confronted by a bewildering array of products that seem to be substantially identical except for styling differences, and is told that this model is almost the same as that model but she can get a better price on this one because it's last year's model, it's not too surprising that she has turned into a cynical bargain hunter. The practice of flooding dealers with "obsolete models" at bargain prices has tended to turn the marketplace into an oriental bazaar.

We are trying to make everything we now produce obsolete by developing something better, but this is far different from face-lifting. Our concept does not tie the introduction of new models to the calendar.

Rather, it ensures that new models will be introduced to the public whenever a new and better way has been developed for the particular appliance to perform its job for the homemaker.

We believe that the prospective customer is motivated to buy a new appliance when she clearly understands that it will do things for her that she cannot do with the equipment she now owns.

While everyone notices and coments on new styles in clothing or new cars, relatively few people see appliances in the home. The homemaker is still primarily concerned with the utility and convenience of home laundry appliances and is apt to be more annoyed than pleased at the transient quality of annual appliance models. The life of a household appliance is measured in a somewhat longer term of years than that applied to fashions or to automobiles.

An even more significant drawback to annual models is that there is no ready market for used appliances that are traded in. Much of an auto dealer's profit comes from resale of trade-ins. A very limited market exists for used appliances.

A Rude Awakening, A Difficult Choice

Fred Maytag inherited a management structure typical of the times. In addition to the CEO, there were officers in charge of manufacturing, marketing, and finance. A secretary and assistant secretary to make routine matters legal with their signatures completed the officer ranks.

When Fred replaced his father as CEO, George Umbreit, who had headed the financial division, was promoted to executive vice president and treasurer, giving him status as the number two player. He also continued to head the financial division until after World War II, when E.G. Higdon was named comptroller. Robert E. Vance was brought on board in 1942 as assistant to the president. He had been in charge of Elmer's estate. He became secretary in 1951 when long-time employee W.I. Sparks died. Attorney Murray Nelson was named assistant secretary.

Lack of a formal management training program or succession planning forced Fred to go outside the company for several high-level positions following World War II. Fred hired Irwin A. Rose, manufacturing vice president at Hotpoint in Chicago, to take the same position at Maytag. To replace a disappointing employee relations manager hired during the war, Fred brought in E.F. (Don) Scoutten from an eastern industrial concern to be director of industrial relations in 1952.

Then came Fred's great awakening. He was deeply involved in Republican politics and greatly flattered when the state's kingmakers came to him and asked him to be a candidate for the U.S. Senate. The offer was practically the position, since Republicans were in control in Iowa at the time.

Fred wanted very much to do it. But he asked for time to meet with his Maytag staff and discuss the offer before accepting it. He needed to give the Republicans an answer immediately, so he called his people together Saturday morning and requested their approval and cooperation. He had barely gotten the proposal out on the table when George Umbreit risked his career by saying, "You can't do it!" George felt the company couldn't survive the loss of the single dominant person in charge. The company was looked upon as a family-controlled, one-man operation. George recognized his own limitations.

In a state of shock and anger, Fred dismissed the meeting. Monday morning he reassembled the group. He told them of his first feelings and that he later came to agree with George's concern, but he still wanted to become involved in political office. In order to be ready should another opportunity present itself, he was determined to restructure the company management along modern professional lines. He no longer wanted the company so dependent on a single individual. Thus began the long, careful process of installing professional management, utilizing the management consulting services of Booz, Allen & Hamilton.

The Creation of a Divisional Structure

The plan adopted by Fred created six operational divisions, each headed by a vice president. Each division head was restricted to his or her own area of responsibility but was more responsible and accountable for decision making within that area. Maytag and executive vice president Umbreit would be responsible for overall policy. Already in place were Irwin Rose in charge of manufacturing and Roy Bradt at the head of marketing. Tom Smith, director of research and development, had been made a vice president in 1953.

The three new vice presidents were E.G. Higdon, vice president and controller, in charge of the financial division; Don Scoutten, vice president and director of industrial relations; and Bob Vance, vice president and secretary, who headed the administrative division. These were the officers named by the board of directors in 1956.

Now Fred was free to do his own thing. But cancer struck before another political opportunity presented itself. In 1959 he fell ill and underwent emergency abdominal surgery at Lowry Air Force Base in Denver while on a tour of air bases for the Air Force's Air Training Command. He served as a member of an advisory board. He underwent a second major operation in St. Louis in 1960 and returned the following year for yet another. Fred Maytag had a total of five major operations and underwent both chemotherapy and radiation treatments.

Although the final outcome was all but certain from the beginning, Fred tried anything his doctors could suggest and became engrossed in the subject of his own illness. He had periods of apparent remission and periods of rapid deterioration.

Ensuring Smooth Leadership Succession

As part of Fred's move toward professional management, he constructed a headquarters building to house the entire management group, except for research, which had its own ivory tower across the street. The new building encompassed the old main office and doubled its size. Fred wanted it called a headquarters building rather than a main office. It contained many of the engineering departments and their labs, as well as the marketing, manufacturing, industrial relations, financial, and administrative divisions.

Fred became chairman of the board in 1960 and George Umbreit was named president. E.G. Higdon became executive vice president in an obvious signal for management succession. Because of Fred's failing health, Umbreit ordered construction of the building expedited so that Fred could preside over its dedication and open house on May 26, 1961. Thus the company was prepared for his death when it came on November 4, 1962. Fred was 51.

As Seen in *Life* Magazine: A Commonplace Lifestyle

In 1949 *Life* magazine sent photographer Leonard McComb to follow Fred Maytag around for several weeks, and a nine-page photo essay resulted. The thrust of the piece was that Fred led a commonplace existence in Newton, operating on a first-name basis around the courthouse square. Even so, the awe of the community toward a Maytag kept Fred and Ellen isolated, with few social invitations outside a close circle of friends.

But Fred's life was anything but commonplace. He followed his grandfather's footsteps in a number of extracurricular activities. In addition to serving as a state senator, he was a trustee of Skiff Hospital from 1937 to 1949, headed the Salvation Army board, and became a trustee of Grinnell College. Like his father, he headed the family banks and the dairy farm.

His hobbies led him to become involved in the Izaak Walton League and Ducks Unlimited. He was a lifelong supporter of the Boy Scouts. Fred presided at the eightieth birthday celebration for former President Herbert Hoover at his birthplace in West Branch, Iowa, and went on to become chairman of the executive committee of the Herbert Hoover Birthplace Founda-

Figure 8-12. Fred Maytag II—an insatiable curiosity—with Roy Bradt (left) and George Umbreit.

tion, instrumental in the preservation of both the Hoover family home and the presidential library at West Branch.

Fred's outside directorships included Equitable Life Insurance Company of Iowa, Northwestern Bell Telephone, Minneapolis-Honeywell, Iowa Power & Light, and the Midwestern Research Institute. He served as a director for the National Industrial Conference Board and served for three years chairman of the taxation committee of the National Association of Manufacturers.

The End of a Family Dynasty

A private memorial service was held at St. Stephens Episcopal church in Newton and a public memorial service the following day at the First Methodist church, site of the funerals of Fred's father, Elmer, and grandfather, F.L. The body was cremated and the ashes strewn over Fred's favorite duck marsh in Canada.

Present-day Maytag company values reflect much of who Fred Maytag II was and what he believed in. If F.L. established the company, it was Fred who set the course that the company still follows. The things he prized in his private life often became adopted as company values. He learned to fly during World War II and got his private license in 1945 (see Figure 8-12). He said flying was the most exciting thing he did, an enthusiasm that led the company to buy a single-engine Cessna 195 airplane in 1949 for business use.

As a natural leader both within the company and in all his outside activities, Fred inspired a tremendous loyalty. For many old-timers, things were never the same after he died. He was a very natural, open person, and unassuming. He possessed the knack of giving his undivided attention, of making a person feel important, as though what he was saying was the most important thing in the world at that moment. He was a gentleman and exuded integrity. Not an orator, he learned to acquit himself adequately at the podium but was much better in a small group or one on one.

Fred was born with a natural curiosity that made him want to probe into things to find out what made them tick, a quality that led him to view everything as an adventure, even the illness that ultimately took his life.

9

Dilemma Decade—
The Sixties

Competitive Challenge Part I—Questing
for Growth in a Mature Market

A Perilous Transition

A long-standing tradition such as that of Maytag quality can successfully
be passed on from generation to generation of the founding family. A
dynasty provides coherence, even if it is comprised mainly of the percep-
tions of others. The corporate entity tends to become personified in the
family tradition. Thus had it been with the Maytags, with the management
philosophy of the founder preserved and enhanced by each succeeding
generation.

But can a concept that is at the same time as ethereal as an unwritten
credo and as eternal as Old Lonely successfully make the transition to
hired management mercenaries? Once captured, can it be transmitted to
successors motivated more by finance than family pride? In the case of the
Maytag company, the answer appears to be yes. One of Maytag's greatest
challenges in its 100 years of existence came not from outside competition, but from the internal need to sustain its quality ethic through the
transition from family to professional management.

The Mercenaries

Of the four professional managers who have so far ascended to the CEO-ship after the last of the Maytag family CEOs, the first two were steeped in the family tradition. The next two barely knew Fred Maytag and came on the scene long after his predecessors were gone. Each of the latter two held the job of company president and later corporate president and CEO of a greatly expanded business empire.

Yet each of the four has held the concept of Maytag quality and dependability as the be-all and end-all of his job. It is every bit as important to current CEO Leonard Hadley as it was to Fred Maytag, whom he saw and heard from afar in the brief time their careers overlapped. Hadley began his Maytag career the year Fred was stricken with cancer.

Deeply conscious of the company's heritage, Hadley told his directors at the dinner the night before he was elected CEO that in all probability he would be the last CEO to know any of the Maytags. He sees it as an important part of his job to pass on that quality heritage to a changing Maytag management so as to ensure that he is not the last quality-consumed leader.

Custodians of the Flame

George Umbreit had run in harness with the young Fred Maytag for 25 years and felt incomplete without him. He had never aspired to the top job but had it thrust upon him by fate. The four years between Fred's death and George's mandatory retirement at age 65 were pretty much devoted to not losing any ground.

As interim caretaker, he reaped the benefit of Fred's recent reorganization creating a professional management team, and little changed during his tenure. The company's interest in Europe and development work on new products went on during his watch but were overseen primarily by E.G. Higdon, who assumed the presidency when Umbreit became chairman.

Umbreit was a very private person. His impact on the company was to keep a steady, no-nonsense hand at the helm and to pass on the company heritage undamaged.

Son of a Milwaukee attorney, Umbreit graduated from the University of Wisconsin a decade before Fred and began his career with Ernst & Ernst in Chicago in 1923. He went on to become a partner in another Chicago accounting firm, Alexander Grant, for four years before coming to Maytag in 1929 as auditor.

Ernst & Ernst, A Longtime Partner and Source of Financial Executives

Maytag's first contact with Ernst & Ernst (now Ernst & Young) was probably in the fall of 1925, when a Mr. Schulte came to Newton to set up a new accounting and materials control system for Maytag. The system didn't prove satisfactory, and most of it was thrown out in the spring of 1926.

The next project, formation of Maytag Sales Corporation following a plan recommended by E&E in 1927, lasted somewhat longer. The separate corporation was formed to handle all interstate sales to avoid state taxes. It was dissolved at the end of 1936.

E&E audited Maytag's 1928 annual report and has continued doing so ever since. Arthur Young & Company was Maytag's previous accounting firm.

Both Umbreit and Higdon had E&E backgrounds. Umbreit came on the scene the year after Maytag's marvelous 1928 recapitalization plan and suffered through sometimes crushing preference dividend requirements until all preference stock was finally recalled in 1959. He joined as auditor and became comptroller in 1932, at the low point of the Depression. He became a vice president and director in 1934, the year Fred Maytag II joined the company, and moved from chief financial officer to executive vice president when Fred assumed the presidency in 1940. He became president 20 years later, after Fred's illness had been diagnosed as terminal, and chairman upon Fred's death. Umbreit himself died of cancer in 1972.

Emerson Granville (E.G.) Higdon of Marshall, Missouri, went to E&E's Chicago office after graduation from the University of Kansas in 1930. He followed Umbreit as internal auditor at Maytag in 1933 and also as chief financial officer in 1941, and became a vice president in 1956 as part of Fred Maytag's management restructuring. He continued to dog Umbreit's career, becoming executive vice president and treasurer and a company director in 1960 and president in 1962.

The office of chairman was left vacant after Umbreit retired, and Higdon became CEO in 1966. Higdon named his successor in 1972 when Dan Krumm became president and Higdon chairman and CEO. The office was vacant again when Higdon reached age 65 and retired in 1974.

Higdon's personality was not unlike Umbreit's. He detested making public appearances almost as much as Umbreit had, although Higdon did learn to make a decent speech. Unlike Umbreit, Higdon didn't stay in Newton all the time. He served as a director of the Federal Reserve Bank of Chicago for six years and was its chairman for three terms. He acquitted himself well before the New York Society of Security Analysts and received an honorary degree from Missouri Valley College in Marshall.

Like Umbreit, Higdon had never aspired to be a chief executive. He had not been particularly close to Fred Maytag and had no close friends among his subordinates. While he kept his own counsel, Higdon was uniquely gregarious. In the office, he would make a daily swing past the desks of several regulars, representing every station of employee. Those who interacted with him regularly called him "Hig." Jokes and banter were exchanged. No business was discussed. Five o'clock regularly found him in an entirely different atmosphere, enjoying the conviviality of the local Elks Club bar, with companions from every walk of life—except Maytag. At home, he was a gourmet cook and took pride in owning an elaborate fish poacher.

Quality: The Price of Admission to Future Business

While neither financially oriented CEO could be described as a dynamic leader, they shared an intense focus on the importance of quality to Maytag's continued existence. They were well aware of the premium price a Maytag product both commanded and required, as well as the hot breath of competition that permitted no slips. To them the only justification for that price tag was to maintain and enhance their quality reputation. The focus was on continued improvement in the laundry field and a toe in the water with other products, but the purse strings were not loose enough to finance expansion.

The New Product Outlook During the Sixties

During the 1960s, while the nation was focused on campus unrest, Maytag found itself in the doldrums. Nothing much was happening in the appliance industry except evolution. Growth was stagnant. Promotions were few and far between. Maytag's management ranks tended to turn over in 20-year cycles. Postwar arrivals began retiring in the 1970s, and the next wave, who had become Maytaggers a decade later, were retiring in the late 1980s and early 1990s. The big difference was that all the action in the 1970s came from retirements, while most of the movement in the 1980s expansion era came from promotions.

While Fred Maytag's short-line specialist philosophy was still valid from a competitive position, he had neglected to consider the effects of a maturing industry with an ever-flattening growth curve. As unlikely as it had seemed in the 1950s, market saturation that topped out at about 80 percent of wired homes had brought year-to-year sales gains to a crawl. Any new business would have to come at the expense of a competitor.

In this environment, new sources of growth were welcome. But management also laid down some guidelines. In line with Fred's philosophy of sticking to your last, the company chose to stay with household appliances, which it knew, and more specifically, water-using appliances, which it knew best.

Dishwashers—A Natural Extension

This line of reasoning led Maytag into the dishwasher market. While the product had been around for a long time, it had not begun to grow until the average homemaker had acquired what were considered the "necessary" appliances—stove, refrigerator, and clothes washer. Even clothes dryers were on the luxury list for a time. But as saturation occurred with the basic appliances, the market for the next level of conveniences began to grow. Dishwashers led the way.

As a practical matter, the dishwasher made a good place to store dirty dishes, after carefully rinsing them off, until a full load accumulated. It also proved to be a good place to store clean dishes until needed again, particularly in a large family. The dishes often went from the table to the dishwasher and then back to the table.

Early Shortcomings: Maytag's Challenge

But dishwashers made for home use generally were short on elbow grease. They lacked an automated Brillo pad. Further, they were not very efficient at getting rid of food residue left on the dishes, and often redeposited food as the wash water was recirculated. Some homeowners thought they wasted water.

One thing dishwashers had going for them was the ability to use much hotter water than could be tolerated by someone doing the dishes by hand. The truism "The hotter the water, the cleaner the clothes" also applied to dishes. For most effective use, the water heater in the dishwasher was often turned up to 160 degrees fahrenheit. Next, the dishwasher detergent could be and was much stronger than a person could tolerate on his or her hands. Finally, dishwashers used far less water than the amount consumed by washing dishes by hand and letting the faucet run during rinsing.

Maytag Makes It Better

Maytag's R&D had dishwashers under development for a number of years, at first sort of on the back burner. As both the need and opportunity became more pronounced, the design was finalized and placed in production in 1966. The slow pace was in keeping with Maytag's policy of not bringing out something until it could make a contribution to the state of the art. Like Maytag's introduction of the automatic washer 18 years earlier, the Maytag dishwasher's performance was vastly superior to anything else on the market.

Breakthrough! Smaller Holes, Finer Filters and a Good Backflush Mechanism, 1967

Maytag found an ingenious way to improve the washing action. The spray arms that circulated wash water top and bottom had much smaller holes, increasing the force of the spray. It was no longer necessary to prerinse everything. After the larger food scraps were scraped off, the powerful washing action did the rest.

The reason Maytag dishwashers had smaller spray holes than others is that they were equipped with a fine-mesh filter to remove food particles that otherwise would clog small openings as the wash water was recirculated. A dishwasher uses only a few gallons of water at a fill, and the water is constantly recirculated during the wash cycle. The reason the fine-mesh circular filter worked so well was a clever spray arm that constantly backflushed the filter and kept it open, washing food particles down the drain.

However, apparently prerinsing the dishes is a hard habit to break. Over 25 years later, with its remarkable new dishwasher design, Maytag still feels compelled to advertise that with a Maytag, dishes don't have to be washed twice.

Taking the Plunge the Painful Way

While some people jump into new markets with a big splash, others enter tentatively, an inch at a time, prolonging the pain. Thus it was with Maytag's bean-counter leadership. They cautiously entered the dishwasher market toe first, introducing only a portable model (see Figure 9-1). It rolled up to the sink on casters, and its hoses quick-connected to a special faucet fitting Of course, it took up valuable floor space in the kitchen, and the top-loading door made it impossible to use the top of the machine for additional storage space. Reaching dishes in the bottom of the dishwasher was sometimes difficult.

The cautious approach probably reasoned that as a free-standing appliance that didn't need to be built in, the dishwasher more closely matched other appliances in the dealer's store. That may well have been true, but the public's tastes ran otherwise and the demand for built-in dishwashers was far greater. So plumbers and kitchen remodelers sold a lot of dishwashers until appliance dealers found ways to handle installation. Today, most dishwashers slip into space vacated by the old unit. Portables never represented more

Figure 9-1. Maytag's first shot at making dishwashers was this top-loading portable model, which freed homemakers to sit on high stools and read cookbooks while the dishes washed themselves.

than a very small share of the total dishwasher market. It took three years for the message to register before Maytag's built-in dishwashers appeared.

But belt-and-suspenders Maytag designers added a best-of-both-worlds wrinkle. They also introduced a convertible dishwasher that could function initially as a portable and later be built in. Such an unusual approach appealed to the logic of some customers, even at a higher price.

Back in the days of wringer washers, Maytag offered dealers a clear plastic tub demonstrator to show the unique Gyrafoam washing action. When filled and set in motion with poker chips in lieu of clothes, the colorful chips swirled handsomely and convincingly. So it was natural that Maytag took the same approach with the powerful dishwashing action. A plastic-enclosed dishwasher didn't need poker chips to convince observers they were watching a tower of power. Such powerful washing action was necessarily noisy, and Maytag had to work out elaborate measures to deaden the sound.

Next, A Logical Companion

The next logical extension of the product line was a food waste disposer. Most built-in dishwashers were installed to drain under the kitchen sink. Drainage into a food waste disposer under the sink made a neat installation. Maytag disposers originally came in two versions: the conventional continuous-feed model with a remote power switch and a batch-feed model whose lid was the switch. Users of the batch-feed model had only to remember to keep the lid on the disposer when the dishwasher was running.

Again, the Maytag contribution was a vast improvement over anything else on the market. Its design practically eliminated jamming, the bane of most competitors. Like the Everready bunny, it just kept going and going, able to grind up pennies or tenpenny nails.

However, not untypically, a Maytag disposer was three times as hefty and three times as costly as the competition. A Maytag of a disposer, it found too few buyers willing to pay the price to grind nails. Never requiring more than a handful of employees to produce, the Maytag food waste disposer saw its volume finally vanish at the end of 1992.

Confronting and Accepting the Myth of Name Transfer

Those customers who identified with Maytag sufficiently to pay the price for its food waste disposer got their money's worth, as with all Maytag products. But the public by and large does not leap to the conclusion that if a Maytag is the best washer it also must be the best dishwasher, disposer, refrigerator, or range. Each product has to earn its own niche to succeed. This was a hard lesson for Maytag to learn, because the company enjoyed the best name identification in the appliance business with its washer. In the case of the clothes dryer, the product was accepted not so much because of name transfer but because a dryer is generally bought to match the washer in appearance. Maytag has tried hard over the years to establish an independent dryer demand, with limited success.

Laundering in Miniature: The Market Cries Wolf

Just as the American consumer didn't cotton to the portable dishwasher, the public has never felt the need for miniaturizing the laundry. Hoover tried introducing its small spinner washer, so popular in England, to the United States but met limited success. Whirlpool tried a version of its Metropolitan automatic washer, 24 inches wide to fit through New York City apartment doors, but it was neither needed nor wanted elsewhere. Frigidaire designed a small stack pair called the Skinni-Mini, introduced at Expo '67 in Montreal. The units were part of *Habitat,* an experiment in prefab apartments that resembled containership modules. Again, the market has been minuscule. Others have approached the minimarket with similar results.

But what caught Maytag's attention was an infusion of Japanese versions of the Hoover concept. Most of the Japanese companies dominating the electronics field also made a small washer that sold in Japan with great success. The small washers were a hit in Japan for the same reasons American washers were a dud. They didn't need the hot-water supply or plumbing, and the Japanese laundry basket, like its counterpart in Europe, just was never that full.

With all the brands advertising their small washers, it seemed to Maytag that there must be a market for a small washer. Maytag's assumption was like that of the entrepreneur who found a swamp loaded with bullfrogs. He contracted to deliver 10,000 pairs of frog legs to a French restaurant chain but, after a week's muddy struggle, had only a bushel basketful for his labor. His plaintive cry: "It sure sounded like 10,000 bullfrogs!"

Maytag engineers responded with the Model A50, similar in design to other spinner washers on the market. Their more significant contribution was a matching electric clothes dryer tailored to handle the A50's halfload. The dryer worked well, could be hung by a bracket to the wall, and featured a nylon sock to capture the lint given off. The pair sold reasonably well in Montreal, but elsewhere it turned out to be a bullfrog market.

The Call of the Lorelei: Complications in Expanding Abroad

Another possible direction for growth was to expand the washer market beyond North America. The prospect was intriguing but the route full of pitfalls. Europe, for example, was full of people who needed to wash but had different ideas about how a washing machine should work. In England, the spinner washer was most popular, but the continent turned up its nose. Each country had its own nationalistic appliance makers. It was difficult to cross borders. Most European washers utilized the tumbler principle, using the least amount of water, like the one Bendix had employed and the one that Maytag had developed with its millrace cabinet washer of 1917. But it wasn't so much water that was scarce as *hot* water, and many European washers contained a built-in water heater element.

Another significant difference between the United States and European markets involved laundering habits. Many Europeans tended to wear an article of clothing more times and to go longer periods between launderings. Bathing was also done less frequently. The heavier soiling that resulted, especially of body oils (ring around the collar), required very hot water, akin to boiling, to remove. This encouraged building in a water heater as part of the washer. Interestingly, Europeans more commonly used oxygen-based bleach, considered mild in the U.S., rather than chlorine bleach. But such bleaches as hydrogen peroxide are effective in very hot water, while chlorine bleach (a 5 percent solution of hydrogen chloride) is far more effective at the temperatures found in U.S. automatic washers.

All European countries shared a dearth of hot water and a plumbing structure that did not permit the use of an American top-loading automatic washer. Only in the United States did the American washer find favor. Germany, France, and Italy all had established appliance industries that pretty much stayed at home. The same was true of Scandinavia. An added complication was the profusion of electric voltages and cycles found throughout Europe.

An Entry-Level Idea

Maytag thought it saw a way to establish a foothold abroad. The concept evolved in 1960 when Fred Maytag was still in charge. The project was Higdon's from start to finish. The toe in the water would come through the Maytag commercial washer. The plan was to establish a commercial superdistributorship in Brussels, from which to open coin laundry markets in various countries.

The drawbacks associated with use of American washers would be solved at the coin laundry, where adequate hot water and plumbing could be provided. The plan has worked to a limited degree. Distributorships were set up in England and in several countries on the continent, and the resulting laundries enjoyed some notoriety. But maintaining an office abroad proved an unnecessary expense when the English distributor was able to serve the continent as well—and still does.

To run the Brussels operation, Higdon looked around the office for a likely prospect. He wanted a comer who had not yet come too far. He asked for suggestions. Recommended highly by his supervisor, Dan Krumm was selected, "Berlitzed," and whisked abroad with wife and two young sons in 1962. Krumm and family spent five years in Europe for Maytag, first in Brussels and later on another assignment. The timing also proved fortuitous.

Opening a Second European Front

Meanwhile, the Maytag strategists were planning a second front. A sure way to get into business is to buy one. They couldn't find a home appliance maker, but in 1964 they did locate a German company owned by Willy Homann that made commercial laundry units used by hotels and hospitals. The firm also made commercial stoves for restaurants and institutions. Another Newton cadre was identified and sent packing to Wupertal. But disaster struck almost immediately. Homann, who it turned out was as much a one-man band as F.L. Maytag had been, died suddenly and without corporate heir.

It took a while to recover, but Maytag persevered and kept Homann-Maytag going while back home the folks in R&D were developing a home washer designed especially for the European market. But it was not to be. The original Maytag representative in Germany departed and was replaced by Dan Krumm, moving over from Brussels. The European economy was in shambles. All in all, it was a tough job to manage. When the economy showed signs of improvement, the Italian washer industry, heavily subsidized by the government, took over the European market and left no foothold for an offshore interloper. It was Krumm's final task to bail out, which he accomplished, returning to Newton in 1967.

Heir Apparent

Daniel J. Krumm grew up in tiny Primghar, Iowa, where his father ran a hardware store, and his folks were instrumental in starting a Lutheran church. Krumm and his sister sang in the choir and soon found themselves singing at weddings and funerals as well.

After a stint as a Navy corpsman near the end of World War II, Krumm went to the University of Iowa's College of Commerce, joined a fraternity, and met Ann Klingner of Chanute, Kansas. The two maintained contact when Krumm took a job in Minneapolis after graduation, and they became engaged there. Ann followed him to Newton when he joined Maytag in 1952, and they were soon married.

Krumm went through Maytag's training program, then joined a rapidly expanding marketing division in the new area of market research. From there he went to Europe to implement Higdon's commercial laundry scheme, and upon his return was named administrative assistant to the president. The job was created because nobody was retiring at the moment, but it also gave Higdon the opportunity to continue taking Krumm's measure. He measured up, becoming a vice president and member of the board of directors in 1970. A year later he was named executive vice president, and in 1972 became president when Higdon assumed the post of chairman. Two years later he was named CEO upon Higdon's retirement.

The Source and Nature of Krumm's Strength

Dan Krumm's values were strongly influenced by his small-town, spartan upbringing, close involvement with the church, and love of music and the arts, which was a product of early training and a musical mother. From this heritage came a firmness of character not unlike that of the company founder. He was determined to achieve the goals he set out for himself and had the discipline to stick it out. It sometimes took him months or even years to achieve an objective, but he always kept the goal in sight until he got his way.

When he chose to, which was most of the time, Krumm could charm the birds out of the trees. When his guard was down, he could show a less gracious side. But few people knew both. Krumm's dedication to the Maytag quality way was every bit as strong as any of his predecessors', but it was apparently generated more from pride and determination than from economic necessity. He simply was not about to permit the vaunted Maytag quality to slip during his watch. He would be instrumental in transmitting the quality imperative to new members of the Maytag family later.

Seeing to Overdue Production Facilities Expansion

Krumm's first task when he took over in 1974 was to take the bold step of investing record amounts of capital in expanding Maytag's production facilities to meet the needs of the next 20 years. In the next couple of years, Plant

2 almost doubled in size. New technologies were embraced in finishing and materials handling. The state of the art remained the Maytag standard.

The growing need had been apparent to Krumm almost as soon as he returned from Europe in 1970. Production facilities often were severely strained when business was good. But the comptroller/CEO wouldn't risk the capital required to provide for needed growth and new processes. Krumm had to wait until he assumed the job of CEO in 1974, and by then it had become a crash program.

Krumm showed from the beginning of his tour as CEO that he had the nerve to take a plunge. He also showed from the first an ability to get others to go along with his programs. If he was a nervous manager, he didn't show it.

A Culture That Overrides Imperfection

Maytag's quality imperative has emerged as a force that overrides the imperfections of individuals. It has a life of its own. It is the collective impact of individuals that counts. Fred Maytag put it this way: "Added together, individual contributions control the patterns of growth."

An example is found in the career of Charlie Gecan, the one who shut down the plant in the late 1950s until a defect was found and corrected. Gecan had obtained the job of head of quality control in competition with an older and somewhat wiser supervisor who lacked Gecan's more nimble mind and tongue. The losing candidate, an old-timer of preautomatic days, had developed during wartime production work an elaborate set of statistical quality-control standards that would have brought a smile to W. Edwards Deming's face. When he took over, Gecan promptly discarded most of the yardsticks that would have saved Maytag time and money if retained. Instead, he focused on measuring the final result and ignored the intermediate checks. The greater Maytag culture survived this instance of what turned out to be shortsightedness, and the company has gradually reinvented the procedures discarded years earlier. As the new wave of Demingitis sweeps the industrialized world, Maytag is recapturing what it was learning but not implementing at the same time Deming was formulating his theories.

The statistical quality control data dumped by Gecan included information on when a tool would need replacing and other maintenance tasks. In 1993, Maytag hired an outside consultant to show them how to tell when a tool needs replacing as part of the concept of Total Planned Maintenance. It operates on the theory that if planned maintenance inspections, repairs, and cleaning are performed as part of a regular daily routine, problems with equipment and tooling can be corrected before a failure or quality problem occurs. This proactive approach has resulted in cost reduction, increased efficiency, improved quality, and optimum production uptime. According to the consultant who helped Maytag, the rationale behind TPM is the belief that it is impossible to consistently produce quality products using unreliable and ineffective equipment. In other words, what goes around comes around.

10
Maytag in the Acquisition Decade

Competitive Challenge Part II— Quality in the Face of Diversification

Finding Comfort in Familiarity

Fred Maytag's short-line specialist philosophy, or perhaps Maytag's inherent financial conservatism, made short shrift of early attempts at diversification. In the late 1959s, Maytag bought and then very shortly sold a controlling interest in a small electronics manufacturing company located in Lawndale, California, called **MAYTAG** American Missile Products Company. The company was a subcontractor of miniaturized electronic components for space-age telemetry systems. Some of its equipment helped send back radio signals from *Pioneer IV*. Needed expansion demanded a substantial increase in the teensy investment, and Maytag was unprepared to do so, sensing it was out of its element. Being in a business it did not understand did not fit Maytag's investment plans.

In the 1960s a scheme more related to Maytag's expertise was Maytag Fabric Centers. The thought was that a perceived trend toward more home sewing might be paired with Maytag's acknowledged expertise in the care of fabrics to produce a viable retail business. Again the venture ran into an unwillingness to invest heavily in unknown waters and faltered.

211

The dawn of the 1980s found Maytaggers sticking to the home appliance business and doing it all themselves under their own roof. In doing so, the company kept control of product quality and stayed on top, even though competitors were improving their quality and narrowing the gap.

Maytag had bought a war-surplus hemp plant at Hampton, Iowa, right after World War II as a place to machine repair parts for obsolete washer models. The purchase freed Plant 1 in Newton to push all-out production on current models in order to meet the tremendous pent-up demand. As the need to supply parts for older washers diminished, other tasks were found for Hampton suitable to the skilled labor pool and involving products readily transportable 90 miles to Newton.

The biggest item was production of powdered metal bearings for both washers and dryers. Powdered iron, stainless steel, or bronze was formed into the part in a press, then run through a sintering furnace to harden the part and make it permeable. The final step was to soak the part in oil to make a permanent bearing.

After a generation, obsolete equipment and new applications forced a major investment in a new facility in Jefferson City, Missouri, and Hampton was abandoned.

Diversification of the Quality Work Ethic

Maytag factory workers, best paid in the appliance industry during the days of F.L. and Elmer Maytag, have kept that distinction, somewhat to their detriment. While Maytag has no intention of moving out of Newton, its labor force has remained static as production has increased through automation and constant improvement.

The work ethic of Iowa Maytaggers has always been a point of pride for the company and the union too. It has been a key element in the ability to produce quality products. Whether fortuitously or not, Maytag discovered an equally compelling work ethic in Missouri and later in both Tennessee and downstate Illinois, the latter locations added to plant cities through merger.

This pleasant fact was discovered with Maytag's first successful appliance industry acquisition in 1981. A small, independent stove company with strong ties to gas utilities was closely held and without a succession plan. Hardwick Stove Company of Cleveland, Tennessee, and Maytag were mutually attractive. Maytag had located a source for reentering the range business.

Sea Changes in the Appliance Industry—
The Acquisitions Decade

The argument for a full line of home appliances took on new significance in light of a rapidly shrinking retail marketplace beginning to be dominated by a handful of mass merchants. The tried-and-true Maytag marketing technique of pulling products through the retail level by virtue of customer demand still had appeal in the marketplace, but some retail giants felt they could safely ignore public demand. These retailers believed that the public would settle for whatever was offered if the price was right. A well-designed quality product benefits most from good retail salesmanship, be it a washer, auto, watch, or camera. As retail salesmanship disappears, customers have to fall back on their own resources, including their own previous experiences. Here's where a reputation like Maytag's pays off. Customer demand for Maytag motivates a retailer to handle the brand.

Contraction of appliance manufacturers in the 1960s and 1970s had reduced retailers' choices to a handful, mainly those offering a full line. General Electric had threatened to pull out of appliances but instead made a major investment in updating Louisville's Appliance Park. White Consolidated gobbled up several brands, including Westinghouse, Frigidaire, and Tappen, and in turn was gobbled by Electrolux of Sweden, probably the world's largest appliance maker. Whirlpool acquired KitchenAid. Raytheon bought Amana, Caloric, and Speed Queen to offer a full line of Amana appliances. Magic Chef added Admiral and Norge. Maytag was the only major short-line player, although there were a few high-end specialty companies like Sub-Zero, maker of built-in refrigeration.

Learning to Swim With the Sharks— The Hardwick Acquisition

Maytag needed ranges and refrigeration. The cost of designing a product line and building production facilities was prohibitive from both a time and money standpoint. Options were increasingly limited. Maytag might have acquired Amana before Raytheon did in the early 1960s, but the folks in Newton were too financially focused at the time. KitchenAid might have made a marriage, but Maytag feared an antitrust ruling from the Federal Trade Commission, so it did its own thing instead, for the last time, by designing and manufacturing dishwashers.

So Hardwick provided an ideal toe-in-the-water investment for Maytag, and the company learned a great deal about acquisition from this first effort. Maytag tried to preserve local pride and culture while inculcating the "Maytag way." The most significant discovery—and one that has held true from Hardwick to Hoover—was that while surprisingly good rank-and-file and middle management personnel came with a merger, top management sometimes left something to be desired. Maytag's management looked better by comparison with every addition.

Jenn-Air—A Jewel in the Crown

Almost before Maytag had its name on a new line of ranges, both gas
and electric, it had acquired another range company. In 1982 the Jenn-
Air Corporation became available. Started in 1965 by Lou Jenn to make
ventilation equipment, it wasn't long before, like early Maytag, the tail
began wagging the dog as Jenn brought out its remark-
MMM° able cook top that permitted outdoor barbecuing
JENN-AIR inside with its patented ventilation system. The Jenn-
Air cook top became the darling of the yuppie generation. Lou, lacking management succession, sold out to a company
later acquired by United Technologies, which was eager to dump a
holding outside its chosen field. So Maytag pilots began flying to Indianapolis.

The smaller Jenn-Air and Hardwick companies both used wholesale distributors to market their products, a form of distribution Maytag had abandoned in the 1960s. But true to Maytag's acquisition philosophy, things
were left as they were for the time being.

The Architect of Acquisition

Neither of these acquisitions happened by chance. They were the result
of a deliberate strategy put in place by CEO Krumm. He created a new
department to study acquisitions, headed by Leonard Hadley, then a
financial division employee marked for the fast track. Until 1979, when
Hadley was named vice president of corporate planning, Maytag had no
formal method of evaluating the opportunities to acquire or be
acquired that are a regular part of corporate life elsewhere. Hadley
had both the general assignment to evaluate opportunities and the
specific assignment to get Maytag into the range and refrigerator business.

Hadley was ideally suited to the assignment. He had joined Maytag in
1959 as a cost accountant. Involved in budgets, he gained a unique
insight into all aspects of the company through financial spectacles.
Placed in charge of data processing, he learned how to use the analytical
tools available from computers. He was named assistant controller in
1975.

Hadley, another small-town Iowa boy and graduate of the University of
Iowa College of Commerce, grew up in a Quaker community. He may have
learned to take the big view when the Army Signal Corps taught him to
climb telephone poles. In any event, for someone brought up in the
parochial financial environment, he has managed to take a catholic view of
business.

Transplanting the Maytag Way

Not only did Hadley have the job of locating and negotiating for acquisitions, and ensuring that Maytag got what it paid for; he also was given the job of operating the acquired companies. This was a totally new experience for both Hadley and Maytag. To its credit, unlike many a takeover parent, Maytag did not throw out the baby with the bathwater and force conformation. The assignment, understood from the first, was to create an environment that permitted a transfer of the Maytag quality culture. Patience paid off, and the concept became transfused. Of course, most companies think of themselves as quality companies. The secret is to keep them believing it as they are transformed into a *real* quality company. For example, Jenn-Air had a quality product reputation but needed the top management dedication to maintain it. Lou Jenn had not successfully created a culture of quality at Jenn-Air that would survive his departure the way the Maytag family had.

The other necessary ingredient at Hardwick and Jenn-Air was an infusion of capital to reach state-of-the-art production. Few companies maintain their facilities like Maytag.

In the five years before major acquisitions forced corporate restructuring, Maytag continued as a company doing business as usual in Newton with only a handful of people involved in the management of the acquired range companies. To outward appearances, Maytag got its range lines but otherwise pretty much let well enough alone. But Maytag was learning all the time, knowledge that would pay off in dealing with finance, information services, marketing, and production synergism.

Magic Chef—A Large Nut to Swallow

Then one day Dan Krumm got a phone call from Skeet Rymer, chairman of Magic Chef. Skeet had built an old-line range company, like Hardwick, also located in Cleveland, Tennessee, into a full-line appliance manufacturer through acquisition of the Admiral  white goods facilities. Included were the Admiral refrigeration plant at Galesburg, Illinois, the Norge washer plant at Herrin, Illinois, and the Admiral freezer plant in South Carolina. Magic Chef also had build its own microwave oven factory in Alabama.

With the Admiral acquisition had come a number of managers from Rockwell, Admiral's former owner, which included John Green, who was named president of the merged firm when Rymer became chairman. Although he had an office in Cleveland, Green retained his office (and focus) at Admiral's Chicago headquarters. It just wasn't going to work out. Once again, there was no management succession to suit Rymer.

Admiral ▟

A Clandestine Meeting

Krumm arranged to meet Rymer in Florida. They got together in a dark and empty ballroom at The Breakers in West Palm Beach. They had previously had no more than a passing acquaintance. Rymer told Krumm what he wanted, and Krumm took the information back to Newton and set Hadley to work.

The deal was put together in secret, and the acquisition sent Maytag into the red for the first time since 1928, when Elmer Maytag vowed never again to be in debt (see the end of Chapter 5). The 1986 news was received positively by the financial community.

A Hard Sell to Internal Customers

The news was received with utter shock by the Maytag organization. Maytag represented the ultimate in product quality and dependability in the appliance business. Magic Chef, although larger, represented a product line that, to Maytaggers, didn't belong in the same ballpark. A merger seemed unthinkable. Even competitors were amazed, one referring to the merger as the "odd couple."

It required imagination to consider Maytag products in the same basket with Magic Chef. However, weighed against the disadvantages of the corporate marriage were some major pluses. Maytag would have its refrigerator line. Strong as the Maytag name was, it dominated only the upper end of the marketplace. Magic Chef was a major player in the broad middle market. Together, they could become a major factor across the board. They also had a good position in the homebuilder market, where Maytag had almost no exposure, other than through Jenn-Air.

Careful analysis eventually produced a favorable response from top management and the board of directors. However, little thought was given to how best to break the news to the rest of the organization, since initially it was thought that Magic Chef would exist as separately as Hardwick and Jenn-Air and with as little disturbance to Maytaggers. It was not to be.

Creating a Corporate Family—The Maytag Corporation

What had been minor skirmishes in the marketplace among Hardwick and Jenn-Air distributors with Maytag turned to bloody battles with Magic Chef, **MAYTAG** which also sold directly to dealers. It was difficult to keep **CORPORATION** a rein on all parties. Sharply focused salespeople couldn't be expected to step back and see the big picture. Other intracorporate disciplines were as much at loggerheads, although perhaps not as publicly.

Necessity forced management to once again seek outside counsel, and an overall corporate structure was the outcome. Initially, the corporate staff was small, dealing only with the obvious issues of finance, legal, and public affairs. Autonomy in production and marketing was maintained.

But the need for corporatewide product planning and interchanges, centralized purchasing opportunities, and overall financial controls and accounting soon began to chip away at autonomy. Once again, attrition of acquired senior management was eventually almost total. Some went immediately, some gave hope for a time and a few remained, none in the post held at the time of the merger. Nowhere in Maytag experience was there the wholesale staff bloodletting so common with takeovers and mergers. Maytag truly hoped it was getting management help along with the rest of the acquired assets. However, in the absence of a deeply ingrained culture of quality and dependability, few measured up. On the other hand, rank-and-file employees measured up admirably and Maytag found that folks from Tennessee and Illinois responded to the challenge of producing quality just as the Iowans had always done. Nevertheless, for many old-timers among Iowa Maytaggers, things would never be the same again. For all of Maytag's carefully nurtured ability to accept change, change had always come from within, and even then, the status quo always had its supporters, albeit mostly among those least likely to make a contribution.

Ultimate Test of the Quality Culture

Krumm and others didn't need the immediate dismay among Maytaggers to enforce their determination to make quality the top concern of those being acquired. They exposed the newly acquired management to Newton's quality culture immediately and took the message to every foreman in each plant through meetings addressed by Krumm himself. He made it very clear that he expected one quality level from *everyone,* and it was to receive top priority.

Krumm made the distinction between quality as in high end, top of the line, creme de la creme, and quality as in meeting the customer's expectations for a given product as it relates to price and features. While overall expectations may differ, all customers expect the product to perform dependably. That became Maytag's quality objective for every brand and every company in the new family. Perhaps surprisingly, it has succeeded.

Maycor—Reaping the Benefits of Consolidation

One immediate challenge to a diverse family of appliance makers was coordinating service and parts availability. Dealers needed centralized

service training and parts for whichever products they handled. With the
range companies had come a separate parts ware-

house combining parts from all companies. It was set
up in Jefferson City, Missouri. Now a more compre-
hensive solution was needed.

The answer was to establish Maycor, a centralized parts and service organization for all brands, products, and companies. It was headquartered in
Cleveland, Tennessee. A new central parts warehouse was established at
Milan, Tennessee, where Maytag parts were moved from Jefferson City and
combined with Magic Chef, Admiral, Norge, and Hardwick parts in a state-
of-the-art facility.

The move toward centralization and coordination was extended to the
international level. In that direction, Maytag International, formerly called
Domicor, was created in 1987 to consolidate all interna-

tional marketing efforts into the former Admiral pro-
gram, which had been inherited by Magic Chef as part of
their merger, and which had the most experience in
world markets. Maytag Financial Services Corporation was formed to provide
both wholesale and retail financing for dealers served by the corporation.

Maytag International is headquartered in Chicago, but the financial
services organization is part of corporate headquarters in Newton. Early
on, there was agitation to locate Maytag Corporation headquarters elsewhere, but Krumm did not heed the proposals. The corporate folks are
probably ambivalent, but Maytag Company people felt some keen reser-
vations about having corporate headquarters on Dependability Square in
Newton.

Investing Big-Time in Quality Production

The first priority following the corporate reorganization was production of a
Maytag refrigerator. While design work was going on, the production facilities at Galesburg, Illinois, were expanded and modernized. Over $90 million
was invested in the plant. It took three years for Maytag to go to market with
its first refrigerators because, again, they were not just face-lifted Admiral
boxes but offered features specifically designed for Maytag.

Hardwick, conveniently located just across the railroad tracks from the
Magic Chef plant in Cleveland, Tennessee, was integrated into a single production facility. The brand name all but disappeared. Maytag wanted a
unique new look to its range line and spent another $50 million to con-
struct a new range production facility within the old one without interrupt-
ing production. New Maytag ranges featuring a seamless back panel
waterfall design reached the market in 1993.

Dixie-Narco—Soft Drink Cash Cow

When acquired, Magic Chef also contained Toastmaster, a small appliance company, and Dixie-Narco, the leading producer of soft drink vending **Dixie-Narco.** machines. Toastmaster was sold off within the year in a leveraged buyout to its management. But Dixie-Narco, a better kind of cow than any of Elmer Maytag's holsteins, has not only been kept but coddled.

Dixie-Narco represents the only departure from Maytag's traditional investment strategy of sticking to the appliance business. Vending machine production and appliance manufacturing share some of the same skills in metal-bending and finishing. More important, the vending machine business shares the income-producing proclivity of the original Maytag Company, especially its commercial laundry division. Production was moved from a decrepit Topsy-like plant in West Virginia to a modern plant in South Carolina that had housed Magic Chef's freezer operations, which were closed out.

In 1992 Dixie-Narco earned $16.3 million on sales of $165.3 million.

Making Management Stretch

In stark contrast to the static days of the 1960s and 1970s, the mergers created unprecedented demands for management, and promotions abounded in every division. Maytaggers responded to the challenge and infiltrated the entire corporate structure with quality-focused managers, even as new managers were gaining experience at home in Newton.

With formation of the corporation in 1986, Krumm vacated his role as company president, albeit with some reluctance, in favor of Hadley, who had the job of refereeing between his company and the corporation, now camped in each other's laps. The financial division was divided into company and corporate groups as well, but not marketing, and only a single manufacturing job existed at the corporate level. A human resources department for the corporation was formed to bring varying personnel practices of the companies closer together. In the rapid growth and promotion, the Peter Principle popped up once or twice, but most of the newly elevated did a remarkably good job of growing to meet the challenge.

Continuous Improvement Made Exponential

The Maytag heritage of divine discontent found fertile ground at all the new facilities. Not only were improvements galore to be made at each plant and with each product, but there soon came a search for situations where commonality might come into play.

Maytag had always designed for interchangeability and rebuildability, meaning parts were held to such close tolerances that any part would fit any assembly without use of a hammer. Thus any product might be rebuilt, using repair parts, and could function as good as new. This means that at Maytag there is no such thing as a lemon. No appliance need ever be discarded because a part wears out. A Maytag can be kept running like new as long as repair parts are available, which is often 25 years or more. Interchangeability and similar concepts became part of the expanded corporate culture.

How Important Is Culture? Very.

In the fall of 1992, a new broom was sweeping the executive suite at R.H. Macy, nationwide department store chain with the flagship store on 34th Street in New York City. Theirs are the inflatables of the Thanksgiving Day parade.

An Associated Press business story reporting on the change quoted the new CEO as saying, "We're trying very hard to personalize the business and take all the baloney out of it and the pomposity out of it." The new leaders want to change the entire Macy culture, eliminating the imperial atmosphere that existed under the predecessor.

The story went on to discuss the importance of culture, reporting that an outdated culture has been blamed for the troubles at IBM, GM, and Sears. A pioneering culture is credited for the successes of Wal-Mart and Apple Computer. While Maytag is not as Johnny-come-lately as either, it could well be said that its shirtsleeves culture is responsible, in large measure, for its success. Preserving that culture at the new corporate level is a primary assignment for corporate management.

11
Going Global

Competitive Challenge Part III—Quality Image Meets the Globalization Imperative

Groping for a Global Strategy

At about the time Maytag successfuly absorbed the Magic Chef aquisition and finally became a full-line appliance manufacturer, a new trend was sweeping corporate boardrooms in the appliance industry. With a European Common Market all but assured and with nearly total product saturation at home, longing eyes were cast abroad. Saturation of home appliances in Europe was substantially less than that in the United States and Canada. The traditional nationalistic trade barriers were about to fall.

The handful of companies remaining in the U.S. appliance industry felt a need to become part of a global concern in order to avoid being swallowed up by the megaconglomerates that would emerge. The focus was on Europe because of the opportunities seen in the common market. It was difficult or impossible to find a meaningful appliance partner in the Pacific Rim, partly because of the incompatability of products.

Already, the former Westinghouse and White Consolidated appliance business was in the hands of Sweden's Electrolux and being directed from abroad. Whirlpool entered into a consortium with the Dutch-owned Phillips, a conglomerate whose appliance business dominated much of Europe. For a number of years Whirlpool had owned a Brazilian subsidiary, but in Central and South America trade barriers exacerbated nationalistic constraints, and for the most part, appliances did not cross borders.

Lifestyles Limit Major Appliance Potential in Foreign Markets

Beyond the strangling trade restrictions found in Japan and other nations in the eastern hemisphere, markets for those appliances that require such amenities as hot water and U.S.-style plumbing are extremely limited worldwide. Refrigerators, while they have constraints of voltage, current, and size, need only to be plugged in. The market for other appliances is severely limited by the realities of overseas housing.

Europe comes closest to having an appetite for a full line of home appliances, and an anticipated rise in the standard of living there made that market most promising. A global strategy also would require new appliance designs better adapted to emerging markets. Maytag strategists felt that a new level of synergism might well emerge by combining the efforts and expertese of companies on both sides of the Atlantic. Companies abroad faced similar limitations in bringing their product lines to America. Above all, everyone wanted room to grow.

If at First You Don't Succeed

Maytag had sought entry into the European market in the 1960s but had been frustrated as described in the previous chapter. Back in the 1920s, as part of the mercurial growth that accompanied introduction of the Gyrafoam washer, Maytag had established distributors in several European countries, as well as in Australia, China, and Colombia, South America. Of course, the wringer washer was better suited for use almost anywhere in the world. All that had disappeared with the Depression. What little international market existed—mainly U.S. citizens living abroad—had been served by a succession of international distributors prior to the formation of Domicor, a combined effort of Admiral, Magic Chef, and Maytag that followed the Magic Chef merger. The name recently was changed to Maytag International.

Other than in Canada, the international market had never seen significant volume. Canada had been a major market for farm equipment, along with South America. Maytag's Canadian subsidiary, dating from 1903, had manufactured wringer washers at Winnipeg for a time. Maytag Ltd. has sales branches at Toronto and Calgary. Quebec and the Maritimes are served by independent distributors, bilingual in the case of Quebec.

Hoover—Acquiring an International Foothold

The Hoover Co. grew up in North Canton, Ohio, and has long dominated the floor care business, just as Maytag owned the prewar wringer

washer market. Hoover established a toehold in the European market a number of years ago and today is a commanding brand in the floor care market. In addition, they developed a spinner washer for the British market that became the leading laundry product in that country. In fact, Hoover imported that washer into the United States. But the highly popular English design had little appeal in this country. While its laundry product was not as popular on the continent as in Britain, Hoover did have distribution throughout Europe both with floor care products and appliances.

While Maytag's goal was a window to the European Common Market, the debt load that came with the 1989 Hoover aquisition also made Maytag unpalatable to merger mania advocates.[1] Conglomeritis was a business curse of the 1980s when companies were being aquired and liquidated without any business logic. In the Wall Street feeding frenzy, many shark-bit companies went under when management lost control to speculators.

While Maytag's historic premium stock price would have made an unfriendly takeover costly, the price might nearly have been recovered from the debt-free company's treasury, certainly with the leverage that borrowing could have produced. Even after going into debt to buy Magic Chef, Maytag was not home free, but the Hoover deal effectively put that concern to rest. Maytag was no longer a cash-rich shiny red apple ripe for the picking.

Hard Times Hound Maytag in Europe

Just as economic hard times had doomed Maytag's earlier European adventure, a severe and lasting recession, particularly in the UK, Hoover's main market abroad, has forced retrenchment instead of expansion in Europe.

Meanwhile, the existing Hoover management in Europe had to be replaced. In contrast, Hoover North American remains in the hands of a Hoover executive. The Ohio company has a history similar to that of Maytag in the pursuit of quality and follows the same tenet of maintaining state-of-the-art production facilities. These investments have kept Hoover

---

[1] Lack of management succession in the Hoover family caused the company to be available for acquisition by Chicago Pacific (once Rock Island railroad) as an investment after the latter company had divested its railroad holdings. It was Chicago Pacific that Maytag aquired, with a mountain of debt, in 1989.

competitive in the highly competitive North American floor-care industry, and Hoover is the market—and profit—leader.

But the similarities end at the ocean. Many Hoover production facilities abroad are aging and require additional investment. Operations there have been a financial drain. Announcing a further restructuring in the fall of 1992, CEO Len Hadley said that Hoover appliance and floor care operations in Europe continue to experience losses, primarily because of excess capacity and the unexpected further deterioration of economic conditions in the United Kingdom and other European countries. Hadley continued:

> In the past two years, we have implemented significant cost reduction activities throughout our Hoover Europe operations, but further reorganization is necessary. Overcapacity is prevalent in manufacturing throughout Europe and Hoover is no exception. This is a serious problem that must eventually be addressed in all industries.
>
> Consequently, our reorganization thrust in the months ahead will be aimed at downsizing production capacity and streamlining sales, marketing, administrative, and distribution operations in Europe.

In early 1993, Maytag Corporation announced plans to close the Hoover floor care plant in Dijon, France, and consolidate all production of floor care products at the Scotland plant.

New European Thrust With German Company

The fall he retired, Krumm engineered yet another opportunity for Maytag in Europe. He formed an alliance with Bosch-Siemens Hausgerate GmbH of Germany. The objective is to jointly explore mutually beneficial business opportunities in the United States, Europe, and other parts of the world, a further reflection of Maytag's corporate strategy to become a global competitor.

BSHG was founded in 1967 as a joint venture between Robert Bosch GmbH and Siemens A.G. It employs about 24,000 people, is headquartered in Munich, and is the largest appliance manufacturer in Germany, and second largest in Europe, behind Electrolux. Products include all white goods, floorcare, electric housewares, air conditioning, and electronic entertainment, with plants in Germany, Spain, and Greece.

Possible Joint Efforts

Unlike a traditional joint venture in which one company financially invests in another, this arrangement is a formal agreement to work together to enhance each other's brands and market each other's products, by means of joint teams to explore various areas of concentration.

In technology, the two could see an exchange of current knowledge, and joint development could take place in product and component design, manufacturing processes, energy savings, and appliance standards. While environmental issues have grown more important among American manufacturers, European consumers have historically been more environmentally conscious.

In Germany, BSHG is a leader in this effort. Their corporate objective states:

> We feel responsible...to help maintain a healthy environment by finding new ways of conserving scarce resources, reducing the consumption of electricity and water, and minimizing the use of polluting substances.

Likewise, Maytag's corporate policy says that it will "conduct its business in a responsible manner reasonably designed to protect the environment and the health of its employees, customers, and the public."

BSHG is expected to provide input in chlorofluorocarbon (CFC) replacement in refrigeration, currently a major governmental issue in the United States. Maytag will share advancements they have made in environmentally sound practices such as recycling.

New Products and Markets

Both Maytag and BSHG are "consumer driven," and have been able to realize marketing strengths in countries where they do business. Of particular interest will be the potential in places where neither firm has a strong presence, such as Southeast Asia, South America, China, the former Soviet Union, Mexico, and India. The possibility also exists of new products to meet consumer needs.

The firms will explore the opportunity to market products made by each other. BSHG has well-established distribution channels throughout Germany and much of Europe that might accept Maytag products, using a Maytag or BSHG brand name, or both. They will explore the possiblity of using Maytag distribution to expand sales of BSHG products. In addition, the alliance will investigate the potential for sourcing BSHG's products, as well as BSHG sourcing products from Hoover Europe.

Both are involved in vending machines, with Neff the German brand.

BSHG's corporate philosophy begins with the statement: "Quality and innovation are the driving forces in our success," a notion Maytag finds totally acceptable.

The Krumm Legacy

Dan Krumm's 40-year tenure at Maytag, half as president, encompassed three main growth spurts. First came the major expansion of production facilities in Newton that kept Maytag in business in a growing economy. Next was the Magic Chef merger and blossoming into a full-line appliance manufacturer. Krumm's final giant step was the Hoover move. Of the three CEOs who contributed most to Maytag's growth—Elmer, Fred, and Dan Krumm—the last has been the architect of greatest change.

Krumm's swan song as CEO came at the 1992 annual meeting of shareowners and subsequent board meeting, when he turned over the reins to Len Hadley. Krumm told shareowners:

> I'm sure a number of you here today were also at Maytag's 1974 annual meeting when I gave my first report to shareowners. We have changed significantly since then—partly because we wanted to, partly because we had to. What is significant, I think, is that Maytag has grown, prospered, and continues to survive as a successful corporation.

At the end of 1992, Krumm, then 66, retired as chairman of the company he had helped turn into a $3 billion global appliance maker, having stayed on an extra year in the vain hope of overseeing a European turnaround.

Leadership and Stewardship Personified

Krumm received many honors during his career—for business leadership, civic contributions, and philanthopy—that would have boggled flamboyant F.L. Maytag's mind. A popular outside director of other firms, Krumm was serving on the boards of Centel Corporation, Snap-On Tools Corporation, and Principal Financial Group when he retired. He is a past chairman of the National Association of Manufacturers, and a member of the board of trustees of the Committee for Economic Development.

He was selected outstanding CEO of the decade in the appliance industry by *Financial World* magazine, and executive of the year by the National Management Association. Krumm was named Iowa's business leader of the year in 1986 by the *Des Moines Register*. He has served on the Iowa governor's task force on ethics in state government, and is past chairman of both the Iowa Venture Capital Fund and Iowa Business Council. In Newton, he was president of Progress Industries, serving handicapped citizens, and headed the 1976 United Way fund drive.

New Direction for Maytag Foundation

Krumm greatly expanded both the scope and funding of the Maytag Company Foundation (now Maytag Corporation Foundation) and used it as a tool for significant aid both to higher education, Maytag's historic interest, and to the performing arts, a new thrust. In the process, he gave leadership to the Iowa College Foundation, Iowa Natural Heritage Foundation, Des Moines Symphony Association, Iowa Peace Institute, University of Iowa Foundation and FINE (First in Nation in Education). Considered one of the leading fund raisers in the state, he has raised outside money for many of the same causes supported through the Maytag Foundation.

Krumm's Lutheran activities included chairing the board of Grandview College in Des Moines, a church-related institution. He continues to direct the choir of First Lutheran church in Newton, considered by many (particularly Lutherans) to be the finest choir in town.

The Baton Passes Officially to Hadley

In his first public appearance for Maytag as the CEO, Leonard A. Hadley, 57, expressed his pleasure at a new educational complex both as a Maytagger of 33 years and as a citizen of the community where he has lived and raised his family. He was probably also expressing the sentiments of his wife, Corine, a long-time school board member and former city councilperson. Together, they formed a unique public/private partnership with his business career, her community service, and their shared parenting of a son and daughter.

Fostering a Future of Training

A remarkable and unique combination of private enterprise, higher education, and municipal government has created a college campus in Newton. Moving far beyond philanthopy, the consortium of Maytag Company and Corporation, Des Moines Area Community College (DMACC), Iowa State University, and the city of Newton will combine to produce a $5.5 million facility at a time when all are undergoing budget restraints.

Scheduled to begin classes in the fall of 1993, the Newton Polytechnic Campus of DMACC is far more than a college campus. In addition to housing expanded educational and training programs from the community college, the facility will provide the community with a large conference center and auditorium and a consolidated location for Maytag training and technology needs, to be leased from DMACC. Iowa State will offer college credit courses at the facility.

Maytag's contribution to the public/private partnership includes six acres of land containing the vintage Tank Track building, a 100,000-square-foot manufacturing space built during the Korean War. The building will be converted to two stories. About a fourth of the new facility will be devoted to expanded Maytag Company and Corporation training functions, both marketing and technical, as well as the skilled trades training program.

Both Maytag and others in the community will make use of the conference center, as well as the opportunities for training and retraining to be offered by DMACC. In a time of national emphasis on training and education, the Maytag community effort is right on cue.

At the press conference, Maytag CEO Hadley said the allegiance

> ...fits perfectly with the four points of our corporate strategy—quality, synergy, profitability, and globalization. Each of these elements must be grounded in the most up-to-date professional and technical training possible for our employees throughout the United States and around the world.

Citing the demands of a highly competitive industry and an ever more sophisticated and diverse customer base, he added, "Maytag's ability to rapidly incorporate training and retraining as a normal aspect of work life will be a major competitive advantage for this corporation in the decades ahead."

He reminded his audience that Newton had been the largest community in Iowa without a postsecondary campus, adding "In addition to filling this gap, a major objective of the Newton Polytechnic campus will be to offer employee training and conference facilities to interested businesses in Newton and the surrounding area, just as it will be doing for Maytag."

Speaking of the newest CEO, a former college recruiter for Maytag recalled that he had spotted Hadley as someone Maytag wanted when he had visited the campus at the University of Iowa, and was delighted when Hadley made it past the screening committee interview. A long-time accounting employee remembers Hadley as a comer from the beginning. Both, of course, had the benefit of hindsight.

Budgets as a Management Tool

His lengthy career in the budget department gave him contact with most of the company's managers in plant and office. While most accounting types come on as Scrooge, Hadley always seemed to be on the department head's side. He was a good listener with a healthy sense of humor. His pleasant demeanor covers an Iowa stubborn streak that gets him the answers he needs.

He remains disarmingly friendly and casual in management style, but underneath, his committment to Maytag and its quality culture is rock-solid and uncompromising. As the one person who can make it happen, Hadley brings a force that is absolutely essential to giving direction to the rest of the corporation while maintaining Maytag pride at the company. The grail of quality and dependability appear safe for the next generation.

An Ever Faster Track

The pace of everything has quickened on the fast double track of keeping Maytag Company profitable while trying to coax profitability out of some of the rest of the appliance family—all in conditions that deny the magic potion of growth and expansion. In response, a recently announced major reorganization is intended, according to Hadley, to "further strengthen our brands in the marketplace, improve operating efficiencies, and enhance margins in the years ahead."

The consolidation combines Magic Chef marketing, accounting, and information services with those of Jenn-Air, which is dropping its distributors in favor of direct marketing to dealers. The combined field sales representatives will sell Jenn-Air, Magic Chef, and Norge products directly to dealers and building suppliers from Jenn-Air's Indianapolis headquarters.

Also starting in 1993, the marketing of Admiral brand appliances, formerly handled by Magic Chef, is to be done by the Maytag sales organization. In Hadley's words:

> One of the principal benefits is that we will be taking our major appliances to the marketplace in a more efficient and a more economical manner. Our two sales organizations will each be offering a high-priced line as well as a mid-priced line that can enhance the position of all our brands on dealers' floors.

Both companies are headed by former sales executives. Dick Haines, president of Maytag Company, and Carl Moe, head of Jenn-Air, both started as Maytag regional sales managers. Illustrating Maytag's multigenerational tendencies, Moe's father was a Maytag regional manager and Haines's father was a Maytag retail dealer.

Hadley had told shareowners at the 1992 annual meeting that he expects the years ahead to be rewarding for Maytag, with help coming from the maturing of the baby boom generation during the 1990s.

> This increasing number of more affluent second- and third-time major appliance customers bodes well for us because they will want high-end products. Maytag and Jenn-Air are the strongest upscale brands in the

industry, so we are well positioned to take advantage of this trend and outperform the industry.

Synergy Versus Brand Loyalty

A new appliance division called Diversified Operations is headed by Don Lorton, who had been in charge of Magic Chef's production facilities at Cleveland, Tennessee. He had headed Jenn-Air when Maytag bought it. Lorton was given the added responsibility for the Admiral refrigeration plant at Galesburg, Illinois, and the corporatewide parts and service organization, Maycor. Thus, he will be producing ranges and refrigerators for all corporate brands. Jenn-Air, whose range line complements those made at Magic Chef, also produces specialized products for Maytag.

Maytag still produces washers and dryers only for the Maytag brand name, but the new dishwasher plant at Jackson, Tennessee, will be making that product for all brands. The Norge laundry facility has become part of Maytag but makes only brands other than Maytag.

"Another benefit of the reorganization," according to Hadley, "is that it unites Jenn-Air and Magic Chef marketing expertise in cooking appliances and their strengths in accessing the builder market." Clearly, Maytag's rash of aquisitions over the past decade or so was intended to broaden the company's horizons, and strengthen its global position as opposed to the "buy-up, carve-up, and sell-off" strategy that so many other companies and investors have pursued. Maytag's focus has been on synergistic combination of aquired firms.

The North American appliance reorganization also includes a redesign of information services that will result in a significantly enhanced common order management and distribution system for goods produced by the manufacturing locations.

While the sophisticated management tools of the computer age are increasingly essential to success, they still come to the P&L statement as an expense, and it is only those things produced in the factories with value added that add wealth to the world. Anything produced in the mushrooming service industries is merely an exchange of dollars.

Maytag Corporation Today

The legacy Krumm turned over to Hadley included a corporate staff of about 120 people, the original Maytag Company, now about 3200 strong[2]

---

[2] Record employment for the Maytag Company was about 4000 during the early automatic washer days.

and total employment of approximately 21,500 at the corporation's 20 manufacturing operations located in 10 states and 6 other countries. In the past four years, more than $300 million has been invested in plant and equipment for Magic Chef, Admiral, Dixie-Narco, the new Jackson dishwasher plant, and Maytag's Newton facilities. Consolidated sales in 1992 totaled just over $3 billion.

How Hadley will fare is a matter of speculation at this point. The protracted business slump on both sides of the Atlantic has kept the debt burden high. Tough management decisions are called for. On the other hand, the corporation is about to cash in on major investments in production facilities, and product design and seems well poised to take advantage of the coming U.S. economic upturn.

The New CEO Speaks

In his first annual report letter, Hadley reported on the unique strengths of the corporation's major brands:

> Maytag, with its legendary reputation for dependability; Hoover, a name synonymous with floor care in North America and Europe; Jenn-Air, on the cutting edge in design of built-in kitchens; Magic Chef, a recognized innovator in cooking features; and Admiral, on the forefront of refrigerator engineering and design. As a result, we have enviable North American market positions: In the upper-price segments, Maytag is No. 1 in laundry equipment and dishwashers, and Jenn-Air is No. 1 in downdraft grill ranges. Hoover is No. 1 in floor care, Magic Chef is No. 2 in gas ranges, and Dixie-Narco is the No. 1 supplier of soft drink vending machines in the world.

He concluded:

> As we enter 1993, Maytag is a better-positioned company, with powerful brands that help consumers manage their homes in five principal areas: laundry, cooking, dishwashing, refrigeration, and floor care. Our brands are consistent leaders in total customer satisfaction, including design, features, price, quality, and service, quite simply because we understand consumer lifestyles and home management needs.

While becoming a global company is still as important as it was when Krumm aquired Hoover, some things have changed. Europe no longer appears to be the best answer to market growth. The prolonged recession there, along with a more realistic appraisal of the potential, removes much of the imperative.

Followers of the appliance industry think Maytag's best bet may well be to bail out of Hoover Europe, surrender the continent to better placed competitors, and look for greener pastures among the rice paddies. The Bosch-

Siemen angle seems a wiser approach to Europe, with little downside risk, and it also offers a shared look at other world markets.

Meanwhile, the domestic potential for synergysm is far from exhausted.

Synergism of People

In addition to the new refrigerator line at Galesburg, the new plant-within-a-plant production line at Cleveland is producing totally redesigned gas and electric ranges of exceptionally high quality and sophisticated appearance. The new dishwasher produced at Jackson, with just the Maytag brand, has enabled Maytag to triple its market share since 1986. And Jenn-Air, Magic Chef, and Admiral brands come on stream in 1993. There also is space available to modernize washer and dryer production in Newton. Not only is everything state of the art, but today's state of the art is far more sophisticated than ever.

Together with the facilities comes all the newest in management technique, computer-aided process control, and sophisticated engineering. No avenue to improve Maytag has been left unexplored. Old-timers may complain now and then, but young turks have the tools and enthusiasm to make things happen.

In fact, Maytag technology has progressed to the point where it now feels it has the capability to generate the statistics necessary to support an application for the Malcolm Baldrige Award, including the data it might have had from the 1930s if Charlie Gecan hadn't dumped all those hand-generated statistics. Up to now, Maytag has had only the incredible quality results, not the means of proving them statistically. Perhaps a winner is in the offing.

Baldrige or not, the most important tool lies not in technology, but with people. And the synergism of people shows the greatest promise for the future. An Old World saying, one that F.L. Maytag probably knew well, translates "No one of us is as smart as all of us." And the new breed of Maytagger has taken the maxim to heart. For example, R&D, marketing, manufacturing, and engineering have formed task forces to put new products into production in a fraction of the time it used to take. They start working together early on the drawing board, and the interactive process can save years in development time. Twenty years ago, the heads of these disciplines barely spoke to one another, and product development progressed at a snail's pace.

Quality: Yesterday, Today, and Tomorrow

As generation after generation of the Maytag family members were creating the company, focusing on dependability to the customer and pride of workmanship in the shop, there were no fancy words turned into acronyms to describe what, and how, and why things were done as they were.

In the 1990s, our comptuter-aided analysis of tools and techniques has come down to an alphabet soup vocabulary that attempts to describe and define those same commonsense concepts that were applied, albeit unidentified, to create what has become the Maytag quality legend. In applying modern terminology to ancient history, however, Maytag has a major failing. It is one of the rare Fortune 500 company that never faced a life-or-death turnaround situation—even in 100 years of operation.

A century ago, F.L. Maytag had a hunger for innovation, and an insatiable desire to develop and implement new technologies. After 100 years in business, fundamental Maytag philosophy hasn't changed. Although many companies are funneling vast amounts of money to information services firms and management consultants, few are driven from their very core by a century-old culture of quality, customer service, and product dependability.

Even Motorola, broadly recognized for its highly successful Six Sigma quality program, describes it's own process of renewal this way:

> Renewal at Motorola not only has meant a change in product focus, but has meant a change in managment emphasis or direction. A significant change in management emphasis—perhaps even in corporate culture—occurred in 1981 when senior management decided the Motorola product quality was not good enough.

Give Motorola credit for recognizing and responding to the quality challenge, as have many other companies. Without a widespread recognition of the value of quality manufacturing and service, quality training, and consulting would not have become the growth industry that it has.

In 100 years of manufacturing, once the company hit its stride, Maytag has managed, through both family and professional management, to evade the fateful moment when company executives need admit that product quality is not good enough. If F.L. Maytag were available today to consult companies on quality manufacturing, he would likely tell the story of how grain harvesters once discarded defective self feeders in the field and stopped making payments.

His bottom line now, as it was then, would probably be to draw a distinction between "sold" and "paid for." Thanks to Elmer, Bud, and Fred Maytag, to Umbreit, Higdon, Krumm, and Hadley, and to thousands of dedicated Maytaggers throughout the years, F.L. could step in front of a present-day executive committee or a plant floor meeting at Maytag and say again, "Nothing is actually *sold* until it is in the hands of a satisfied customer." and everybody would know exactly what he was talking about!

Companies without a century-old culture of quality can pick up the trail at any time. Over time, the presence or absence of a faithful customer base will indicate whether the commitment to quality and dependability has been taken to heart by everyone at every level of the organization. It starts at the top and it ends with a truly satisfied customer.

All the contemporary technological and theoretical innovation in worldwide industry notwithstanding, Maytag's success, more than anything else, is a story about people. At any company, successfully serving the needs of internal and external customers determines prosperity at the bottom line.

If F.L. Maytag were alive today, he and Old Lonely would be drinking bud-dies. Moreover, setting all his eccentricities aside, F.L. would strive, just as current Maytaggers do, to make sure than the only place people see the Maytag repairman is in a Maytag television commercial. The pride of the past, the pace of the present, and the promise of the future combine to make Old Lonely's prospects look desolate indeed.

Index

About the Authors

Robert Hoover is a 38-year veteran (retired) of the Maytag Company. As public relations director, he was in a unique position to both witness and participate in Maytag's decisions to automate, diversify, and go global. **John Hoover,** a southern California-based entrepreneur who produces entertainment, educational, and corporate training sales programs for a wide range of clients, is the coauthor of the highly acclaimed book, *Leadership When the Heat's On.*